HEAVY IS THE RAIN
STELLA ADAMS

To Robin:

Thanks for your
support.
    Happy reading!
        Stella Adams

HEAVY IS THE RAIN
STELLA ADAMS

For the women whose inner little girl screams for authentic love.

Heavy is the Rain

No need to shutter the windows from the stormy gloom,
The vanished sun and driving rain have darkened the room,
Darken my spirit, assaulted my brain.

Heavy is the rain.

Heavy the heart, the mind troubled with guilt and sorrow,
Damaged self, violated and bruised, praying for tomorrow,
Praying for life without pain.

Heavy is the rain.

Heavy is the cruel torrent, showering down on my head,
No soft pitter-patter that soothes my soul when nestled in bed,
No soothing sunlight to heal and keep me sane.

Heavy is the rain.

—*Stella Adams*

PROLOGUE

The choir swayed from side to side, singing, in call and response, "I'll be caught up to meet Him, I'll be caught up to meet Him," while the family slowly filed into the sanctuary. The church was filled with well-dressed mourners. Some fanned furiously, some craned to see whose company they shared, some were bored as they waited for the service to begin, and a few honored the dearly departed.

It was the attractive and smartly dressed young woman's turn to view the remains. *Remains,* the young woman thought. *A lifetime of trying to be somebody, only to end up as remains for all eternity.*

She noticed his hair. As he had gotten older, he stopped using the potato and lye concoction to conk his hair. But much to the surprise of his immediate family, he had good hair—real good. Miscegenation was alive and well in the Old South.

A concerned church lady in a stiff, starched uniform put her arm around the young woman and nudged her on. *Not a moment too soon,* the young woman thought, because she suddenly had the urge to spit on the remains.

She looked past the two people behind her in line to the sister of the deceased, who was bawling her eyes out. *To be expected I guess, the young woman thought. She is his blood. I, on the other hand, am not, and I'm glad the son-of-a-bitch is dead.*

1

1948

The Southern Railway train started to chug to a slow grind as it began to make its umpteenth stop, this time at Mount Royal Station in Baltimore. There must have been a thousand-one horse towns and whistle stops between South Carolina and Maryland. Lilly Ann, a slim and strikingly beautiful woman of twenty-three, sat in the colored car of the train, with her equally skinny, seven-year-old daughter, sleeping on her shoulder.

It was hot and crowded in the colored car, and Lilly Ann knew her daughter was hungry. They had eaten all the fried chicken, ham sandwiches, and apples that her mother Gertie had packed for them for the long trip from Fairfield to Baltimore. Coloreds weren't allowed to eat in the dining cars; Jim Crow made sure of that. You packed your own food or went hungry. Funny more people didn't die of food poisoning.

Lilly Ann had named her daughter Billie in honor of her favorite singer. But unlike Ms. Holiday, her daughter had never been much farther than the front yard of Gertie's old shack, and the awesomeness of a world never seen had completely exhausted her.

Baltimore was the destination, partly because Billie Holiday grew up there in the twenties. Lilly Ann had made the trip up North several times: a couple of times to visit her brother in New Jersey, and other times to visit her sister in Baltimore. It was during one of those visits that she met her future husband.

The train whistle signaled that it was pulling into the station, and Lilly Ann gently shook Billie to rouse her. "Wake up, honey chile, wake up," Lilly Ann said. Disoriented at first, the child stared wide-eyed at her, then pressed her forehead against the train window. "Grab you knapsack, and let's go chile."

"Yes 'um, I'm coming," Billie said, rolling her tongue around her mouth.

Lilly Ann straightened her dress over her slim, but curvy figure, and smoothed her finger-waved hair. The dress had been practically brand new when Miss Branford, one of her old employers, gave it to her.

Lilly Ann was used to turning heads everywhere she went. She was a smidge under five-feet ten inches tall, with long limbs and high cheekbones inherited from some distant and unknown Native American ancestor. You would think she owned the world the way she walked with her head held high. And that was her plan—that is, before Billie—but she hadn't given up on that dream entirely.

She gathered her beat-up old suitcase and an assortment of bags and boxes as best she could. "Here, Billie. Tote this," she said, pushing a worn paisley satchel toward the child.

"Yes, 'um," Billie said, suddenly wide awake and curiously looking around her new surroundings.

"Hurry up, hurry up! We gotta git off this train before it takes us clean to Philadelphia," Lilly Ann urged.

They hurried off the train and passed the porter, who tipped his hat. Lilly Ann felt his eyes following them as they departed and stood on the platform.

As the train picked up steam and started to chug out of the station, Lilly Ann suddenly remembered that she had forgotten to grab her hatbox. It contained a navy blue silk straw hat that had a matching navy blue silk ribbon circling the crown of the wide brim, and a rhinestone brooch where the two ends of the ribbon met.

"Oh no, no! I done left my navy blue silkstraw," Lilly Ann said as the train picked up speed. "That was for my weddin."

Not a good omen, she thought.

2

Gertrude Cunningham—Gertie, to most folks—sat on her porch, slowly rocking in her weatherworn chair and chewing reflectively on her corncob pipe. She wore a dirty, loose-fitting cotton print dress, with an equally dirty apron over it. Her hose were rolled up on her wizened bowlegs and knotted at her knees, and her gray hair hung in two braids over her shoulders. Her rheumy eyes were the color of her hair, and they sometimes appeared as cold as steel. Her eyes had chilled many to the bone when she chose to direct her steely gaze their way.

Some people thought she was blind, and others were frightened of her or called her a witch. But she had a gift. She knew it, and she used it. It was an innate ability to see into the souls of folk, to glean their true intentions, their real pain, their darkest secrets. What she had, others paid money to acquire—they were called psychologists and therapists—but the gift had just been dropped on her. She didn't know why, but she used it. It was, after all, God's way of helping her provide for herself. She did readings, handed out potions, and sometimes cast spells for a small fee. She personally didn't believe in those things, but she knew what she knew, and that people accepted her gift only when it was packaged with a gimmick.

As Gertie rocked, she thought about her granddaughter. "Gwine miss my baby," she said out loud. Sure, she'd miss her daughter, Lilly Ann, the youngest of her six children, but not like she'd miss Billie.

Billie had taken the monotony out of her days. They picked wild strawberries, chased the chickens, and made hoecake bread, and Billie's lines and squiggles on her notebook from the little one-room schoolhouse fascinated Gertie. She couldn't help Billie with her schoolwork, so she pretended to be busy bustling around the kitchen, but she silently prayed that the little girl did well and learned all she could. And besides, Billie was also another source of income. When Lilly Ann went on her trips up North, she often got some days' work and sent money home for Billie's care.

Gertie was shaken out of her reverie when she spotted Laura, her neighbor, coming through Mr. Blackshear's tobacco field and frantically waving like a semaphore flagman. Gertie acknowledged her by nodding, knowing full well that Laura could not see her head moving from that distance.

No need wasting any motion, she thought. *She be here soon enough with her usual greetin'.*

Sure enough, Laura approached the porch, dabbing her forehead and neck with a red-checkered gingham handkerchief. She also carried a small burlap sack that she gingerly rested against a porch support.

"Mornin', Miz Gertrude. How do you do this fine mornin'? Where's the lemonade?" Laura said in one breath.

"I be fine for an ol' lady, and the lemonade where it always be, Miz Laura."

"Mind if I have a glass?"

"No ma'am, and don't mind if I have one, too!"

The porch was at the back of the house, so Laura entered the kitchen and fetched freshly squeezed lemonade, which was already poured into two glasses, from Gertie's icebox. To the left of the door sat a wood-burning stove, and a small window overlooked the porch.

On the other side of the window were shelves full of Gertie's mysterious ingredients. Some she threw in various stews and soups, and others in concoctions for her clients. To the right of the door was a rough-hewn, small wooden table with four straw bottom chairs where the family took their meals, Billie did her homework, and Gertie received clients. In the far corner, opposite the table, sat Gertie's rocking chair, which she often pulled to the center of the room to catch the warmth of the pot-bellied stove that resided there. In the chill of the autumn and the cold of the winter, it was the focal point of all activity until everyone was snug in their beds. The far side of the kitchen led to a short hall. To the left was Gertie's room, and to the right was the room Lilly Ann and Billie had shared.

Backing out of the dilapidated screen door, Laura handed Gertie a glass of lemonade and sat down on a straw-bottomed chair next to her.

"Did Lilly Ann and Billie git off all right?"

"They did. Miss 'em already, 'specially Billie."

"Now, Gertie, don't be selfish. Billie needed to get away from here, and I know you don't begrudge Lilly Ann a husband."

"No, Laura, I don't, but I never met the man. Never even talked to him on the telephone contraption down at the general store. I did see a picture of him, but I didn't like what I saw. The marriage just ain't sittin' well with me. My spirit is restless 'bout it."

"What did you see? What do you think it is, Gertie?"

"Don't know … Ain't be revealed to me yet."

"Gertie, I know you not usually wrong 'bout these things, but maybe this—"

Gertie cut her off, not wanting to give voice and life to her fears. "Maybe you right. Just a mother not wantin' to let go."

Gertie was very troubled, and she knew Laura wanted to help put her mind at ease, but didn't know what to say. Gertie, after all, was the one with the third eye, but she couldn't put her finger on what was amiss in Baltimore. She glanced over at Laura, who patted her on the hand, and, for a moment, they sipped their lemonade in silence.

Laura broke the silence. "I'm sho' you'll figure it out and find a way to fix it. When you think 'bout it, you know James Hayes wasn't much of a choice, either. Besides, his daddy woulda cut him off if he had married Lilly Ann."

"You right, Laura. Won't no need to buy the cow anyway. He already had the milk. He was nice enough, I reckon, and quiet, but despite his daddy, he weren't about much."

Laura nodded without speaking and Gertie continued. "Lilly Ann never did talk much about James before she asked to take company with him. I didn't know she was already seein' him on the sly befo' she asked permission to bring him home. I took one look at the grown man, and dared her to see him again or I'd take a switch to her little fresh tail. Little good that did."

Gertie's third eye never revealed the time and place of their rendezvous.

After the two women had sat for a while longer, Laura started to take her leave when Gertie reminded her of her task. "Don't you have somethin' for me?"

"Almost forgot," Laura said. She picked up a burlap sack from its resting place and gingerly handed it to Gertie. "Your goose egg."

"Appreciate it," Gertie said as she carefully took the sack.

"I started to boil it, so I wouldn't break it, but I thought better of it."

"Boil it! Damn you, Laura. I ain't told you to boil my goose egg."

Laura laughed it off. "See, I knew it was a raw goose egg spell," she said as she headed down the steps, smiling. "See you in church tomorrow?"

Gertie grunted and waved a dismissive goodbye. After Laura took off toward the tobacco field, Gertie gathered her small, but spry, sixty-two-year-old frame and started for the screen door. She had to mix a potion for her first appointment of the day.

3

Billie was too busy absorbing the sights on Howard Street and catching the rhythm of Baltimore to notice her mother's distress. Now she knew why her mother came up North so often to look for work and to find a husband. It was an amazing place, with buildings so tall she couldn't see their tops, clanking trolley cars, scampering black motor cars, and people everywhere.

Mesmerized, Billie followed behind Lilly Ann, who, with bags and boxes falling, scurried to the colored taxi stand. "How could I leave my navy blue silkstraw?" Billie heard her mother moan as they climbed into a waiting cab.

The yellow cab made its way southward from Howard Street to an address on Clayton Street. Billie held her breath as the Baltimore landscape whizzed by. She had never seen houses—she guessed they were houses—so close together, some with porches and some with marble steps.

Billie didn't know why her mother was so worried about her hat. She had plenty of them. She loved hats, and spent every spare dime she could get on hats and clothes. That's why, according to Grandma Gertie, the old biddies at church called her mother that fresh-tail gal. But Grandma Gertie said the real reason was that their husbands, all devoted men, couldn't keep their eyes off of her mother.

Billie had heard that her mother was marrying an *old* man, but she wasn't sure what getting married meant. She just knew that there were some weddings at her church—she had never been to one—and that sometimes they weren't at church. Reb Barnes would go to a house, say some words in front of a small crowd, and the next thing you knew, two people who didn't live together before suddenly did. But then there were times when Reb Barnes wouldn't get there until after the living arrangements had changed. If her mother was getting married, Billie didn't know how she would accomplish it without Reb Barnes.

Billie had once heard that her mother was going to marry her father, James Hayes, but that didn't happen. Her father was *older*. Billie didn't know which was better: old or older.

She didn't know her father very well. She took her mother at her word when she said James Hayes was her father, even though she didn't have his last name, and he didn't come around much. But when he did, they sat on Grandma Gertie's steps, talking about nothing—sometimes they didn't talk at all—and watching the chickens strut across the dirt front yard. After several long periods of silence, he'd give her a nickel, brush his rawhide hat across his knee to remove some invisible particles, and rest it jauntily on his head. He'd mumble a farewell greeting and take off down the dirt road.

Billie didn't know to where; she'd never been to where he stayed. For all she knew, he might have vanished when he was out of her sight. But what she knew for sure was that he was five years *older* than her mother. She caught that in snatches of Grandma Gertie's conversation with Miz Laura.

Eavesdropping on old folks' conversation was one of Billie's pastimes. A quiet, precocious child, she processed all she surveyed, filtered it through her childish lens, bumped it against Grandma

Gertie's imparted wisdom, and came up with Billie Cunningham's Worldview.

As the taxi slowed, Billie felt the excitement rising, and she could hardly contain herself.

* * *

A few doors down from where the cab stopped, Thomas McNeal, Jr. sat on his marble steps in deep thought. He watched disinterestedly as the scene up the street unfolded. On Saturdays, he usually slipped out of the house early to roam the neighborhood with his younger brothers, David and John. Their ultimate goal was to stay out of sight of their father, Thomas Sr. But this morning, he hadn't felt like dealing with his brothers or having them tag along with him. So, he just sat on the front steps, melancholy, and lost in his own reflections.

His neighbor, Miss Wilma Taylor, had told him her sister and niece were coming to visit, and that she wanted him and his brothers to meet "little Billie." The last time he checked, a niece was a girl, and he had no use for girls. And Billie was a curious name for a girl.

But forgetting his own words, Tom's melancholia lifted a bit as a tall woman and a little girl stumbled out of the cab with boxes, bags, and a beat-up suitcase. He watched as the woman paid the taxi driver, and the girl looked up and down the street. Their eyes locked for an instant.

So that's the niece, Tom thought. *Looks like a regular girl. Who needs 'em? I don't. I got enough friends.*

Apparently, the Taylor household was waiting for the guests, because Tom heard squeals of laughter as they approached the front stoop. He went back to his thoughts.

* * *

"Oh, look at you, look at you!" Wilma Taylor cooed as she reached out to hug her sister. "We so glad you here. Come on in, come on in.

And this must be Billie," she said, nodding toward the little girl. "It's been a spell since I seed you honey. My, have you growed."

An ample woman, Wilma engulfed Billie with a bear hug while her husband, Larry, a tall man with friendly eyes and a warm grin, stood in the background and watched the goings-on. When it was his turn, Larry hugged Lilly Ann and patted Billie on the head.

Billie peered around Uncle Larry and saw a set of stairs. Standing at the top of them was a girl of about eleven, who glared down at Billie with her sturdy legs firmly planted and arms folded. Unperturbed, Billie took in the house. It was a small Baltimore row house, but it looked like a mansion to her with its three rooms and an upstairs. Later, she would find the best surprise of all: an indoor toilet.

"Carletha," Wilma called up the stairs. "Come on down here and met yo' cousin all the way from South Carolina."

"Yes ma'am," Carletha said as she stomped down the steps.

Billie knew what she would do if she wasn't in the presence of grown folks: *whup her ass*. But she wasn't sure of herself in her present situation. *Who does she think she is?* Billie wondered.

Suddenly, Carletha leaped over the last step and landed directly in front of Billie. Before a shocked Billie could react, Carletha bear-hugged her and slightly lifted her off the floor.

"Hello, country cousin. How do you do?"

Everyone laughed heartily.

Billy watched as her newfound cousin headed back up the stairs. "Bring your knapsack and come on upstairs. You're gonna share my room," Carletha boomed.

Share her room? Billie thought. *She has a room all her own?*

"Where do the white folks stay?" Billie asked, and Carletha doubled over with laughter.

Wilma and Larry chuckled to themselves.

As the girls disappeared into Carletha's room, Wilma turned to Lilly Ann and smiled. "Lil, you know where to put yo' things. Gone up and freshen up, and I'll fix you somethin' to eat. I know y'all hungry after that long ride."

"Indeed we are," Lilly Ann called over her shoulder as she took the stairs. "And guess what sister? I left my blue silkstraw on the train."

4

On Sunday, one week and a day after they arrived, Billie was to meet her new daddy-to-be, who was coming to dinner at Aunt Wilma's after church. Billie wasn't the least bit interested, but her mother was all atwitter.

Billie's week had been full of sensory overload. She was perfectly willing to give up unfettered access to open fields, familiar fauna, and flora growing wild, for things new and different. She missed the animals and walking barefoot in her grandmother's front yard, but her new surroundings had promise.

One day, she ran into three rough and tumble brothers down the street and was completely ignored. Carletha had introduced her to the two sisters across the street, but they were too prissy for Billie's taste. There were still more neighbors to meet, a park not too far away, and a general store in short walking distance from the house.

Billie was happy to be preoccupied because she couldn't quite put the grown folks' pieces together. She knew once her mother was married, they would live with her daddy-to-be—that is, Herbert Brown—but what would James Hayes be?

"Daddy-was," she chuckled to herself. *Daddy-never* was closer to the truth. She didn't know where her daddy-to-be lived, or where he worked, or even how he looked, but the fear of the unknown manifested itself into nonchalance.

Billie liked living in Aunt Wilma's house, and she had determined that they were rich, but her mother said they were "comfortable." In 1940's Baltimore, colored people who were laborers and maids made a decent living, she'd explained. Aunt Wilma cleaned houses, and Uncle Larry worked at Bethlehem Steel.

Then there was Carletha. She was a mystery and gave Billie pause for thought. Which Carletha was the real one? The arms-folded-stomping Carletha, or the hello-cousin-bear-hugging Carletha? As Grandma Gertie would say, "She bears watchin.'"

How Billie missed Grandma Gertie! They could walk through the backfield and discuss these weighty matters.

After church, Aunt Wilma and her mother donned aprons over their Sunday-go-to-meetin' clothes and headed straight for the kitchen. The grown folks stayed all gussied up waiting for dinner, while Billie and Carletha headed upstairs to change.

"You not going to put on that countrified jumper to meet your new daddy are you?" Carletha smugly asked as Billie fished a pinafore out of the closet.

Billie frowned. "You worry about what you gonna put on and leave me alone."

"I don't know why your momma don't buy you some new clothes."

"It ain't none of your business, and you need to shut up!"

"Momma says Aunt Lilly Ann ought to take some of that good money she spends on herself and spent it on you instead of gettin' Grandma Gertie to make your clothes, even if you do grow like a weed."

"You *and* your momma gossip too much!" Billie tapped her eyes, nose, and mouth with her fist, a silent threat to do bodily harm.

* * *

Lilly Ann Cunningham was, by all accounts, a beautiful woman. She bore striking features: high cheekbones, full, but not too full, lips, and piercing black eyes. She knew she was beautiful, and she carried herself with a poise and grace—some would call it haughtiness—that belied her station in life.

People made assumptions, generally erroneous, about her personality based on her physical appearance. It was inconceivable for some of them to believe that any woman who looked and carried herself the way she did could be anything other than stuck-up. The attitude they presumed she had, got her in trouble with her siblings and misunderstood by lots of people, mostly women.

But she was never at a loss for suitors. Though her older brothers watched her like a hawk, they weren't always around. They got married, moved North, or got drafted. At the tender age of fifteen, she found herself beguiled by a twenty-one year old suitor. At sixteen, she had Billie, and she was very careful not to make that mistake again. Not that she didn't love her daughter and didn't want the best for her; Billie just made her own goals a little harder to achieve. Men could wait.

Then along came Herbert Brown. She met him on one of her many trips to Baltimore to visit Wilma. She couldn't honestly say she was in love with him, but at age thirty-five, he had what her younger suitors didn't: a steady source of income and his own place.

Theirs had been a chance meeting. Mr. Branford, father of the family for whom Lilly Ann sometimes did domestic work when she was in Baltimore, had just dropped her off at her bus transfer point when the sky opened up. Fearing for her croquignole curls, Lilly Ann took refuge in the doorway of a barbershop.

A patron had excused himself as he brushed by her and headed out into the rain. Hearing the door open again, Lilly Ann moved slightly to the right to let the next man by, but instead, the man stopped beside her and spoke.

"Late spring rain. We can use it," the man had said, wiping his hands on his white smock.

"Yeah, a good soakin' rain, but I didn't want to get wet," Lilly Ann replied.

"Why don't you step inside until it lets up?"

Up to that point, Lilly Ann had been facing Edmondson Avenue, but when she turned to reply, she had come face-to-face with Herbert Brown. There was nothing particularly striking about him, or any pheromonal interplay, but his stare was engaging.

"Don't mind if I do," Lilly Ann had said. Herb held the door so she could step inside the shop.

The scene that ensued was the classic, Lilly Ann-just-walked-by reaction, with men momentarily freezing in place when they saw her. Females never entered this venerable, male inner sanctum, and if they did, they were never as strikingly beautiful.

As quickly as it had begun, the rain stopped. Lilly Ann took her leave, thanking Herb as she departed.

"My pleasure," Herb said, escorting her to the door. "You brought sunshine to my shop."

With false modesty, Lilly Ann had smiled, lowered her head, and whispered, "Thank you," before heading for the bus stop.

A couple of days later, and not so modestly, Lilly Ann got off her bus and slowly strolled past the barbershop before going into the grocery store next door.

"Can I help you?" the clerk asked.

"Yes," she responded while positioning herself to keep an eye on the door. "I'll take an RC Cola and a bag of chips." She took her purchase and sashayed back to the bus stop, but she did not see the barber.

Finally, after her third visit to the grocery store, the barber stepped out and stood on his stoop, smoking.

As Lilly Ann approached, he said, "Why, if it ain't the sunshine lady!"

"Good Morning. Just call me Lilly Ann."

"Lilly Ann," he said, extending his hand. "Just call me Herb."

"Herb, please to meet you. Gotta get to my bus. Beautiful day though, ain't it?"

"That it is, that it is," Herb said with an approving eye.

She gave him a toodle-doo wave and headed for the bus stop, basking in the knowledge that Herb appreciated what he saw.

On the next couple of visits, the grocery clerk would disappear into the back of the store, and, within a few seconds, Herb would coincidently enter the store. After these accidental meetings, Herb asked Lilly Ann out and she had graciously accepted.

* * *

At exactly three o'clock, the Taylor's doorbell chimed. Lilly Ann went to answer it, with Billie close behind and Wilma and Larry pulling up the rear. Unperturbed, Carletha had already taken her place at the children's table in the kitchen.

"Oh, Herb. Come in, come in," Lilly Ann said as she opened the front door.

"Good afternoon, Lilly Ann," Herb replied. He removed his hat and stepped into the vestibule. He took a quick peek around her and hurriedly kissed her on the cheek.

Once in the living room, Lilly Ann made introductions all around. "Herb, this is my sister, Wilma," she said, pointing to her sister. "And her husband, Larry."

Herb extended his right hand to Wilma and covered her right hand with his left. "A pleasure to meet you, ma'am," he said, shaking her hand.

"Oh, the pleasure is all mine. Welcome to our house."

Then Herb extended his right hand to Larry, and they grasped each other at the elbow. "Pleasure to meet you too, sir," the charming Herb said.

"Mine too, mine too," Larry replied with a big grin. "Come on in son. Make yo' self at home."

"And this," Lilly Ann said as she stepped aside with a fling of her arm, "is Billie."

As Billie moved from the safety of her mother's dress, she extended her hand. While the grown folks were exchanging greetings, she had taken in her daddy-to-be. He was barely taller than her mother, and neither good-looking nor ugly. He wore his hair in the slick, pasted down fashion of the day. His pointed-toe shoes were spit-shined, and his suit was pressed to perfection.

"How you do, sir?" Billie asked in her most polite voice.

Instead of taking her hand, Herbert swooped her up and planted a kiss on her cheek. "We gonna be family, girl. No hand shakin' for us."

The grown-ups laughed, but Billie did not find the humor. For some strange reason, she thought of Grandma Gertie.

* * *

It was about three-thirty when Gertrude Cunningham walked her only client of the day to the door and began to settle in for the rest of the afternoon. She really didn't like seeing clients on Sunday.

"My Lawd, that Brenda Mae Johnson is a dumb heifer," she mumbled to herself. "How many ways do that old man of hers have to cheat 'fore she wake up and see the light? I ain't got no potions for stupid! If I did, they'd be wasted on her," she laughed.

It was a hot August afternoon, but as she made hoecake bread for her dinner, she thought about Billie and got a cold chill.

* * *

After planting Billie back on her feet, Herb had put his arms around her mother's waist and kissed her on the cheek. Billie was immediately uncomfortable. She had never seen a man touch her mother in such a way and was put off by it. In fact, she had never thought of her mother as an affectionate person. She was mother with a capital "M."

There was an invisible line between them that Billie did not cross. Not for hugs or kisses, or boo-boo soothing, or bedtime stories. Those she got from Grandma Gertie. Her mother set rules, gave instructions, and set parameters for her life, but she was not intimately involved in it.

"Herb," Uncle Larry began after the round of greetings, "maybe you'd like to freshen up 'fore dinner. Bathroom is left at the top of the stairs."

"Don't mind if I do, sir," Herb replied and headed up the stairs.

Billie watched her mother and aunt exchange glances and hug their bodies, slightly rocking from side-to-side, faces scrunched up as they grinned in silent, girlish glee. Billie headed for the kitchen.

"What's takin' y'all so long?" an impatient and hungry Carletha asked when Billie came into the kitchen.

"Don't ask me. I ain't got nothin' to do with it," Billie retorted as she took her seat across from Carletha at the small kitchen table.

The dining room was big enough to accommodate all of them, but the girls were relegated to the kitchen so as not to interfere with grown folks' business. Despite that, Billie made sure she positioned herself so that she could eavesdrop and spy on the goings-on.

The dining room table, set with all the trappings of a southern Sunday dinner, reminded Billie of church socials back home. There was plenty of hot fried gospel bird, a steaming bowl of collard greens with ham hocks, gooey macaroni and cheese, candied yams, steamed rice, and Aunt Wilma's famous yeast rolls.

"My, my, this sho do look and smell good," Herb said as Uncle Larry showed him to his place at the table.

"Hope it tastes as good as it look and smell," Aunt Wilma chimed in with false modesty. "I couldn't decide whether to make rolls or corn bread. I hope—"

"Oh now, Wilma," Billie's mother said, cutting her off. "You know this is just fine."

Aunt Wilma smiled and dropped her head.

"Aw y'all, please come on!" Billie heard Carletha mumble under her breath as she swung her right foot to kick the leg of the kitchen table.

"Bow yo' heads girls, while we say grace," Uncle Larry called from the dining room. "Gracious Lawd, make us truly thankful for the food we 'bout to eat for the nourishment of our bodies. And thank you for the hands that prepared it. In Jesus name ..." Uncle Larry paused so they could all chorus, "Amen." Then he summoned the girls. "Billie, Carletha. Come on in here to get your plates."

"'Bout time," Carletha whispered as she got up.

One day she's gwine git hers, Billie thought. *Grandma Gertie would whup her ass.*

As Billie waited for Aunt Wilma to fix her food, she stole a quick glance at her mother and Herb, and watched Herb as he piled a little of everything onto his plate.

"Miz Wilma, I ain't had a meal this good since I left home," Herb said.

"Now Herb, you flatter, but thank you and call me Wilma. Like you said, we gwine be family."

"Yes, ma'am. I hope your sister can cook like this!"

Everyone laughed, but Billie rolled her eyes and followed Carletha back to the kitchen. "I think Grandma Gertie would say Herb is as full of stuff as a Christmas turkey," Billie said as she sat down.

Carletha looked like she wasn't quite sure what that meant, but she nodded her head in agreement anyway. They were quiet for the rest of the meal, trying to hear what was being discussed in the dining room.

* * *

Herb expected to be grilled—after all he was marrying into the family—and it started before he could hardly get a morsel down.

"Herb," Larry began tentatively. "What you do for a living?"

"Aw Larry, mind yo' manners," said Wilma. "It ain't polite to—"

Herb watched Larry hold up his hand to silence Wilma. "I jest wanted to know what he do so I can get a job there and buy me a sharp suit of clothes like the ones he got on. No offense."

The women smiled nervously while a laughing Herb responded, "No offense taken. Me and my brother own a barber shop and grocery store on Edmondson Avenue."

Amused, Herb watched the expression on their faces. Wilma and Larry raised their eyebrows but said nothing, and Lilly Ann unsuccessfully tried to conceal her delight. Herb was accustomed to these reactions, so he volunteered, "My brother Leon saved up a lot of money when he was in the Army, so we—he—invested in the businesses. He supplied the capital, and I supply the labor and the smarts."

By this time, Herb had taken on a slightly arrogant tone. With a slight twist of his head, he could see into the kitchen, and he was almost positive that the look on Billie's face was a smirk.

* * *

After dinner, the girls quickly scraped their plates so they could head outside.

"Told you he was full of stuff," Billie whispered as she sat her dishes in the sink.

"Uh huh," Carletha nodded. She drained her glass of sweet tea and followed Billie through the dining room and out the front door.

Generally, certain activities were restricted on Sundays. No stepball, Mother-May-I, Hot Butterbeans, or the like, but this was a special day and the girls were left to their own devices. They ran down the street, where Thomas, John, and David—the McNeal brothers—had congregated. Too curious to ignore Billie for very long, and tired of Carletha's badgering, they had let Billie into their circle.

* * *

Larry and Herb chatted in the living room while Wilma and Lilly Ann did the dishes.

"Whatcha' think, sister?" Lilly Ann prodded Wilma.

"He certainly is a fine lookin' man, and so mannerly."

"Come on, Wilma. What do you really think?"

"I think you could do worse. And you better reel this one in, but keep yo' dress down 'til you git him."

"I already got him! You just had to say that, didn't you?" Lilly Ann hissed through clenched teeth. She tossed the dish towel she was holding on the table and stormed out of the kitchen and into the living room.

"'Cuse me, Larry," Lilly Ann said as she grabbed Herb's hand and pulled him from the sofa. "Herb and I gwine to take a walk, if you don't mind."

"Ah sure, sure," Larry said as a puzzled Herb got to his feet.

"'Cuse me for a minute, Larry ..." Herb's voice trailed off as a seething Lilly Ann led him out of the front door.

Taking her hand as they headed down the block, a concerned and perplexed Herb asked, "What's wrong, baby girl?"

"Nothin.' Sometimes two women just can't be in the same kitchen, 'specially if one's yo self-righteous older sister."

"Was it somethin' I said?"

"No, no," Lilly Ann said, momentarily resting her head on Herb's shoulder. She hadn't given any thought to where they were walking and found herself headed toward Woodley Park.

* * *

Tom and Billie were in a conversation about marbles when she noticed her mother and Herb approaching. Her brain screamed, *Take yo' hands off my mother! Take yo' hands off my mother!*

Billie had no idea where the thoughts came from, but she knew they were ones she would never ever verbalize. She had no business in grown folks' business.

"Don't y'all leave the block," her mother called over her shoulder as she and Herb strolled by.

As the children watched the couple continue their walk, the McNeals' screen door flew open and the boys jumped to attention as if they were shot out of a cannon. A man, still in his pajamas late in the afternoon, stood barefoot in the doorway and barked, "What y'all doin' out here?"

Before the boys could chorus, "Nothin' daddy," the man abruptly turned and went back in the house, slamming the screen door. The boys were visibly shaken, while Carletha was defiant, and Billie wild-eyed.

"W-who was that?" Billie stammered.

"That's they crazy daddy," Carletha whispered in Billie's ear as she grabbed her cousin's dress sleeve and pulled her up the street.

* * *

Larry walked into the kitchen with a scowl on his face and accosted Wilma as she prepared to do the dinner dishes.

"What was that all about?" Larry asked. He was usually unflappable, but his second tenor voice had risen a couple of decibels above normal.

"Oh, nothing. Just girl ta—"

"Don't tell me nothin," Larry said, tightening his jaw muscles. "What did you say to Lilly Ann?"

"If you must know …"

"Yes, I must know!"

"I jest told her not to let this one get away."

"And?"

"You know how they talk about her down home, and call her the fresh tail—"

"You don't call your sister what those jealous biddies down home call her. Lilly Ann ain't the first young girl to make a mistake. I don't wanna hear you talk to your sister or about your sister like that nary another time! Do I make myself clear?"

Stunned speechless, Wilma nervously twisted the dishcloth. *What got into him?* she thought. Larry had never spoken to her in such a tone. Angry and hurt, Wilma started to speak, but she was preempted by Larry's staccato interrogative.

"*Do you understand?*" he yelled.

"Yes, yes," Wilma mumbled as she brushed past him and retreated to the stairs, heading for her bedroom.

* * *

Billie and Carletha entered the house to find Uncle Larry standing in the kitchen doorway, shaking his head as Aunt Wilma fled up the stairs as fast as her chubby legs would allow.

Carletha looked taken aback. "Momma and Daddy sure look mad with each other about somethin.' That's somethin' I ain't used to, and I don't like it!"

Billie didn't know what to make of any of it. She just knew she'd seen enough upset grown folks for one day.

5

1948

Larry had watched as plans for the wedding, scheduled for a month after the dinner at his house, became a bone of contention for the betrothed. Lilly Ann and Wilma were set on a small wedding at church after Sunday Service. Herb, who had not been in a church for decades, swore he would be struck by lightning if he entered one. He was adamantly opposed to a church wedding, and courthouse nuptials suited him just fine.

Larry was not surprised that Lilly Ann was the first to yield, with Wilma's words echoing in her head. It was ultimately decided that the wedding would take place in the Taylor's living room on Sunday, September 12, 1948.

Larry knew Wilma consoled herself with the mistaken notion that once married, the family's religious habits would automatically rub off on Herb. Larry had no such illusion, but he kept it to himself. He liked Herb well enough to overlook this chink in his armor, even though there was something about Herb that he couldn't put his finger on. *But the upside,* Larry thought, *is that Lilly Ann might be one of Wilma's relatives I won't have to help support at some point in her life.*

The Taylor household was a temporary refuge for family members in need of a hand-up. Larry was a good man with a kind heart, and he did not mind it, but it did get old.

* * *

Saturday, the day before the wedding, was filled with a strange atmosphere. It rained, but it did not dampen the spirits of at least two people: Lilly Ann and Wilma. Larry watched the woman busily decorating and rearranging the house to accommodate the small number of expected guests. He thought the courting had resulted in marriage a little too soon, but he said nothing and tried to stay out of the way except when he was called to do heavy lifting—furniture, that is. His mood was something else.

* * *

Tired of hearing about the wedding for the last month, a bored Billie stared out of the kitchen window, watching the rain and taking in the panoramic view clear down to Woodley Park. She wished she could be there running free. Failing that, she thought about getting back to school after the weekend.

She could hardly wait. Her first week had been delightful. There were so many children, at least in comparison to back home, and so many teachers. And books she couldn't wait to get her hands on. And if that wasn't enough, she had five new dresses with socks and ribbons to match, sent to her by her daddy's sister. *Imagine that*, she thought. *I don't even know her.*

She was going to stay with Carletha until her mother and Herb returned from their honeymoon. She had no idea what a honeymoon was, and she wasn't sure who to ask about it or whether she should ask anybody. Tom was smart about grown-up things, so she thought she might ask him.

Billie continued to watch the rain. It was a soft, gentle rain that some might have found soothing, but for some inexplicable reason, rain up North made Billie uneasy. When she was outside and attempted to cross the street, she could see her reflection in the shining wet asphalt and felt like she would fall in. She knew it didn't make sense, but when the street was wet, she ran zigzag across it to prevent being sucked in.

* * *

Back in South Carolina on that same Saturday afternoon, Gertie wandered aimlessly around her tiny shack of a house. It was an unsettling day. Her spirit was troubled, and she was disappointed that she couldn't make the trip to Baltimore for the wedding. But on Friday, Laura had taken her to the general store. She called Lilly Ann and gave her daughter her blessing, and had briefly spoken to Billie, which made her heart sing.

Later that night, her sleep was disturbed by an Incubus, the mythical demon believed to assault sleeping women. It ignited passions that were not yet dead in her, and rode her until she moaned and gyrated in ecstasy. Spent, she started to sink deeper into the stages of sleep when she began mumbling and flailing her arms.

"No, no, leave me be," she mumbled as she fought off the invisible thing. "No, no, not tonight."

Suddenly, zombie-like, Gertie rose from her bed and walked barefoot through the kitchen and out the door through the tobacco field. From the recesses of her diaphragm came a lament reminiscent of the call and response of a slave song. But when the notes took flight, they echoed back the sorrowful chant of dead Native American spirits. Bent over from the waist and hopping from one foot to the other, Gertie danced around in a circle for several minutes.

As the trance state started to dissipate, she shivered in the light rain that had begun to fall. Though the night was pitch black, she easily made her way back to the house on a well-worn trail carved by many nights of tortured sleep. Tortured sleep put her on notice to beware. Tortured sleep confounded her mind and vexed her soul. Pray or chant? Prayer or potions? Heaven or Hell?

Gertie climbed the stairs to the porch, walked into the kitchen, wiped her feet on the goose-egg burlap bag that had never been moved, and fell, exhausted into bed. She stayed there most of Sunday listening to Mahalia Jackson on the phonograph.

Didn't it rain, chirrun
Talkin' bout rained
Oh, my Lord
Didn't it
Didn't it
Didn't it oh, oh my Lord
Didn't it rain?

* * *

The wedding was held on Sunday, and attended by a few church members, a couple of neighbors, Herb's brother, and two of their patrons with their wives. Even Tom's mother and father were among the guests.

Billie and Carletha made sure they cut a wide path around Mr. McNeal. Mrs. McNeal, a petite, timid woman, had offended her families' high-brow sensibilities by marrying the likes of Thomas McNeal, Sr. It was from her that Tom Jr. had acquired a modicum of refinement, but it rarely surfaced, concealed by the seething anger that festered beneath his young exterior.

So this is a wedding, Billie thought as she listened closely to the preacher's words. Her mother was beautiful. She wore a navy blue, mid-length silk shantung dress that had a wide belt encircling her narrow waist. The form-fitting dress had a wide, standup collar that was lined with a white ruffle that ended in a "V" at the décolletage, and she wore white lace gloves on her hands. In her hair, absent the blue silkstraw hat, she wore a white gardenia in the style of her idol, Billie Holiday.

"I pronounce you man and wife. You may salute your bride," Billie heard the preacher say. Then she watched in horror as Herb kissed her mother squarely on the lips, contrary to the reaction of the guests who clapped and giggled. In that instant, she knew her relationship with her mother would be forever changed. The invisible line widened.

While the adults kissed her mother and pumped Herb's hand, Billie grabbed a small plate of potato salad, turkey, and ham, and headed down the street looking for Tom. Carletha was nowhere to be found, so Billie left without her.

Tom was perched on the steps, biting his nails and looking furtively up the street.

"Tom, I brung you some food."

"Brought. Brought me some food."

"Brought? Anyway, here," Billie said, pushing the plate toward him. "You can stop eatin' your fingernails now. What's wrong?"

"Nothin'," Tom said defensively.

"Well …" She knew something was wrong, but she had more pressing matters to discuss. "Well, the weddin's over. Now they gwine on a honeymoon."

"Going. Going, not—"

"Okay, I know, I know. But I don't have time to think about the right way to say it. This ain't school," Billie said defiantly, putting her hands on her hips. "What's a honeymoon?"

"Now your mother is Mrs. Brown, and they'll go off someplace for a vacation and get to know each other."

"They already know each other."

"Yeah, but they get to know each other better," Tom mused.

"What y'all talkin' about?" Carletha quipped as she rounded the corner, disheveled and coming from who-knows-where.

"Nothin'," Billie and Tom chorused.

"Is your father serving liquor up there?" Tom asked, nodding up the street.

"*My father?* Deacon Larry Cornelius Taylor?" Carletha asked incredulously. "Hell no!" she said as she skipped and twirled up the street toward the house.

Tom and Billie exchanged disapproving glances and sat quietly for a while, lost in their individual thoughts.

* * *

The thought of his father getting drunk tied Tom's stomach in knots as he recalled the unpleasant experience of Saturday night. It was an all too familiar scene.

He and his younger brothers, David and John, had cowered in the corner of their tiny darkened bedroom. The two younger boys stooped in the corner facing each other, while Tom, with his back to them, stretched his arms behind his body to shield the boys. Crippling fear froze them in this position almost every Saturday night.

Instinctively, Tom was willing to sacrifice himself for his brothers. But there was really no need. Even though their father scared the brothers until they peed in their pants, he never touched the younger ones. Tom was always the object of his drunken tirades. He was big for ten, but not big enough to protect himself, his brothers, or his mother from the darkness that fell over his father when he had been drinking.

"Little Tom!"

He hated being called that.

"Git yo' ass over here!" his father had demanded as he burst through the door of the tiny room.

As Tom had half-crawled, half-walked to obey his father's command, he thought about his mother. He felt sorry for her and hated her at the same time. At that very moment, she was probably laying in a battered and bruised heap on the kitchen floor, or worse, tearfully shaking as she fixed his father's dinner.

Why doesn't she help us? Why doesn't she run away and take us to Grandma? He always asked himself these questions, and just as the belt had assailed him, he took himself away to the exotic places he saw in books at the library. He became oblivious to the pain and refused to cry. This only fanned the fire of his father's drunken demons, but luckily, his father's energy was spent quickly and he had passed out, exhausted by his all-consuming rage. Otherwise, buff from stevedoring at the Baltimore shipyard, he could have killed them.

The shrill sound of somebody calling Billie brought Tom crashing back to reality.

* * *

"Billie, Billie, come on here," someone called from up the street.

"Yes 'um, I'm comin.'"

Billie bade Tom goodbye and headed for the sound of the voice. When she reached the porch of Aunt Wilma's house, her mother and Herb were standing there, beaming, with suitcases nearby.

"Billie, me and your daddy are about to leave for our honeymoon."

My daddy's here? Billie thought. *Oh, she means Herbert Brown. I hope he don't think he's my daddy.*

"I want you to mind Aunt Wilma and Uncle Larry 'til we git back," her mother said.

Billie stole a quick glance at Carletha and rolled her eyes as Carletha tapped her chest and mouthed, "*And me too.*"

"Yes 'um," Billie replied, looking down at her feet.

"She'll be jest fine," Aunt Wilma chimed, putting her arm around Billie's shoulder.

Billie was used to her mother leaving her from time to time, but she generally spent those absences with Grandma Gertie. She loved Aunt Wilma and Uncle Larry, and being at their house, and she was sure they loved her. She knew she'd be fine, but she hoped Carletha did not push her to show her other side. Little did Carletha know, she could, and would, *whup her ass.*

When her mother bent down to kiss her goodbye, Billie asked, "Momma, what's a honeymoon?"

Herb patted Billie on the shoulder as he picked up the suitcases. "It's a trip where me and yo' mother git to know one another," he said with a wink. The other adults laughed.

So, Billie thought, *Tom was right.*

6

The day after the wedding, all anxiety and curiosity about it was forgotten, and Billie and Carletha found themselves back into their regular routine.

"Come on, Carletha. Come on," Billie impatiently called as she headed out the door for school.

"Hold yo horses. I'm comin.' I git tired of you rushin' me to school every day," Carletha said, smashing the last piece of toast in her mouth.

"Then you need to be on time," Billie replied as she skipped down the steps.

Billie saw the McNeal boys up ahead, but she knew better than to try to catch up to them. Surprisingly, she and Tom had become good friends in a very short time, but she knew he would rather be dead than be seen walking to school with girls. And definitely not at recess. He completely ignored her on the playground.

In the time that Billie had attended Public School #110, she was thriving. When her mother went to enroll her, the counselor had mistakenly assumed Billie's southern accent was indicative of a slow mind, but she was quickly disabused of the notion. Billie was more advanced than the average students on her grade level, and she was on par with the handful that was considered advanced.

As had become their daily custom, once at school, the girls did a silent Miss Mary Mack, wordlessly smacking hands and clapping. Then they went to their respective classrooms: Billie to the second, and Carletha to the fifth.

* * *

Oddly, it was November, two months after the wedding, before Billie actually transitioned to the apartment where her mother and Herb lived. Prior to that, the subject never really came up. Billie was not eager to leave the house on Clayton Street, and the occupants were not inconvenienced by her presence. Her mother visited, but she had never insisted on taking her home until the day she stopped by after work, and Billie showed her that Aunt Wilma had packed her things in a valise and left them at the front door. Luckily for Billie, Herb's house was also in walking distance of her school, so she would not have to transfer. P.S. #110 was between the two residences, near Lexington and Payson.

To Billie's disappointment though, Herb's house was not a house at all, but something called an apartment. It was over a shoe repair shop in a building next to an alley on Bryson Street. The front of the shop faced Bryson, but the entry was on the side of the building facing the alley. From the alley, Billie entered a small foyer, and the shoe shop was straight ahead. To the right was a long flight of stairs that led to the apartment. At the top of the stairs, a door on the left opened into a hallway that led to all the rooms in the apartment.

The apartment was longer than it was wide. Once inside the door, a few steps to the left led to a small living room, which was the width of the narrow building. Along the hallway to the right were two bedrooms and a bathroom. At the end of the hall was the kitchen, which was also the width of the building and parallel to the living room. Billie took some small comfort in knowing she would have her own room.

Most days, Billie walked home with Carletha and waited there until her mother or Herb came to walk her home after work so she wouldn't have to let herself into the apartment and stay by herself. When her mother walked her home, they held hands, but didn't talk much. When Herb walked her home, they didn't hold hands, and she had to practically run to keep up with his long strides. But he talked incessantly and told her funny stories.

Eventually, she was directed to go straight home every day because increasingly, she and Carletha did not "set horses," an expression Grandma Gertie used when people couldn't get along. When Billie and Carletha weren't sniping at one another, they were making Carletha-led mischief: going to Woodley Park after school instead of going straight home, opening backyard gates so that neighborhood dogs escaped, and taking three penny-candies from the corner store while only paying for two.

Now, after school, Billie and Carletha walked one block west together, then went in opposite directions home.

* * *

Today was the day Billie decided she would give somebody the what-for because of all the teasing she had endured at the hands of some of her schoolmates. She had tried to exercise Grandma Gertie's turn-the-other-cheek philosophy, but that had gotten her nowhere and served to infuriate Carletha, who was willing and able to take them all on in defense of her country cousin.

Billie chose her victim with care. One of the prissy girls would be an empty victory. A boy her size might be risky, but a smaller boy would work. Beating up a boy, no matter what his size, would quiet the taunters. And she was smart enough to stage her attack away from school grounds.

The school bell promptly rang at three, and a raucous bunch of children flung themselves out of the school's front door and dispersed in every direction. Billie quickly ran a block toward a red maple tree, dropped her books and coat, and took her position behind the tree. An unsuspecting Carletha milled around the front of the school, waiting for Billie.

As a group of boys passed, Billie circled the tree and immediately jumped on Leroy Ellis' back, knocking him to the ground. With her right arm wound tightly around his neck, she yelled in his ear.

"What you call me boy? What you call me?"

"Git off me, girl!"

Billie yelled the question again. "I said, what you call me?"

"And I said git—"

Before he could finish, Billie tightened the hold on his neck. By this time, a crowd had begun to gather and laugh at poor Leroy. This fit Billie's game plan to a tee. She was firmly on his back, like roping a calf, and he could not move her. To avoid further embarrassment, Leroy acquiesced.

"I ain't called you nothing. Now git up off me girl before I hurt you."

"That's what I thought! You ain't call me nothing, and you bet not call me nothin,' or I'll whup your ass," Billie said as she let him up. "Yourn and anybody else's. It'll be a country ass whupping, too!"

"You heard my cousin," Carletha shouted, breaking through the crowd.

A defiant Leroy stared at Carletha, who stood in front of him, arms akimbo. He must have thought better of challenging her because she was older and bigger. Billie knew he did not want to chance any more embarrassment. Besides, Billie saw Tom McNeal gathering her books and coat and figured Leroy must have realized they were friends. He certainly wouldn't want to tangle with Tom.

"Now I know we're blood!" Carletha said, slapping Billie on the back as she adjusted her dress and discovered that one of the sashes had gotten ripped off in the fight. She was famous for coming home with one sash in her hand and one hanging from the side of the dress.

Billie said nothing, but her heart was smiling as she took her things from Tom.

"Didn't expect that out of you. Carletha, yeah, but not you," Tom said, relinquishing the books.

"I was tired of being called country and other stuff," Billie said as the trio left for home.

"Okay, okay, I understand. Can't let people walk all over you. I'm just surprised is all." Then she heard Tom whisper under his breath, "I wish Momma would stand up for herself."

They came to the point where they had to go their separate ways, and they said their goodbyes. Billie continued on alone and briskly walked in the November chill. Reaching her destination, she quickly ran up the long flight of stairs to the apartment. When she reached the top, she started to feel around her neck.

"Oh no," Billie whispered, feeling for the key she normally wore on a shoestring.

"Oh no," she repeated, frantically searching herself for the missing key. After a minute, in her mind's eye, she could see the key hanging from the bathroom doorknob. She breathed a sigh of relief.

"At least I didn't lose it," she said as she walked back to the bottom of the steps. She decided to sit there since there was no light at the top of the staircase.

As she sat, hoping that her mother or Herb would show up soon, Red, the shoemaker's helper, came out of the shop and walked to the steps. He rested his right foot on the third step where Billie sat, unladylike, and he leaned on his elbow so that his face was directly opposite Billie's.

"Billie, is it?" His breath smelled of stale cigarettes.

"Yes … yes, sir," she said as she tilted her head back to avoid his foul-smelling mouth.

"Watcha doin' sittin' on the steps?"

Billie hesitantly replied, "Waiting for my parents."

"You mean your mother and what's his name—Herbert? Yeah, Herbert."

"Yes sir," she said, nodding vigorously as if that would ensure their imminent appearance.

"Okay, guess they'll be along directly."

Without warning, he reached under Billie's coat and dress and patted her on the underside of her thigh. As quickly as he had done it, he went back into the shop.

Shocked and frightened, Billie retreated up the steps backwards on her butt. Ten minutes later, she was ecstatic to hear Herb's footsteps taking the stairs two at a time. Not expecting to encounter anybody on the stairway, Herb jumped when he made out Billie's form.

"Holy shi …" he started. "Girl, you scared ten years off my life. Why you sittin' on the steps?"

"Forgot my key."

"Forgot it or lost it?"

"Forgot it."

"How can you be so sure?"

"I know where I l-l-left it," Billie stammered.

"If you know where you left it, why did you leave it?"

She didn't have the energy to try to explain to him. All she wanted was to be alone in her room. Besides, she knew he was trying to trick her with word games the way he always did.

"Well?" Herb asked as he let her into the apartment.

Heart pounding, Billie said nothing and prayed as she went straight to the bathroom, hoping to find the key on the doorknob.

"See, here it is!" she called to Herb, who had gone into the kitchen for a glass of water. "I told you so," was on the tip of her tongue, but she thought better of it.

"So it is, so it is. You need to be mo' careful, little girl. Suppose you had lost it? Somebody coulda found it and come in here and took all we got," he said to her as she walked into the kitchen.

"But I didn't lose it, and if I did, how would somebody know which house …" She stopped, realizing she was back-talking a grown up. She turned and headed for her room.

"I'll let yo' momma figure out yo' punishment," Herb called after her retreating back.

In the privacy of her room, Billie poked her tongue out at Herb, the embarrassment of the invasion of her person by the shoemaker's helper temporarily forgotten in the lost key drama.

* * *

It was Friday night, and to his credit, Herb had started dinner. In fact, cooking didn't seem to bother him. By the time Lilly Ann got home, the fish was fried and the cabbage and cornbread were done.

"Hi, I'm home," Lilly Ann cheerily called as she came into the apartment. "Somethin' smells mighty good." She poked her head into Billie's room, blew her a kiss, and headed for the kitchen.

"Hey handsome, whatcha doin' in here?" Lilly Ann sing-songed.

"Hey, baby girl," Herb said, circling Lilly Ann's waist as she kissed him. "Gone get ready for dinner so we can eat whilst it's hot."

"Um, can't wait," Lilly Ann said as she went to the bathroom to wash her hands.

"You think we can leave Billie wid yo' sister while we go celebrate tonight?" Herb called after her.

"Oh yeah, I already asked Wilma. It's all right. I told her we won't be long."

"Maybe *you* won't be long, but I intend to be out all night!"

* * *

Overhearing the conversation, Billie was not at all concerned about where they were going or why they were going, especially since she would get to spend the night at her Aunt Wilma's. She hurried to the kitchen and took her seat.

Once they were all seated, Herb mumbled a grace and passed the rice. He stared at Billie but addressed her mother. "Lilly Ann, Billie left her key this morning. Left it on the bathroom door. That's gettin' pretty careless to me. You need to punish her."

"At least I didn't lose it. I just forgot it," Billie faltered.

"Told you about back-talking," he said, pointing a finger at Billie. She dropped her head.

"I told you about rollin' your eyes, little girl," her mother added. "Billie, you got to be more careful. Suppose Herb and me were going to be late gettin' home? You'd have to sit on the steps in the dark and the cold. You too old to be so careless!"

Here it comes, Billie thought.

"You do the dishes tonight," her mother continued. "Then go to your room and pack an overnight bag. I'm gonna let you slide this time 'cause I'm too excited about tonight, but you better not let it happen again! You hear me?"

"Yes, ma'am," Billie replied in disbelief. *No punishment? Tonight must be the Rapture!*

* * *

Later that night, Billie lay awake in bed at the Taylor's and thought about the incident at the bottom of the steps. *What grown-up can I go to to tell on another grown-up?* She was supposed to be seen and not heard. *Anyway, how would I explain it?*

To further complicate the matter, she was ambivalent about whether it was bad or not. *But it did not feel right. If Grandma Gertie was here, I could talk to her about it.*

* * *

Although it was not necessary, Larry got up early on Saturday morning to walk Billie home. It was a time when little thought was given to letting young children walk the streets alone in their own neighborhoods. They were safe, for the most part. But Larry was an early riser, and he wanted to see the child safely deposited on her own doorstep. Besides, he was going to the barbershop anyway.

Since Lilly Ann married Herb, he had switched barbers, a hard decision not made lightly. Herb's patrons were generally younger, talked about things he knew nothing about, and used words that had no meaning to him. Some of them were even jazz musicians, a lot he did not think much of, but being a genuinely warm person and a Christian man, he exchanged pleasantries and did not criticize or condescend.

Because Larry was not planning to return directly home, Carletha was left out of the equation. That, and the fact that she had to get her hair *fried*, a grueling, multi-hour Saturday ritual.

As Larry and Billie ascended the steps to her apartment, they caught snatches of a rich alto voice singing Mahalia Jackson's "How I Got Over." Captivated, they paused to take it in.

"How I got over ... How did I make it over? ... You know my soul look back and wonder ... How did I make it over? ... How I made it over ... Coming on over all these years ... You know my soul look back and wonder ... How did I make it over?

"Tell me how we got over, Lord ... Had a mighty hard time ... Coming on over ... You know my soul look back and wonder ... How did we make it over? ... Tell me how we got over Lord ... I'm falling and rising all these years ... But you know my soul look aback and wonder ... How I got over ..."

"That's your momma," Larry told Billie with a smile on his lips and a mist in his eyes. He gingerly knocked on the door, waited, then knocked more loudly.

Billie produced her key and let them in. They walked toward the kitchen, where Lilly Ann was busy washing breakfast dishes.

"Um um." Larry softly cleared his throat so as not to startle Lilly Ann.

Without hesitation, Billie ran and threw herself against her mother, wrapping her arms around her legs. Lilly Ann jumped slightly, turned around, and uncharacteristically kissed Billie on the forehead.

"Oh, little girl. Good Mornin,'" Lilly Ann said with a lilting laugh.

"My, my, Lilly Ann," Larry said. "It's been many a year since I heard you sing. Does my heart good. I know you gonna git on the choir at church now that you done finally settled down in Ballamore." It was more of a statement than a question.

"I'll certainly give it some thought. You just missed Herb by a few minutes," Lilly Ann said, deftly changing the subject.

"No matter. I'm headed that way anyway. I know he gits out early on Saturdey. So, y'all had a celebration of some sort last night?"

"Oh yeah. We plan to tell everybody about it. No big deal really. It's just that I won't be doin' any more day's work. I'll be working in the grocery store in the evenings to relieve Leon, and then I can be home in the mornings when Billie goes to school." Lilly Ann's words came out in a hurried jumble.

Without thinking, Larry blurted out a remark more typical of Wilma than himself. "Guess young people find any excuse to celebrate—not that … I mean, that's good, good. Like you were singin,' looks like you done got over. New husband, new life and all. You need to thank God."

As Larry processed what he was saying in his own head, he realized that it was indeed something to be happy about, but not necessarily a reason for a night out to do it. *Oh well*, he thought. *Must be gettin' old.* Then he remembered that at forty, he was only a few years older than Herb. Five, to be exact. *Five years might as well be a generation. Guess I'm old befo' my time*, Larry thought as he chuckled to himself.

"Oh, don't worry, Larry. I'm thankful. Do you want a cup of coffee? I still have some left."

"No, no. I'd better be on my way. Stuff to do. You know how Saturdey's are. Look, I'll let you tell yo' sister the good news yo'self."

"All right. Good. I'll tell her tomorrow when I see her." She dried her hands and started behind Larry as he walked to the door. "Thanks for keepin' Billie last night and bringin' her home."

Larry threw up his right hand and waved as he headed down the steps.

* * *

Billie was still amazed that the magnificent, rich, and vibrant sound that she had heard came from her mother. She had never heard her mother sing, and she had heard that she had not sung since Reb Barnes sat her down from the choir at the insistence of the Mothers'

Board. They had demanded her removal for her indiscretion. This, of course, Billie knew from eavesdropping on Grandma Gertie and Miss Laura, who did not tire of gossip even if the event was seven years old.

They had also said her mother's voice was soul-stirring. Billie did not know what an indiscretion was, but she assumed that since her mother was singing, she must have rid herself of it. *I wish Momma had lost her indiscretion sooner,* Billie thought.

Billie was even more delighted to learn that her mother was giving up days' work. This meant her mother, not Herb, would do her hair each day before school.

When her mother did day's work, she left too early to do Billie's hair, so at night she would carefully comb it and tie it with a scarf before Billie went to bed. This did not always work as intended. Some nights, the scarf came off while Billie slept, and Herb was obliged to repair the damage in the morning. Combing a little girl's hair was not his strong suit, and his ineptness had added to the teasing Billie had endured before her encounter with Leroy Ellis.

* * *

Lilly Ann was indeed ecstatic over her new station in life, but she had not been entirely honest with Larry, nor did she intend to be. Sure, she would work in the store to help Leon—sometimes.

But what she *did not* tell Larry was the big news. Herb and Leon had just completed renovations on the back of the barbershop and grocery store by demolishing the wall that separated them. It created an open space for a small private juke joint, where the featured Saturday night singer would be Lilly Ann Brown.

7

P rivate or not, it did not take long for word of the Brown brothers' juke joint to spread in the tight-knit community. It was hushed conversation for the churchgoers, and matter-of-fact gossip for those who had yet to seek salvation. Then there were those, like Lilly Ann, who had their feet in both worlds.

For months, Lilly Ann denied to her sister that she was singing at Brownies, as the place was called, until she could no longer sing on Saturday nights and show up in church on Sunday. She made sure, however, that Billie at least went to church with a neighbor. Lilly Ann's lack of attendance at Baltimore Street Baptist Church widened the gulf between her and Wilma even more, and pretty much killed the notion that she and Larry would convince Herbert Brown to seek the Lord.

Brownies served fried chicken, pigs' feet, collard greens, potato salad, candied yams, sweet tea, and lemonade. Patrons brought their own liquor. They ate, danced, drank, sometimes fought, and listened to the rich, soulful sounds of Lilly Ann Brown singing the standards of the day: Billie Holiday's "Good Morning Heartache," Sarah Vaughn's,

"I've Got a Crush on You," Dinah Washington's "Teach Me Tonight," and Ella Fitzgerald's "How High the Moon." Sometimes, she would even throw in some Mahalia Jackson and Sister Rosetta Tharpe.

Lilly Ann loved singing anything and anywhere. Had she not been under Herb's influence, she may have ended up as the featured soloist in the church choir, even though the rejection from her home church in South Carolina still stung and made her skittish about church.

Things were good with Herb—mostly. She had to work harder in the grocery store than she had been led to believe amid Herb's jokes about her earning her keep. She came to realize that she disdained her total dependence on a man and missed making her own money. She had sworn to herself when Billie was born that she would never put herself in such a position, but life had a way of getting in the way of her plans.

Since they left Billie home alone on Saturday nights, Lilly Ann would not go to Brownies until half an hour before her set, and she returned shortly after it. When she left, she did so reluctantly, because Herb sometimes drank too much, and bold female patrons openly flirted with him.

One Saturday night, she had doubled back to find Herb leaning against the bar as if he had been asked to assume the position by some invisible cop. Trapped between his splayed arms and legs was *Sister* Florence, who sat cross-legged on a bar stool, dress hiked up way above her knees as she swung her crossed leg between Herb's. Lilly Ann had swiftly walked to the bar. She would have preferred snatching Florence by her greasy pompadour, but she had grabbed Herb by the collar and asked him to join her in the kitchen, where they had it out.

"Look, baby girl," Herb had said. "It means nothing. You know I have to keep the patrons happy so they keep comin' back. Besides, Flo has a husband, and I'm scared of that big nigger. You got nothin' to worry 'bout."

Then he kissed her and tried to laugh it off. That was when she realized that she had traded some of her self-respect for creature comforts. One of the creature comforts would later manifest itself as a 1948 Chevy Impala.

8

Gertie scurried around the shack, getting herself ready to go uptown. She had to be by the road when Mr. Pickett came by with his mule-drawn wagon to pick up all who wanted to make the trip uptown to spend the day shopping, catching up on gossip, and just enjoying the fellowship of neighbors not seen for a week or more.

Carrying her shoes, she started for the door and heard a motorcar on the road. Wagon riders carried their shoes so that their footwear would not get dirty as they walked along the road waiting to be picked up. She peered out the window, and, to her surprise, a car—a Packard—turned onto the dirt trail leading to her shack.

She certainly did not recognize the car, but an image of the driver flashed in her mind seconds before the lankly figure of James Hayes stepped out and slammed the door. Clad in overalls and a straw hat, James effortlessly strode toward the shack and took the six porch steps two at a time. Gertie came out to meet him, gingerly closing the screen door behind her. To do otherwise would have dislodged it from its last remaining hinge.

"Mornin', Miz Cunningham," James said, removing his hat and putting it under his left arm. "How do you do this fine mornin'?"

I didn't know the boy could talk, Gertie laughed to herself, but she said, "I be just fine, James, just fine. What brings you out this way?"

"Well," he started, "I came out to see how you were doing, and to inquire about Billie."

Right proper, too. "I be fine for an ol' lady. I heard tell you pappy has been sick a spell. How he gettin' on now?"

"Just fine now, Miz Cunningham, but he's not running the farm like he used to. Over the last few years, it's been up to my brothers and me—at least the ones who haven't moved up north."

"Well," Gertie said, "Billie's been gone almost a year now, and you jest—"

"Yes ma'am, I know," James said, putting his hands up to interrupt her. "I know, Miz Cunningham. I'm sorry about that. I'm sorry about a lot of things. It was an unfortunate set of circumstances—"

Riled, Gertie said, "I wouldn't call my granddaughter an 'unfortunate set of circumstances'!"

"No ma'am, no ma'am," James stammered. "That's not what I meant. Billie's a fine child—"

Gertie cut in again. "A fine chile? A fine chile? She yo' daughter!"

"Yes ma'am, I know. I d-didn't …" James continued to stammer. He nervously laughed under Gertie's steely gray gaze and said, "Let's start over. Good mornin' Miz Cunningham. How are you doing this fine mornin'?"

Gertie could not help but smile and replied, "I be fine for a ol' lady. Last I heard, Billie was doin' jest fine." She did not share that she had some reservations about this being the absolute truth.

"How about I take you uptown today and you can call her?"

"Oh, I'd jest love that," Gertie smiled with delight. "But, as far as I know, Lilly Ann and them don't have no telephone thing. My daughter Wilma do, and I got that number."

She went back inside, walked to a shelf over the sink, and removed a neatly folded piece of paper from one of the jars there. She stepped back out onto the porch and handed the paper to James. "Here. The number right here on this letter from Lilly Ann."

The letter contained few words because Lilly Ann knew Miz Laura, who had to read the letter to her mother, knew few words. Wilma's phone number was written in large block letters, which Gertie had memorized from hearing it repeated to the telephone operator.

"The number is Madison 6–4239. Maybe we can call Wilma, and Billie might jest be there since its Saturdey and all."

"Yes ma'am. We can give it a try."

Seeming to be in thought for a moment, Gertie paused and said, "I'm not sho' I want to ride uptown in that motor car. I'll catch a ride with Mr. Pickett and meet you there."

"Miz Cunningham, you don't have to worry. The motor car is safe, and I'm a good driver. We'll be uptown long before Mr. Pickett gets there."

"That's what I'ma scared of," she replied.

James stifled a laugh. "No ma'am. Since I won't have to stop and pick up people, we'll get there first. And besides, you can wear your shoes."

"All right. Let me shut the do.' Guess I can ride wid my eyes closed and pray."

Gertie opened the screen door just enough to reach in and close the kitchen door. "All right. I'm ready to meet my Maker."

James laughed out loud as they walked toward the Packard. "How 'bout I come back and fix that screen for you?"

* * *

James Hayes and his eight siblings were the offspring of a quadroon mother who had defied her mulatto mother and married a dark-hued Mandingo of a man. The union resulted in hazel or amber-eyed children ranging in color from pecan to Brazil nut. His mother had no regrets about her marriage, and despite what her parents had initially believed, the senior Hayes had developed his land into a successful, prosperous farm.

James' father was a farmer from sun up to sun down, and he expected his sons to be the same. His greatest joy was to walk the acres where only skinny South Carolina pines grew at dusk in early spring and summer. It gave him great peace and connected him with his God who had granted him stewardship over 300 acres of prime land.

Of the five boys and four girls, James fell in the middle, where he often felt forgotten. He had been taken with Lilly Ann because she showered him with the attention and adoration that he craved from his large family. His father was busy running the farm and interacting with the older boys, and his mother was too busy keeping the home running smoothly, making sure they spoke and behaved properly, and grooming the girls to marry well.

James was quiet and spent a lot of time in his own head, reading the many books his mother kept around the house and thinking about greatness. Mrs. Hayes was very literate as a result of her mother's relationship with a plantation owner, and she had passed that love of learning on to her children. James had even spent eighteen months at South Carolina State University, but his father had forced him to come home because, in his newfound freedom and connection to a peer group, he neglected his studies.

His failure was a bitter disappointment to his mother, but it enraged his father as a waste of time and money. The senior Hayes was further angered when he heard—and not from James, either—the news of James' impending fatherhood. Since Lilly Ann had no father to protect her honor, Mr. Hayes took it upon himself to do so and was willing to put a shotgun, if necessary, to his own son's head. He demanded that his son marry Lilly Ann.

After much wringing of hands and pacing the floor, Mrs. Hayes finally disabused him of the marriage notion. At first, he had reminded her of how her parents had attempted to keep her from marrying the man she loved. But after she convinced him that "Love had not been invited to the party," he acquiesced. He did insist, however, that in addition to working on the farm, James had to get a job uptown to support his child. James found work, but he did not give Lilly Ann money regularly, a constant bone of contention between them. Instead, unbeknownst to his parents or Lilly Ann, he put it in a bank account for Billie's eighteenth birthday.

9

Herb drove the 1948 sky blue Chevrolet Impala in front of the apartment and parked along the curb where Billie was jumping rope. She jumped as he loudly honked the horn, and, not knowing it was Herb behind the wheel, she moved farther from the curb. Herb got out of the car, stood in the driver's side doorway, and leaned across the roof with his arms folded.

"Hey Billie," he yelled. "How you like this?"

Surprised, Billie squealed with delight, ran around to the driver's side, and grabbed the door handle.

"Whoa. Wait a minute, girl," Herb cautioned her as he stepped aside to let her peer in.

By now, the shoemaker, his helper, and two neighbors came out to surround the car, "Oo-ing" and "ah-ing" as they circled. It wasn't unusual to hear a car horn on Bryson Street, but if not for the muffled sounds of male voices and a squealing child, Lilly Ann would never have looked out of the window.

As she raised it higher to look out, she saw a shiny new car and heard Herb say, "I wanted to wait for the '49 Caddie, 'cause it's suppose to have a new engine called the V8, but it probably won't come out 'til November. Besides, $3,500 is a little out of my price range, and the Impala's a good car."

Lilly Ann saw the men nodding in agreement as they continued to walk around the car and look under the hood. She dropped what she was doing and raced down the stairs. "Herb! Herb, oh Herb!" she said excitedly. "Where did you get that car?"

"Where do you think, baby girl? From the Chevrolet car dealer." His response elicited snorts and chuckles from the men.

Lilly Ann began to ask, "But how—"

"Lock up the house and let's go for a ride," Herb interrupted.

"Now?"

"Yes, now! Go'an lock up!"

Billie, with a smile as wide as a Cheshire cat, was already in the backseat bouncing up and down. "Can we show Carletha, can we?"

"Don't be bouncin' in my car, chile," Herb scolded her.

Still grinning broadly, Billie replied, "Yes sir!"

As Lilly Ann went inside to lock up, she heard the shoemaker's helper say to his boss out of the side of his mouth, "Wonder what old Herbert's up to now?"

* * *

Herb drove the few feet to the end of the street, took a left at Edmondson Avenue, another at Fulton Avenue, and headed to northwest Baltimore. Fulton Avenue was the Old West Baltimore demarcation between blacks and whites, with blacks generally living east of Fulton Avenue. More aptly, Fulton Avenue was a boulevard where streetcars clanked along each side on its wide, tree-lined median. There were a few trees on Clayton Street, but nothing like Fulton Avenue, and certainly no streetcars. Through the rearview mirror, a proud Herb caught the wonder in Billie's eyes as they cruised through town.

From Fulton Avenue, Herb went east on North Avenue, then north on Madison Avenue through the Etruscan triple arch entranceway to Druid Hill Park. The inscription over the archway read, "Druid Hill Park, Thom Swann Mayor, Inaugurated 1860." Herb effortlessly maneuvered the Impala through the park's narrow winding roads and came to rest near a grassy spot under a grove of trees in the Colored section. On a distant playground, children were swinging, climbing the monkey bars, and riding the teeter-totter. Herb had scouted out the spot.

When they got out of the car, Herb retrieved a blanket, a picnic basket, and a thermos of sweet tea from the trunk with the exaggerated motions of a magician about to pull a rabbit from his hat. He spread the blanket on the ground, grinning from ear to ear as Lilly Ann squealed with delight.

The spring day was gently warmed by the spears of sunlight that broke through the grove of trees. For the moment, in this idyllic setting, Lilly Ann forgot Friday night's argument with Herb about the hours he was keeping.

"Herb, I just can't believe this," Lilly Ann gushed. "You packed this lunch … and a new car … Why, I'm speechless."

"Don't be, baby girl. Git used to the good life," Herb proudly cooed as he stretched out on the blanket with his arms folded behind his head and his legs crossed at the ankles. His brown and white spats gleamed in the spring sunshine, and the razor sharp creases in his trousers were undisturbed.

It always amazed and delighted Lilly Ann that no matter what he did, he was always spit-shined and polished. It did occasionally give her pause, though, because the condition of his clothing would never reveal any misbehavior on his part.

* * *

Billie forgave Herb for not swinging by Aunt Wilma's to pick up Carletha. She reveled in the moment, realizing she would rather have

Carletha enjoy the moment secondhand, through her eyes, than have her experience it firsthand for herself.

"Can I go to the playground?" Billie asked, mouth full of bologna sandwich.

"I'll take you down," Herb replied before Lilly Ann could answer.

Billie started skipping toward the swings before Herb could get up from the blanket. "Whoa, little girl. I'll give you a piggy-back ride."

Billie stopped and waited for Herb to catch up to her. He stooped and hoisted her onto his shoulders. After they had gone a few yards, Herb's breathing became slow and pronounced.

"Herb, if you tired, let me down," Billie called. She didn't think his breathing sounded like tired breathing. It was different. She thought Herb was a strong man. After all, men were strong, but maybe he wasn't as strong as he should be.

"I ain't tired," he said in a low, hoarse voice as he continued on.

* * *

After about an hour, Billie's mother beckoned her from the playground. Billie reluctantly scurried to the spot where they had had lunch and found the mood of the grownups decidedly different than it had been. Except for a strand of conked hair that fell down over his eye, Herb still looked like he had stepped out of a bandbox, but he worked his jaw muscles as he folded the blanket and gathered the lunch trash. Her mother, on the other hand, was disheveled, and one cheek appeared slightly bruised.

Though the trees defused the sunlight, Billie surmised her mother's reddened cheek was the result of too much sun. She wasn't left to ponder the situation for too long when, much to her delight, Herb announced he wanted to show the car to Uncle Larry. Her mother gave a shrug of her shoulders in nonchalant agreement, got into the car, and somberly stared out of the window.

The ride back downtown was different from the ride uptown, but all of it was quickly lost on Billie, who couldn't wait to step out of the motorcar in front of Aunt Wilma's house. Even the light spring rain that had begun to fall did not dampen her enthusiasm. She asked her mother a million questions as they rode homeward, until Herb told her to hush and enjoy the ride.

As they rounded the corner to Clayton Street, no one expected to see the site they encountered. Two black police cars, with red lights spinning, a paddy wagon—Black Mariah as it was known—and an ambulance had taken over the street from the Taylor's house to the McNeal's house.

Neighbors milled around but kept a respectful distance from the scene of the action. Two burly white policemen exited the McNeal house, half-dragging a barefoot Thomas Sr., who had his hands handcuffed behind his back. A frail figure on a gurney was being lifted into the ambulance as Tom Jr., David, and John helplessly looked on. A female voice somewhere in the crowd shouted, "'Bout time you locked his ass up."

Unnoticed, Herb parked the car, and they hurriedly climbed out to find out what was going on. Since people were standing in the way of Billie opening her door, she got out on the street side. Impervious to the rain and her fear of sinking into the wet asphalt, she started to dash down the street, when a strong arm gently restrained her.

"No, Billie," Uncle Larry said. "You best stay here."

"But Uncle Larry," she protested, "Tom's hurt. He needs me." As she tried to break free, she stared at Tom's bloody nose and shirt and began to cry.

"Gone over there with yo' momma while I go see what's gwine become of these children," Uncle Larry said with authority.

As Uncle Larry approached the scene, an ambulance attendant cleaned up Tom while an officer questioned David and John. "'Cuse me, suh, what is gonna become of the children?" he asked the officer who seemed to be in charge.

"Who are you?" the officer curtly responded.

"Just a well-meaning neighbor is all."

"Is that so?" the officer said sarcastically. "We have to take them to the Child Welfare Office for temporary custody, seeing as their daddy will be in jail for a few days and their momma will be in the hospital for I don't know how long."

"Suh, I don't think you have to do—"

"I'm their mother's first cousin," Mrs. Dorothy Black interrupted. It was a lie. She was the McNeal's next-door neighbor. "They'll be staying here with me until their momma gets out of the hospital." Before the officer could comment, Mrs. Black had gathered the boys and shooed them into her house. Tom Jr. was battered, but had no broken bones.

"Just as well," the officer replied. "We don't need no more colored boys in the system anyway."

Uncle Larry nodded, half in agreement with the officer, and half in approval of Mrs. Black's action.

The officers filed back into their cars, and Aunt Wilma rode in the ambulance to Sacred Heart Hospital with Mrs. McNeal. The neighbors dispersed to their various homes.

Carletha met Billie as she climbed the steps to the porch. "Guess what?" she shouted.

Billie, who was hardly in the mood for guessing games, answered with a half-hearted, "What?"

"Grandma Gertie called today, and you missed it!"

If this was another time and she had been on her game, Billie would have shouted back, "And you missed a ride in a motor car!"

Instead, Billie broke down into gut-wrenching sobs.

* * *

"Whew!" Gertie exclaimed as James helped her out of the Packard. She had half a mind to kiss the ground. "Got to git my land legs back."

"Yes ma'am, but you'll be fine," James responded, half-carrying her up the steps and into her shack.

"Let me sit for a spell," Gertie said as she flopped down on the chair nearest the door.

"Yes ma'am," James repeated, smiling to himself. "Didn't mean to shake you up, Miz Cunningham."

"Oh son, you didn't shake me up. It was that damn ... that motor-car. But I thank you for takin' me to town."

"My pleasure, but I'm sorry you—we—didn't get to talk to Billie."

"Me too. Me too. Maybe one day they can git one of them telephones theyself."

"Yes ma'am, but to make it work better, you have to get one, too."

"Hum, hadn't thought that far. Too much new fangled stuff to worry 'bout, but I'll think on it."

"If you don't mind, I can call Wilma and tell her to have Billie there next Saturday at noon, and I can take you to town again."

"Don't mind at all, but I'll catch a ride with Mr. Pickett," Gertie said emphatically.

James chuckled as he headed out the door and thought, *Suit yourself. Don't want any roots on me.* But he said, "Think about it, and let me know next week when I come to fix the screen."

James forgot the precarious position of the door and strode through it at his usual gait. The door slammed behind him, broke free of its last hinge, and crashed to the porch floor.

10

Billie had only seen Tom once in the three weeks since his father was arrested and his mother hospitalized. In customary fashion, the grownups did not share any information about the incident or the people involved. Billie and Carletha got as much as they could by their usual eavesdropping.

Tom was as reticent as ever and refused to talk about what happened. He had missed two weeks of school, and there was talk that the family, sans Mr. McNeal, was moving to another country. At least that was what the children heard. In the interim, Mrs. Black cared for the brothers, and the rest of the neighbors pitched in to buy food and whatever else Mrs. Black needed.

Tom seemed humiliated for having been put in such a situation. Though he was happy to see Billie on his first day back to school and appeared to want to talk to her about it, he did not. He left the school grounds promptly after the last bell and successfully avoided her during the school day. He had avoided recess all together.

Tom's welfare was constantly on Billie's mind, and it occupied her thoughts as she absently climbed the stairs to the apartment after school. "Momma, I'm home," Billie yelled.

It was her usual greeting, and she was taken aback when Herb called from the living room, "Yo' momma ain't here."

"Oh," Billie said, mentally retracing her steps. She didn't recall seeing the Impala outside. She walked into the living room and found Herb laying on the sofa.

"What's the matter Herb, you sick?"

Although Herb and her mother insisted she call him Daddy, she could not bring herself to do so. And a good thing too, because when she spoke to her real father two weeks ago, she would have felt as if she had betrayed him.

Never mind that he was absent and rarely in communication with her. Herb was not her real father, as Carletha reminded her on so many occasions. But what to call Herb was a serious issue, because little children simply did not call grownups by their first names without a handle: Miss, Mister, Uncle—something.

"Yeah, got a headache," Herb replied. "So Leon's fillin' in for me, and yo' momma's fillin' in for Leon."

"Oh, I see …" Billie began, delighted to have been given so much grownup information, but Herb often did that. Even so, she would never bring up a grownup subject with him. "I didn't see the Impala, so I didn't know you was here."

"Yeah, I took it to the service station. Had a flat tire. Billie, git me a cold rag from the bathroom."

"Yes sir," she mumbled. This was the Herb she did not like. Always demanding things. She asked Carletha if Uncle Larry was equally helpless, and Carletha had replied, "Yeah, but it's my mother's job to wait on him hand and foot. You have to do it 'cause he ain't yo' real father."

Billie went to the bathroom and ran cold water over Herb's washcloth. She returned to the living room and attempted to hand it to him.

"Fold it and put it on my forehead," Herb said, his eyes closed.

Billie frowned as she folded the cloth and started to place it on Herb's forehead, but he reached out and encircled her tiny waist with his right arm. Taken by surprise, Billie momentarily froze, expecting to be released as soon as the cloth was applied. She patted it on Herb's head, but he did not release his grip. She wiggled to free herself, but he still held her.

"Now hold still, little girl. I won't hurt you," Herb replied in that voice she remembered from the park. And in one motion, he raised her dress, stuck his hand in her panties and groped her private parts. After what seemed like an eternity, he released her. Billie ran to her room and slammed the door.

Once in the room, she stood, face to the wall, in the corner by the window, tears streaming down her face. Her brain could not grasp what had just happened or why. *It had to be wrong and nasty,* she thought. But Herb was an adult. She faced the wall until she heard a noise in the hallway. Frightened, she looked over her shoulder to see two one-dollar bills being pushed under her door.

"I gotta get back to the shop. Yo' momma will be here soon. Don't forget, we got us a secret. Buy some ice cream when the truck comes," Herb called from the other side of the door.

When Billie heard Herb leave, she removed her panties, balled them up and hid them in the back of her closet. From that day until her mother complained about how much underwear she dirtied, she wore two pairs of panties at one time.

* * *

"See you gotta new screen door," Miz Laura observed as she had her usual lemonade on the porch with Gertie.

"Yep, my woulda-been son-in-law put it up fo' me," Gertie replied.

"Maybe you shoulda' put some roots on him befo' now," Laurie joked in her usual fashion.

"I ain't put no roots on that boy. Guess his upbringin' finally kicked in," Gertie replied. "You know I still ain't met the one that *is* my son-in-law. I think *he* the one that needs the roots."

"Gertie, you been sayin' that for almost a year now. Whatcha gwine do about it?"

"Don't know, don't know, but when I walk the tobacco field tonight, somethin' might come to me."

Laura laughed. "If it does, I hope it's somethin' you can handle."

"Dey you go, makin' fun. You know better," Gertie said a little menacingly, her eyes gone cold.

11

1950

The joint was jumping and business was booming. Brownies'
reputation had spread far and wide, and the place was packed
every Friday and Saturday night.

Leon and Herb were as proud as peacocks at the success of their
endeavor and expanded the enterprise. There was no room to expand
Brownies' at their current location, and they did not think it wise to
buy another storefront. Instead, they decided to expand their regular
hours of 9:00 p.m. to 2:00 a.m. on Fridays and Saturdays to include
8:00 p.m. to midnight on Thursdays, and 4:00 p.m. to 9:00 p.m. on
Sundays.

The expansion necessitated hiring extra help. After rejecting the
shoemaker's helper, whom Herb did not like, Leon suggested Tom
McNeal, Sr., who had been fired while serving his sixty-day sentence
in jail. Tom Sr. desperately needed the work, and he eagerly accepted
it. He was to stock shelves, set up tables, run errands and clean-up.
Whenever necessary, he waited tables and helped in the kitchen.
Because he was a muscular, well-built man, he became the bouncer

by default. Never mind that he was a man with a quick temper and a short fuse.

Lilly Ann had started to have mixed emotions about the place. She loved the lifestyle it afforded her. She went to the beauty parlor regularly, kept Billie and herself in stylish clothes, and was even learning to drive the Impala.

She also loved singing at Brownies, but she did not get the opportunity to spend much time enjoying the music, dancing, and socializing with the patrons because she had to get home to Billie. She especially did not like the fact that since the expansion, Brownies was taking up more and more of Herb's time.

She did not relish going home directly after her set and leaving Herb free to flirt with the female patrons. She was a commanding presence when she was there, and the on-the-prowl, loose women cut a wide path around her. But the moment she left, it was open season on Herb. It did not matter to them that he was married; after all, it did not seem to matter to him.

Whenever Lilly Ann contemplated confronting Herb with an issue, he had the uncanny ability to detect her intentions and would perform some act, make some promise, or say some sweet-nothing that would dissuade her from the confrontation until another time that never came. On this particular Saturday night, he allowed her to be a patron and not the hired help.

"Baby girl," he had beckoned to her after her set. "Why don't you stay awhile, and I'll go on home? Enjoy yo'self for a change. Maybe we can look into gittin' somebody to sit with Billie a few hours on Frideys and Saturdeys. Befo' long, she won't need no babysitter. Whatcha think?"

"Herb, would you do that?" Lilly Ann answered, pleased. "You know I love to sing, but I would like to jest hang out for awhile. You right about Billie, though she is just asleep and probably don't really need anybody in the apartment with her. But better safe than sorry."

Lilly Ann rarely asked Wilma to keep Billie on Friday or Saturday nights anymore because of her sister's criticism of her lifestyle. And if her lifestyle had not been such a good target, Wilma would have been on her about her clothes, hair, makeup, *anything*.

"Yeah ... you stay and enjoy yo'self. I'm a little tired anyway." Herb kissed her and headed for the door, acknowledging patrons as he worked his way through the crowd.

For a split second, Lilly Ann was suspicious of his actions and watched the door to be sure no unaccompanied woman left behind him. Who knew marriage would require so much vigilance and energy.

* * *

Despite what her mother and Herb thought, Billie hardly slept at all on Friday and Saturday nights until she heard her mother's key in the door. This Saturday was no different. Tossing and turning, she breathed a sigh of relief as she heard the door being unlocked and immediately begun to spiral into sleep.

But she quickly realized the footfalls did not sound like her mother's. They were heavier. It was Herb. She pulled the covers over her head and feigned sleep. After a few minutes, with no further sounds, she relaxed and tried to sleep.

Suddenly, her door creaked open.

"Billie, Billie, you sleep?" Herb called from the doorway. When she didn't respond, Herb said, "I know you not sleep. I can tell by yo' breathing."

Billie did not respond.

"Billie," Herb continued as he moved into the room and sat on the bed. "How 'bout I read you a story?"

"No sir, I'm too sleepy," Billie replied, frightened.

"All right then," Herb said as he got up from the bed and started for the door.

The room was filled with his presence. The smell of his Old Spice, his gin breath, the heat from his body, and the aura of his predatory nature. Billie held her breath, waiting for the door to close behind him. The door closed quietly, but he had not left the room.

"Bill-ee ... Bill-ee," Herb sing-songed as he pulled her covers back and got in the bed beside her. "You remember when yo' momma and me got married?" Without waiting for an answer, Herb said, "You wanted to know what a honeymoon was, well tonight I'm gonna teach you about a honeymoon."

Billie had an out-of-body experience. She was no longer in her bed, but walking through the tobacco field with Grandma Gertie. First she sang a hymn in her mother's voice, then she howled a Native American battle cry.

The next morning, Billie had a vague memory of washing some sticky substance from between her legs during the night and falling into a deep sleep.

She had buried Herb's violation deep into the recesses of her mind.

* * *

As was her practice after singing in the club on Saturday nights, Billie's mother slept late on Sunday mornings. This morning was no different, especially since she stayed later than usual. As a result, Billie was careful to wait until she heard her mother in the kitchen. In the interim, she quietly dressed for church. As soon as she heard water running in the kitchen, she dashed down the hall, fully dressed.

"Momma, I'm ready for church. I'll jest gone over to Miz Barbara's and wait for them," Billie said in a rush of words.

"My, you up early, and dressed too! What's happenin' at that church today? Need some coffee before I can think ... Now you hold yo' horses, Billie. You need some breakfast."

"No ma'am, I don't," Billie protested. "I ain't hungry. I can eat when I get back." She felt compelled to leave the apartment and, from nowhere, a plan just popped into her head.

"Suit yo'self, but you know I don't cook breakfast twice. Go ahead."

Before she could finish, Billie was down the hall and out the door. She crossed the street and headed to Miss Barbara's house, which was catercorner to the apartment.

Miss Barbara came to the door, still in her bathrobe. "Billie, you're a bit early this morning," she said, yawning.

"Yes ma'am, I know, but my momma said you don't have to take me to church with you this mornin'. I'll be going with my family to Ballamore Street Baptist, so thank you kindly anyway."

Before the half-awake woman could comment, Billie was down the steps and headed back up the street. When she heard the door slam, she turned around and retraced her steps past Miss Barbara's to the end of the street. She turned the corner and u-turned around the block. She didn't want to pass the apartment and chance being seen.

She swiftly made her way to the alley behind Clayton Street, where she entered from the west end to avoid being seen by anybody in the Taylor household who might have been in the kitchen. Once inside the McNeal's backyard, she whistled for Tom, confident that he would hear. He slept lightly and always kept his window slightly open.

* * *

Tom's bed was flush with the window, so he rolled over and answered the whistle. "Billie, what are you and Carletha doin' this time of a Sunday morning?"

"It's just me. Carletha ain't here," Billie replied in a hush.

Perplexed, Tom asked, "Just you? What are you doin' down there? Why are you down there?"

"Kin you jest come down here now, Tom?"

"Are you just crazy or girl-stupid?"

"Tom—"

"Shut up before you git me in trouble! I'll be right there."

In a matter of minutes, Tom came through the basement door to the backyard. He had only taken the time to hook one suspender of his too short coveralls, and he walked on the backs of his too small tennis shoes.

"Billie, what in the world are you doin' here all dressed for church?"

"Can we walk down to Woodley Park?" she asked.

"Walk to the park? Why? What for? Are you looney?"

"No, I jest want to walk to the park. Momma thinks I'm at church with Miz Barbara."

"What is your momma gonna do when she finds out you ain't at church with Miz Barbara?"

"How is Momma gonna know?"

"How about, Miz Barbara is gonna tell her?"

"Nope, I told Miz Barbara I was goin' to Ballamore Baptist Church, so no need for her to say nothin.'"

"That was a lot of lying on your part. So what you do it all for?"

"I was worried about you, and I wanted to talk."

"Worried about me? Worried about me? I saw you in school Friday, so whatcha worryin' about? You better worry about what my mother is gonna say when she finds us out here."

"You right, but I can't go back home 'til church is over. Y'all don't go to church, so can't you just tell yo' momma you going to the park?"

"I guess I can, but I'll tell her when I get back, not before I go."

Tom's mother was accustomed to him getting up and out of the house first thing in the morning and, in all likelihood, she would not be looking for him. Besides, she was still nursing a broken arm and other bruises inflicted on her by his father.

"You goin' lookin' like that?" Billie asked Tom.

"What's wrong with the way I look? I'm going to the park, not church. You the one overdressed."

They laughed and headed for Woodley Park. At the park, they played tag and swung on the swings. Tom noticed that Billie occasionally stopped playing and sat on a bench, staring off into space, but Tom didn't think much about it.

The two kept track of the morning by asking the time of anybody who showed up at the park with a watch. Billie decided to head home after what she thought was the appropriate hour.

Tom punched her on the arm and told her to be careful. As he made his way back to Clayton Street, he wondered what the morning had been about.

12

As the spring of 1950 turned into summer, Herb found several opportunities to *honeymoon* with Billie, with Lilly Ann oblivious to all of it. He was masterful and covered his tracks well.

Billie's only response was passive-aggressive behavior, some of it turned onto herself. She had little appetite most of the time, her countenance was often sad, and the sparkle and innocence in her eyes was gone. When she played stepball outside, she purposely hit players, and she and Carletha had a couple of catfights after she deliberately tore up some of Carletha's paper dolls and lost the saucers to her tea set. Despite her attempt to be indifferent, she loved the bicycle Herb bought her.

But Herb had not bought the bicycle to assuage any guilt or buy silence, or as payment for complicity in humiliating acts. It was a business investment in another one of the Brown brothers' enterprises: number running.

After Herb taught Billie to ride the bicycle, he made her very familiar with the neighborhood and taught her special routes. She was instructed to pick up slips of paper—ribbons they were called—

and sometimes money from each of the designated houses, and deliver them to the barbershop. These were the players who hoped to hit and win some extra cash. Billie had no idea what the slips were, or why Herb even needed them, but she dutifully made her rounds.

Herb had instructed Billie to always wear dungarees when she did her pick-ups because they had lots of pockets to hold the slips and change people gave her, some of which was often tied in rags or dirty handkerchiefs. Sometimes, people gave Billie as little as a penny. Herb hated the "one-centers," but he did not refuse his fifty-cent tip when a one-center hit for a penny combination that yielded the player four dollars and fifty cents.

Always the schemer, Herb's ultimate goal was to go from being a writer to a banker. While a backer or godfather financed the whole operation and was a silent partner, the banker controlled the day-to-day activities and stood to gain much more than a mere writer.

13

Gertie paced back and forth on her porch, a stingy-brimmed straw hat resting jauntily on her head, and a brand new valise parked by the steps. On top of the valise sat a shoe box carefully tied with twine that contained Gertie's sustenance for the journey: fried chicken, a couple of apples, an orange, a small jar of canned green beans, and ham carefully inserted into hoecake bread.

"For God's sake, Gertie, calm down," Laura cautioned. "He'll be here directly. He ain't gone back on his word so far."

"I know, Miz Laura. Besides, I ain't nervous. Jest excited. If anybody woulda told me I woulda been waitin' for a ride to the train station in James Hayes' Packard, I woulda called them a liar," Gertie laughed as she smacked her thigh.

"Life takes strange twists and turns, don't it, Gertie?"

"Yes ma'am! You ain't never lied! Wonder what's keepin' him though?"

"He'll be on. You got everything you need?"

"Mostly. Some things I ought to be able to git in Ballamor,' but if I can't, well, I jest have to make do. I jest need you to feed my chickens and gather my eggs. And make sure that pig stays in the pen."

"Don't you worry none 'bout this place Gertie. You jest take care of business in Ballomor.'"

The place had taken on a brand new look since James had started his relatively frequent visits. Besides the new screen door, he had rewired the chicken coup, whitewashed the picket fence around Gertie's vegetable garden, patched a hole in her roof, puttied air leaks around the windows, replaced worn, squeaky floor boards, and even replaced the newspaper on the wall with real wallpaper. Gertie didn't care too much for the pattern he chose—*too dainty*, she thought—but she agreed it was better than newspaper. James wanted to add a room, but Gertie declined, sighting her lack of need for additional space.

"Oh, I know you'll take good care of things," Gertie told Laura.

Just then, they heard a car horn honk outside and saw James step out of the Packard and head for the porch.

"Good mornin', ladies," James said, taking off his hat as he approached the porch. "Are you ready for your trip, Miz Cunningham?"

"Indeed, son. Question is, is the trip ready for me!" Gertie winked at Laura and took James' arm. With his free hand, James grabbed Gertie's valise, which was surprisingly light, and walked her to the car. Once she was settled, he slowly started backing out of the driveway. Gertie stuck her hand out of the window to wave a goodbye to Laura, then she immediately gripped the door handle and shut her eyes tight.

* * *

James saw Gertie safely situated in the colored car of the Southern Railways train and headed for home. Over the last several months, he had grown fond of the old woman, and was amazed at the paradox of her. On one hand, she was this innocent, childlike creature who was afraid to ride in his motorcar and who had never been out of South Carolina. On the other, she was the cold, steely-eyed hag whose stare could make your blood run cold. Luckily, he had never been the recipient of her darker side.

On occasion, he thought about Lilly Ann and deeply regretted the folly of his youth. She had been more woman than any of the women his own age who were demure and properly behaved because they desperately wanted to be Mrs. James Hayes.

Lilly Ann, he realized, wanted nothing more than his attention, and she had followed him around like a lost puppy, showering him with smoldering passion whenever she managed to get him alone. So in love was she, that she was putty in his hand.

The cold rational dictates of his Christian morals had melted in the face of his hot desire. Her age—fifteen—had not been an issue. After all, many southern women were married at that age.

Now, at age twenty-nine, James had learned that life could not be well-lived when guided by the flesh, and he deeply regretted having succumbed to his sin nature. But, as Miz Cunningham reminded him, there was Billie, who was an innocent by-product—his word. He did not have any experience with small children, and he had failed miserably at trying to bond with her. But he found himself missing the haphazard, awkward visits they once shared.

* * *

As the train began to gather steam and chug down the track, Gertie removed her hat and settled in her berth for the long ride to Baltimore. The countryside sped by in a blur: coniferous trees, farmland, farm houses, undulating hills, rivers, cows, pigs, horses, barns, distant mountains, and dark tunnels. The steady motion and rhythm of the train was like a mantra and, surprisingly, it lulled her to sleep. Her soul was at peace for the first time in a very long time, and the trip was not at all the drudgery she had anticipated.

Fourteen hours after leaving Fairfield, Gertie's train pulled into Mount Royal Station in Baltimore. Donning her hat and gloves, Gertie retrieved her valise and headed for the exit. Once out of the station and onto the sidewalk, she slowly walked in small circles, mouth agape as she looked up at the Baltimore skyline of monuments, church steeples and spirals, and very tall buildings. A few dizzying minutes later, she went back inside the Renaissance-styled building, with its striking red tile roof, and flopped down on the first available bench.

"My Lawd," she said to herself. "This is too much for an old lady!"

She laughed at herself, quickly recovered, and headed for the colored taxi stand, too preoccupied with her surroundings to be overly concerned about the taxi ride. As was the custom, the taxi driver gently attempted to take her valise from her in order to put it in the trunk, but Gertie slapped his hand and tightened her grip. The driver shrugged, wordlessly, and got behind the wheel.

As the taxi headed toward Clayton Street, Gertie continued to take in the Baltimore skyline. *My my,* she thought, smiling. *Wid all these churches, everybody in Ballamore must be saved!* She took great pleasure in amusing herself.

She had a love-hate relationship with churches in general, and her own in particular. Gertie liked the ones where congregants did the holy dance in the spirit. She could relate, having danced with spirits herself, albeit in a tobacco field. She hated the fire and brimstone sermons, but most of all, she hated that the preachers could not answer her questions. For instance, how was what Pharaoh's magicians and sorcerers did with their staffs any different from what Moses did with Aaron's staff? Why did a God of love create people with so many differences that it was easy for them to hate each other? As she rode, she concluded that the preachers worthy of occupying such majestic and imposing churches that dotted the Baltimore skyline would surely have the answers.

Twenty minutes later, the taxi pulled in front of 2220 Clayton Street, and Gertie climbed out before the driver could come around to open the door for her. The driver walked around to the passenger side, slammed the door, cleared his throat, and looked down at Gertie.

"Yes, suh?" she asked.

The driver cleared his throat again and said, "Tip, ma'am?"

"Here a good tip fo' you. Next time, don't try to take an ol' lady's valise!"

The driver glared at her, got back in the cab, and sped away.

Gertie stood at the bottom of the steps and waited for her family to come rushing out of the front door as she made them telepathically aware of her presence. They did not disappoint.

As if on cue, they stumbled onto the porch amid calls of "Momma," "Grandma Gertie," and "Mother Cunningham." An impeccably dressed Herb, hand on his chin liked Rodin's statue of the Thinker, hung back from the group, taking it all in.

Gertie observed him from the corner of her eye. *Ah so*, she thought. *That city slicker must be him.*

The welcoming went on for a few minutes. Needless to say, Carletha was not as close to Gertie as was Billie, who had lived with her all of her life. Gertie hugged and kissed both girls, but Billie would not let go of her.

* * *

Lilly Ann and Wilma had called a truce for their mother's visit, and both were genuinely happy to see her. But then there was Herb. He had not given the visit much thought, but he felt his skin crawl as the old woman gave him an icy stare. It was now or never.

He walked down the steps to Lilly Ann, put his arm around her waist, and nodded in Gertie's direction. Lilly Ann took him by the hand and pulled him to her mother.

"Momma, this is my husband, Herbert Brown." It was obvious that Lilly Ann still loved the sound of those words.

Herb extended his hand and tried not to look the old woman directly in the eye. He felt her slowly taking him in, from head to foot, before she spoke. "You don't say now? I come a long way for this moment, Mr. Brown."

The family laughed, and nobody noticed that neither Gertie nor Herb joined in. With his hand still extended, Herb considered hugging her, but he thought better of it and waited for a cue from her.

She finally said, "Glad to meet chu, son-in-law," and grabbed his outstretched hand.

If her grip had not been so firm, Herb would have instantly withdrawn his hand, because he experienced a split-second of searing heat when their palms met.

* * *

Gertie made it quite clear from the beginning of the trip planning that she could not be away from home for too long. She got there on Thursday afternoon and was leaving promptly on Monday morning. Gertie knew Billie was disappointed that she was staying with Wilma and Larry, so she had negotiated for her to stay too.

Wilma had planned a big Sunday dinner and announced that she hoped they would all go to her church together. But again, Gertie made her wishes quite clear. She did not bring clothes for church and, therefore, would not be going. She had gotten the word that Lilly Ann's visits to church were few and far between, so her plan was to spend Sunday morning at Lilly Ann's. That, she told them, would give her a chance to see where Lilly Ann and Billie stayed.

"But Momma," Wilma argued. "You come all this way, and you ain't goin' to church with us. I am certainly disappointed."

"I understand, honey," Gertie retorted. "But I had to travel light. If anybody from home go to yo' church, and want to see me, tell 'em to come on by yo' house."

* * *

Sunday morning came and Herb made some excuse about not being able to pick up Gertie and bring her to the apartment. Undaunted, Gertie said she'd take a cab so that Herb could take care of his pressing business. Thanks to James, she wasn't as queasy about riding in motorcars as she had been.

When the cab let her out on Bryson Street, Gertie walked directly toward the shoe shop as if she had been there before, entered the foyer, and effortlessly took the stairs to the apartment. Billie and Lilly Ann had been watching at the window for her cab so that they could direct her to the stairway to the apartment, but obviously, and oddly, she did not need their assistance.

Billie flung the door open and greeted her. "Grandma Gertie, Grandma Gertie, come on in and see my room!"

Lilly Ann intervened, laughing, "Hold on a minute, chile. Give Momma a chance to git in the door."

"Yes ma'am, yes ma'am," Billie excitedly replied.

"Here baby, take my valise to yo' room for me, please," Gertie said, handing Billie the practically empty bag.

"Come on in the front room and sit down, Momma," Lilly Ann instructed. Gertie followed her. "I'll git you some coffee if you want it."

The two women talked for nearly two hours, with Gertie regaling Lilly Ann with tales about home and home folks, and even mentioning James Hayes. It did not escape Gertie's notice that Lilly Ann had artfully dodged any significant conversation that would shed light on her life and marriage.

A contented Billie sat as close to Gertie as she could get without saying a word. Gertie knew she was afraid of being banned from the grown folks' conversation if she spoke.

"Momma, I got to run across the street for a minute so Barbara can put some curls in my hair," Lilly Ann suddenly said.

Gertie saw Billie's face fall as she asked Lilly Ann if she could go too.

"No, you stay here wid your grandmother. I'll be back directly," Lilly Ann said.

Gertie said, "Oh, take her wid you. I need a little cat nap anyway."

"But Momma, she don't need—"

"Take her wid you," Gertie emphatically repeated.

"Yes ma'am. Come on Billie."

As soon as Gertie saw them cross the street, she went down the hall to Billie's room. She slowly stepped into the darkened room and sniffed the air like a bloodhound after prey. Then she walked to the corner, and, facing the wall, smelled the pain and sorrow of Billie's tears and the stench of debauchery. She inhaled deeply, as if to take the humiliation into herself, then she walked over to the bed, sat down, and opened her valise.

It contained two changes of clothes, a comb, hairbrush, and toothbrush, but nothing else in the way of toiletries. She removed a rawhide pouch, which was buried under one faded print dress. In it was a small ceramic dish, matches, white sage leaves, and a braid of sweetgrass. The sage was to vanquish bad spirits and ward off trouble, and the sweetgrass to invite good spirits.

Gertie lowered herself to the floor and sat cross-legged, carefully placing the herbs in the dish and setting them on fire. As she softly chanted, she fanned the smoke and the aroma filled the room.

* * *

Billie, Lilly Ann, and Herb got back to the apartment at the same time. As they unlocked the door, Gertie knew they would be assailed by the pungent odor.

Herb was the first to respond. "What the hell is burnin' in here?"

"Momma," Lilly Ann called. "Where are you?"

Gertie started down the hall from the bathroom. "I was smoking my pipe," she said. "Didn't see as to how I could git outdoors to smoke it wid no porch or nothing. Didn't want to leave the apartment. Guess I shoulda tried to raise one of dem windows, but I didn't. Sorry."

"Pipe ..." Herb began incredulously. "I ain't never smelled ..." He stopped abruptly when Lilly Ann forcefully patted his arm.

Gertie sheepishly dropped her head. "Won't happen again." She could almost feel the intensity of Herb's displeasure as he glared at the top of her bowed head. *Bet he got a few choice words for me,* Gertie mused.

When Gertie raised her head and gave Herb her icy stare, he simply muttered, "No harm, no foul."

"Okay," Lilly Ann said, breaking the tension. "Let's freshen up so we can git to dinner. Herb, in the meantime, put the windows up for awhile."

Thirty minutes later, they piled into the Impala to head to Wilma and Larry's for dinner. The sun had retreated and it was threatening rain.

"Oh shoot," Lilly Ann replied, after everybody was in the car. "I forgot to put the windows down."

"Okay. Gimme a minute. I'll put 'em down," Herb said as he bolted out of the car.

A minute passed, then two, then three, then four. Billie and Lilly Ann chorused, "What's takin' him so long?"

"Billie, go see what's keepin' Herb," Lilly Ann instructed.

"Yes ma'am," Billie began, but Gertie cut her off.

"You better go yo'self."

Gertie's tone told Lilly Ann not to question the suggestion. She hurriedly exited the car and quickly walked up the sidewalk to the entrance of the building.

* * *

To Lilly Ann's dismay, a dazed Herb was sitting at the bottom of the steps, holding his left arm.

"Oh my goodness, Herb! What happened?" she asked, walking over to him.

"I don't know," Herb stammered. "Guess I lost my balance. One minute I was walking down the steps, the next minute, I was at the bottom of the steps. I don't remember stumblin' or trippin.'"

"Are you hurt?"

"My left harm hurts pretty bad, but it ain't broke. Think you could get me some ice?"

Herb was in a lot of pain. Before they left for dinner, he changed his shirt, downed a Stanback powder, and swigged a jigger of gin.

After they arrived for dinner, Larry convinced Herb to go to Sacred Heart Hospital to get an X-ray.

Herb was seen after a lengthy wait. The emergency doctor confirmed no broken bones, but he said Herb's arm was badly bruised and his wrist was sprained. He recommended that Herb wear a sling for a few days.

* * *

True to her word, Gertie got up bright and early on Monday, ready for the long trip back home. As Larry whisked her to the train station, she sat smugly, arms folded, satisfied that her mission was accomplished. She had found out what she needed to know and done what she needed to do. She was confident that her remedy would suffice until she figured out a more permanent solution.

When the taxi pulled into Gertie's shack in the wee hours of Tuesday morning, Laura was waiting in the kitchen for her friend.

"How did things go in Ballamore?" Laura asked.

"Guess, that 'pends on who you ask," Gertie devilishly replied.

"Bet you glad to be home."

"Probably not as glad as some people in Ballamore!"

The two women laughed heartily.

* * *

Herb had worn the sling on his bruised arm for a couple of days when it started to itch madly, and he developed an inexplicable rash. The dermatologist who examined him was perplexed and said he had never seen such a rash.

During his examination, he asked Herb a series of questions: Have you changed soaps? No. Has your wife changed laundry detergents? No. Are you using a new cologne or aftershave? No. New dry cleaners, products in the barbershop, cleaning supplies? No, no, no! Gardening? Hell no!

Unable to determine the precise cause of the rash, the doctor gave it the catch-all diagnosis of contact dermatitis. He prescribed a series of creams and salves before he found one that worked. The rash eventually went away, but it left its calling card: a patch of reddish, purplish discolored skin that stretched from Herb's wrist to his elbow.

To add to the conundrum, Herb discovered, much to his chagrin, that whenever he touched Billie's doorknob, it became as hot as a poker and the rash flared up. At first he thought his mind was playing tricks on him, but his thinking was not sophisticated enough to consider that the phenomenon could possibly be an attempt by his subconscious to lead him back to some redeeming moral high ground.

But what he finally concluded was that the old hag must have worked some roots on him. For the life of him, he could not figure out why. After all, he was doing no harm, and the acts were pleasurable to both parties. How would the old hag know about any of it anyway?

Despite how much he tried to rationalize it, he no longer felt comfortable in the apartment and decided moving was the answer. He believed his new station in life warranted it. Although he was not bona fide colored upper-class, lacking education, a professional occupation, and breeding, he did have the means. So he decided to move the family to Upton, a premier Baltimore neighborhood and one of the most affluent colored neighborhoods in the United States.

He and his beautiful and talented wife could easily afford the upscale jazz clubs, dance halls, and theaters that graced Pennsylvania Avenue, Upton's principal thoroughfare. Even though he planned to discuss it with Lilly Ann, he had already made up his mind.

14

During their two years of operating Brownies and running numbers, the Brown brothers managed to stay under the legal radar. There was the occasional skirmish and drunken revelry, but Herb and Tom Sr. kept it in check. Tom Sr. continued to work at Brownies even after he managed to get his job back on the docks because he loved the atmosphere and flexing his muscles.

Lilly Ann continued to sing but, not having any formal vocal training, she abused her voice. She realized that she needed to give it a rest, and limited her singing to an occasional set. Besides, the clientele wanted variety, so the brothers booked other singers. But the biggest hit was the Wurlitzer model 1015-Bubbler jukebox, which played the hits of the day. As a result, she rarely sang at the club anymore.

Lilly Ann was also growing tired of sparring with Herb, who spent a lot of time away from home, ostensibly managing the various enterprises. She didn't think he was having an affair per se, but she believed he took his pleasure with whomever he wanted, whenever he wanted to. After all, Brownies was frequented by shameless hussies who would lift their frocks at the slightest urging.

After playing housewife for a while, Lilly Ann went back to work because she needed her own money. Herb protested, saying his wife didn't need to clean white folks' houses, but it fell on deaf ears. Lilly Ann eventually decided to go to nursing school so that she could be done with domestic work—and maybe even Herb.

* * *

On this particular Saturday night, Herb, Leon, and Tom Sr. were performing their sundry chores to close the club when Herb spotted Red, the shoemaker's helper, sitting in the shadows at the back of the club.

"Hey, Red. Closin' time. Gotta go, Daddy O," Herb called across the room.

"Don't think so. Daddy O yo' damn self!" Red replied, tongue thick with liquor.

"Okay, Red. What's wrong with you? Time to go, cat."

"I ain't goin' no place 'til you gimme my money."

"What the hell you talkin' about, Red? I don't owe you no money!"

"I say you do! You know my number hit, the one I play all the time, every day. You know I played my number wid you, but you say I didn't. I gave my slip to your runner. Maybe you need to get a more mature runner. She is cute, but that ain't got nothin' to do with business. I ain't goin' nowhere 'til I get my motherfuckin' money!"

Just then, Tom Sr. came in from putting out the trash, and Leon, hearing the loud voices, came in from the kitchen. "What's goin' on out here?" Leon asked.

Red got up from the table and started walking toward Herb, pointing his finger. "That nigger better give me what he owes me, or I'm gonna cut his throat."

"Whoa now, Red," Tom Sr. said, motioning for Red to calm down. As Tom Sr. started toward Red, Herb started backing away.

"Whoa, shit," Red said.

There was a clicking sound, and the dim light caught a glint of a blade as Red lunged for Tom Sr., who jumped back, but not fast enough to prevent the blade from grazing his left arm and drawing blood. Tom Sr. momentarily lost his footing, and Leon started across the floor just as Red wildly lunged again. In an instant, a shot rang out and Red stumbled against a table, then fell to the floor.

Standing over Red, Herb snarled, "Get up, nigger. You ain't dead yet. This .22 won't kill you … Just do enough damage to stop yo' ass. I don't owe you no money! From now on, play yo' numbers with another writer. Now git the fuck outta my club and don't come back!"

"Don't worry, you sonofabitch. I won't come back to yo' club, but I will get my money, one way or another," Red said as he struggled to his feet, holding his right shoulder in an attempt to stop the blood that was trickling down his sleeve. The small caliber bullet was enough to stop the menace without maiming.

Tom Sr. recovered his footing, grabbed Red by the right arm, bent it behind his back and shoved him out the door. "Git the hell out, and don't come back!"

"Starting tomorrow, Billie does no mo' pick-ups," Herb loudly announced, brushing a shock of hair from his eye and pocketing the pearl-handled .22.

15

Without ceremony or explanation, Herb announced at home that Billie would no longer do pick-ups and deliver them to the barbershop. Lilly Ann was neutral about the decision, but Billie was silently upset, though she feigned indifference and casually asked what she could now do to earn her allowance. She had come to learn the value of money very early.

Herb assured her he would think of something.

Unbeknownst to the two adults, Billie kept two boxes buried under the clothing in one of her bureau drawers. One box was for *good money*: her allowance for collecting the mysterious slips. The other box was for *bad money*: the hush money she received from upstanding members of the community who bribed her to keep their number-playing a secret.

True to his duplicitous word, Herb came up with a plan for Billie to earn money. Every now and then, Lilly Ann would go out in the evening to a movie, shopping with Wilma, to get her hair done, run some errand, or, without anybody's knowledge, to prayer meeting.

On one such evening, while they were still in the kitchen after dinner, Herb presented Billie with a juice glass with a half-inch of clear liquid.

"You want to earn some money, little girl?" It was more of a statement than a question.

"Yes sir," Billie innocently replied.

"I'll give you these five one dollar bills if you drink this," Herb said, pushing the glass toward her.

"What is it?"

"Oh, nothin' that'll hurt you. Jest hold your nose and drink it down in one gulp," he said as he picked up the money and spread it out over the table as if he were dealing cards. "Go 'head. Do it quick, and you won't taste a thing. I dare you."

Billie wanted the money, and Herb had said the magic words, "I dare you." She always took a dare.

After she gathered up the money and stuffed it in her sock, she held her nose and gulped down the liquid, which burned the back of her mouth and her throat. She remembered gagging and asking for water, but that's all she remembered.

The next morning, she woke up in her bed without knowing how she got there or how she got her pajamas on. As hard as she tried, she could remember nothing after gagging on whatever it was that was in the glass. The five ones were still in her sock.

The second time she took the dare, she was convinced that she could will herself to stay awake so that she could see what went on after she drank the disgusting liquid. To no avail, the same thing happened. She awoke in her own bed in her nightclothes, with money in her sock.

The third time was the charm. When she refused to play the game, Herb upped the ante. Billie pocketed the ten-dollar bill, poured the liquid down the sink and quickly left the room. A surprised, but amused Herb did not follow.

Into which box would this money go? Billie wondered.

16

1952

A nother summer in Baltimore was coming to an end, and Billie, Carletha, and Tom were trying to wring every inch of fun they could squeeze from it. Since Billie was no longer a runner for Herb, she could ride her bike with her friends.

Occasionally, Tom took a break from the antics of the boys in the neighborhood and indulged the girls by gracing them with his presence. The trio biked with a vengeance all over the neighborhood. Ordinarily, they had to get home before the street lights came on, but today they were trying to beat the threatening late summer storm. Billie, with well-developed muscles from her runner days, led the pack, cycling like an Olympic biker closing in on the finish line. Carletha and Tom always escorted Billie home, then headed home themselves.

Tom was not worried about getting into trouble if he missed his curfew. His father was just as likely to get angry whether he was early, on-time or late, but he didn't want to get the girls in trouble. It was his duty to protect them.

* * *

Billie rounded the corner to Bryson Street and approached the alley. In a flash and out of nowhere, a strong arm encircled her waist, covered her mouth, and snatched her off her bike, which skid across the sidewalk.

The assailant, trying to move quickly, struggled to carry a squirming, kicking Billie up the alley. His getaway was also made more difficult by the sudden deluge of rain, which hampered his traction.

* * *

Tom rounded the corner and braked hard to avoid hitting Billie's bike, which rested on the ground, its tires spinning.

"Billie, whatcha do that for ..." Tom began, trying to process what was going on. *Why did she drop her bike here, and where did she go that fast?* he thought. Carletha, pulling up the rear, ran smack into Tom, lost her balance, and fell.

"What's goin' on? What's the matter Tom? Where's Billie?" Carletha asked.

Tom didn't answer, and as he headed for Billie's apartment, he heard muffled sounds coming from the alley.

"Bill-ee, Bill-ee," he called as he headed into the alley. That's when he saw a figure with a kicking girl in tow, trying to make his way up the alley. He immediately took off running, shouting Billie's name.

* * *

The assailant had not planned for such resistance or any witnesses. When the girl bit his hand, he unceremoniously dropped her and beat it out of the alley to a waiting car. He got in, and the driver sped off.

Carletha joined Tom in the alley as they ran to help a frightened, crying Billie.

* * *

Marvin Friedman, who owned a deli on Edmondson Avenue, was putting out his trash when he heard the commotion and saw the three children huddled in the alley in the rain. He immediately went to investigate, but he could hardly make out what they were trying to tell him amid the crying and agitation. However, he recognized Billie and coaxed them to her apartment.

* * *

An unsuspecting Lilly Ann, who had heard nothing in the alley below the apartment, was shocked when she saw the children in such a state and heard Mr. Friedman's account of what he gleaned had occurred. She hurriedly got towels for them as they flopped down on the moving boxes strewn all over the living room.

"Do you have a telephone, Mrs. Brown? You need to call the police."

"I do, I do. My husband should be here in a few minutes. He'll call the police," Lilly Ann nervously responded.

"All right, will you all be okay?"

"Yes, yes, we'll be fine."

"All right then. I'll gather up the bicycles and put them in the foyer," Mr. Friedman said as he headed for the door.

"Thank you so much, Mr. Friedman," Lilly Ann said as she showed him out.

As Mr. Friedman headed down the steps, he met Herb heading up. Seeing the deep, questioning furrow in Herb's forehead, Mr. Friedman knew he was the last person Herb expected to encounter.

"I know, I know. Mr. Brown, your wife will explain it all. You better get up upstairs." And he was gone.

* * *

Herb bolted up the steps to find three wet children, two of whom were crying, and the third one pacing the floor. Lilly Ann immediately told the story of Billie's abduction attempt.

"I can't believe that somebody would try to just take a child off the street—"

Herb interrupted her. "Whether you believe it or not, that's what happened." Then he turned to the trio. "What did he look like? Y'all see him?"

"No sir," Tom said. "It all happened so fast, and he ran pretty fast outta the alley."

"Herb, we better call the police if what they say is true."

"We ain't calling no police. I'll take—"

The telephone rang, interrupting Herb as Lilly Ann looked at him questioningly. She picked up the phone, and heard the crisp, Southern accent of a long-distance operator. "Collect call for Mrs. Lilly Ann Brown from Mrs. Gertrude Cunningham. Will you accept the call?"

"Uh yes. Yes, of course."

"Hello, hello," Gertie yelled.

"Momma? Hello, Momma? I can hear you. Don't yell. We havin' a little situation here. Can you call back?"

"Situation? Situation? No, I can't call back. How Billie doin'?"

"Ma'am?"

"You heard me. How Billie doin'?"

"Momma, Billie is fine. Can I call you back in jest a minute?"

"Nope! That's all right, I be jest a minute. Pack some of Billie's clothes and have her at Mount Royal Station tomorrow mornin' at eleven thirty. Her daddy gwine meet her there and bring her back to Fairfield for the rest of the summer."

"What? Her daddy gonna do what? What are you talkin' about, old lady? Her daddy ain't gonna do no such thing," Lilly Ann shouted into the phone.

"What she sayin'?" Herb asked, agitated. "What daddy? I'm her daddy. I'm the one who feeds her and puts clothes on her back. Where the hell he been?" he asked, grabbing for the phone.

Lilly Ann abruptly turned away from him and waved him off with her free hand.

"Do Herbert Brown have somethin' to say to me?" Gertie yelled, and when no response was immediate, she asked the question again. "Do Herbert Brown have somethin' to say to me?"

Cupping the mouthpiece, Lilly Ann asked, "Herb you want to talk to Momma?"

Herb opened his mouth to respond as he reached for the phone, but the words stuck in his throat. The harder he tried, the more constricted his vocal cords became. He clutched his throat with his left hand and futilely pointed to his mouth with his right finger.

In slow motion and disbelief, Lilly Ann put the receiver back up to her ear and stammered, "When is James gonna git here?"

"Oh, James already there. He been there for two days takin' care of business. Jest pack a few things for Billie. One of James' sisters gonna take her uptown to shop. Billie be wid me most the time, but she be spendin' some time with her daddy's people. She be back to Ballamor' in time for school, so jest have her at the station tomorrow at eleven thirty like I say."

Lilly Ann was in shock, but she realized the situation had taken a strange turn. *Why didn't Herb want to call the police? Why didn't her mother call her before now to tell her James was in town? And what kind of business? And how dare her mother tell her what to do with her child!*

But she knew better than to question her mother at a time like this. She felt so helpless, and could only mutter a feeble, "Yes, ma'am."

"Oh, by the way. Tell Herb to get a little bit of Vicks Salve on the tip of his little finger, eat it befo' he go to bed tonight, and his voice will be fine in the morning.'"

Then the phone went dead.

17

Herb swallowed a fingertip of Vicks Salve before he went to bed—never mind that it was not for internal use—and, as *the old hag* diagnosed, his voice returned on Wednesday morning. He had gotten up a little before sunrise, and dressed quickly and quietly. While talking to himself in the bathroom, he discovered his voice had returned.

Once dressed, he removed a key from around his neck and unlocked a small chest that was buried on his side of the closet. Momentarily distracted, he thought of bigger closets when he moved to Upton. Refocused on the task at hand, he reached into the chest and uncovered a .38, which he tucked into his waistband. He quietly slipped out of the apartment and into the Impala, and headed for Dover Street. First things first, then he had a business appointment at eleven thirty that he wanted to be sure to keep.

He eased the Impala out of the block and headed downtown. When he reached Dover Street, he parked a few doors down from house number 750 and got out of the car. In the pre-dawn light, he crouched down beside the car to hide in its shadow until he saw a woman in a white uniform come out of the house. He walked swiftly and silently to the steps, where he grabbed her and put the gun to her head.

"Is Red in there?" he snapped.

"No, no. I ain't seen him," the frightened woman stammered. "He didn't come home last night."

"Oh yeah? Let's go back in and see."

"I'm tellin' you, he didn't come here last night. Maybe he went home to his wife."

"Maybe, but git yo' ass back in the house and let me see!"

With Herb twisting her arm behind her back, the woman walked back up the steps and unlocked the door. They went in, and he forced her to lead him around the small house. No Red. Herb shoved the woman, sandwiching her between the wall and himself. He kissed her on her neck and ran the gun down the full length of her body.

"If you let on to Red that I'm looking for him, or I hear tell you told anybody I was here, I will shoot yo' ass. That is, after I git me some. You got it?"

"Yeah, you sonofabitch. I got it."

Herb left the frightened, trembling woman, jumped into the Impala, and headed toward the McCulloh Homes, the last known address of Red's wife. He hastily parked the car and proceeded to run up the eleven flights of stairs without even considering the elevator, which probably didn't work anyway. He repeatedly banged on the door of unit number 1105, until an irate, obese woman opened the door. She wore a robe that was hardly big enough to cover her ample figure, and a print bandana over a mass of unprocessed, unkempt hair.

"Who the hell are you, and why you be knockin' at my door at this time of the morning? You must be crayzee boy!" the woman said with a thick Jamaican accent as she stood in the doorway with her hands behind her back.

"I'm lookin' for Red. Is he here?" Herb asked as he tried to get in the door, but he was met with an unmovable mass of flesh.

"So you are, are you?"

Herb took a step back and went for his waistband. But not quick enough. The Jamaican woman produced a Bowie knife from behind her back and glared at Herb.

"Red ain't been here in six months, and if he come, I gut hem. And I gut anybody come 'ear askin' about 'em!"

With that, the woman slammed the door, causing Herb to stumble backwards against the balcony rail. By this time, beads of perspiration had formed on his forehead, and his heart raced. When he regained his composure, he glanced at his watch and reckoned he had time to scour a few more of Red's haunts before going back to the apartment to pick up Lilly Ann and Billie for the trip to Mount Royal Station.

Thinking about Mount Royal Station gave him pause. *Sure is funny James what's-his-name showed up on the same day Red tried to snatch Billie. Maybe he—naw, he wouldn't try to kidnap his own kid, would he? What for?*

Red was nowhere to be found. When Herb got home, he immediately went to the shoe shop and asked the shoemaker if Red was at work. And, like everybody else, the shoemaker had not seen or heard from him. Herb was forced to put his pursuit of Red on the back burner in lieu of another confrontation he anticipated, or rather, planned to instigate.

* * *

Lilly Ann had dutifully packed a suitcase for Billie amid a jumble of emotions: anger at her mother for springing this on her; bewilderment as to why James picked this particular time to take an interest in his daughter; and relief that if Herb's lifestyle had put her daughter at risk, she would be out of harm's way until he could take care of the situation, whatever that meant.

* * *

Billie was also a mass of conflicting emotions: fear that somebody wanted to steal her for some reason; excitement about going home to see her grandmother; and uncertainty about seeing her real father and having to endure a long and silent train ride with him. She expected it to be silent because they never really talked on the rare occasions he had visited her. What would they say during all the long miles to South Carolina?

* * *

Herb was the only one with a firm grip on his emotions. Seething rage. Rage that Red had the balls to first accuse him of stealing, even though the accusation was true, and then to threaten his stepdaughter; rage at Gertrude Cunningham for jinxing his life; and rage at James Hayes on general principle.

As Herb wound his way to the apartment, he realized how his morning escapades and adrenaline rush had exhausted him. All he wanted to do was catch a nap and relax at his place on Carey Street, but first, James Hayes.

Too tired to be a gentleman, and rationalizing that they did not need any help with luggage, Herb honked when he pulled up to the apartment and waited for Lilly Ann and Billie to come down. The two climbed into the car, and he headed for Mount Royal Station, planning what he would say to James.

* * *

James was a jumble of nerves as well, and he paced back and forth in front of the station as he waited for Lilly Ann and his daughter. On the occasions when he thought of Billie, he thought of her as just Billie, and not as his daughter. The time had come to change his thinking.

* * *

Herb slowed the car in the drop-off lane and craned his neck, looking for the country bumpkin that was James Hayes. He looked past the pecan-colored, six-foot-three, lanky man pacing in front of the station.

"Stop. Stop here, Herb," Lilly Ann said, trying to conceal the excitement in her voice. "There's James."

"James, where?" Herb responded.

"There in the tan suit, walkin' back and forth."

"That's James?" Herb asked, incredulously. "I be damn," he muttered to himself. "Not quite a hay seed."

Billie peered out of the window at the man in the tan suit and Panama hat. He vaguely looked like someone she remembered, but she had not seen her father in over two years. He looked different, but she had to believe her mother. This was her real father.

Herb stopped the car and Lilly Ann got out. "Oh, James, James. Here we are, over here," she said, wildly beckoning with her right hand.

In his long easy stride, James walked to the car, smiling. He extended his hand to Lilly Ann as he approached, and, to her surprise, her knees buckled. She never really thought about James anymore. Herb was mature in ways James had not been, though she was often uncomfortable with his demands. She surely believed herself over James, but her knees had buckled nevertheless.

Herb got out of the car as quickly as he could in order to put himself between Lilly Ann and the outstretched hand, which he ignored. But he was a little taken aback by James, who towered over his barely five-foot-eleven frame. And then there were those amber eyes, which he was sure women called bedroom eyes.

"I'm Herbert Brown, Lilly Ann's husband. I guess you must be James."

"You guessed right. How do you do? Lilly Ann, good to see you," James said. His expression said he thought she was still as beautiful as ever.

"Oh, you too Ja—"

"Look cat," Herb interrupted, a little more uncertain than he had planned. "Be sure to take care of *my* daughter down the country."

James grinned. "*Your* daughter?" he said as he leaned back and put both hands in his pockets. He continued to smile as he sized-up Herb.

What's this cat up to? Herb thought, his gun weighing heavily on his mind and against his side.

"Rest easy, Billie will be just fine. Her grandmother will see to that," James said, giving Herb a conspiratorial wink.

Herb had expected some guff when he said "my daughter," but the mention of Gertie took the wind out of his sails. All he could do was nod and uncomfortably shift his weight from side to side.

Billie was still in the car, watching the adults without being able to hear what they were saying.

"Billie," Lilly Ann said, tapping on the window. "Come see yo' fath—see James. Git out, honey. You got a train to catch."

Billie reluctantly exited the car. She slowly walked toward the adults and extended her hand. James took her small hand in his massive one and said, "Little Miss Billie Hayes. So nice to see you after such a long time."

He was a grownup, and she certainly was not going to correct him. She was sure he would get her name right by the time her two weeks were up. But suddenly, all her reservations vanished, and she was ready to board the train.

"I'll go git her suitcase," Herb said as he started toward the back of the car.

"Let me," James said, taking Herb's keys and restraining him with a gentle, but firm hand on his shoulder.

18

Billie thought the circus had come to town. A representative sample of the South Carolina Hayes family had gathered at the train station in high anticipation of seeing James' daughter. They had even managed to get Gertie there for the welcoming party.

Billie's existence was not a surprise to James' parents and siblings, who knew her as a baby. But their interaction with her had been limited to chance meetings in town, and at their church if Reverend Barnes' congregation visited for a revival or big meeting. Many of the nieces, nephews, and cousins did not know anything about her at all until now.

The sea of faces that greeted Billie as she and her father exited the train made her light-headed and giddy, so she clung to her father's hand. But when she caught sight of her grandmother, she broke free and ran to embrace her.

In her grandmother's embrace was a peace and comfort that transcended any words the nine-year old could express. For a moment, she could not distinguish where her body ended and

Grandma Gertie's began. The essence of Billie became the essence of Gertie.

"Billie, meet your family," James said with a wide sweep of his arm. At second look, the crowd did not seem as large as Billie had first perceived, but all she could do was muster a faint smile and hang onto her grandmother for dear life.

"Thank y'all for coming out," James continued. "There'll be time for getting better acquainted later. It's been a long trip. Right now, I have to drive Billie and Miz Cunningham home. They'll be down at the farm on Saturday for the family outing."

After they had milled around a bit longer, family members boarded their various modes of transportation—wagon, horse, motorcar—said their goodbyes, and headed back to their respective houses. One of James' brothers had driven the Packard to the station so that James could drive Gertie and Billie home. Once James put Billie's suitcase in the car and grandmother and granddaughter were settled, he walked over to his parents, who had not yet departed with the throng. He shook his father's hand and kissed his teary-eyed mother on the cheek.

"Papa, Momma, thanks for this."

James' father nodded in silence while his mother said, "Gangly little thing, isn't she? But she's got your eyes, James. There's sadness behind them, but they're your eyes."

"Yes ma'am," James said a little wistfully as he waved goodbye and took off in the Packard. He made a mental note to call Lilly Ann when they got back home to let her know that they had arrived safely, and that all was well.

* * *

"We here. Wake up, Billie," Grandma Gertie coaxed as James wheeled the Packard into the front yard of the shack.

"Here? Here, where?" Billie groggily asked.

"Home, baby," Grandma Gertie said as James helped her out of the car.

As Billie got out of the car, she saw Miss Laura standing on the porch. The porch furniture was familiar, but it wasn't the shack she remembered. Perplexed, Billie asked, "Grandma Gertie, where's the shack?"

Grandma Gertie laughed and replied, "This it, honey chile. This it! Thank yo' daddy for the fixin' up!"

Miss Laura and James joined in the laughter as Billie headed toward the kitchen door.

"Come on in and git some lemonade 'for you head back," Miss Laura beckoned to James.

"Thank you, but no ma'am. I need to get back home. I have some work to catch up on. But I'll see y'all on Saturday morning."

And with that, he got back in the Packard and was gone.

Billie remembered watching her father walk down the road when she was a little girl and thinking he vanished when he was out of her sight. Now she knew he would be back.

19

James picked up Grandma Gertie, Billie, and Miss Laura early on Saturday morning for an all-day Hayes family outing at the farm. Billie would spend the night and go back to Grandma Gertie's on Sunday after church and dinner.

The food was nonstop all day long: chicken, ribs, sausages, ham, greens, potato salad, beans and rice, yams, corn pudding, macaroni and cheese, dumplings, corn bread, banana pudding, sweet potato pie, peach cobbler, and pecan pie. There were sack races, horseshoes, checkers, and tag. Billie easily mixed with the host of cousins she had suddenly acquired. She even endured their endless questions and innocent, but cruel, comments, such as:

"Where is your mother?"

"How can Uncle James be your daddy and he ain't married?"

"How can Uncle James even be a daddy without a wife?"

"Why are you so citified?"

"Why your momma give you a boy's name?"

"You not a Hayes. You a Cunningham."

Finally, Billie put her foot down and told them the story of Leroy Ellis, and she threatened to do the same to anybody who asked her another question. Not doubting her, the questions and comments ended and the children played until they wore themselves out.

The adults—at least the men—sat around late in the evening, smoking pipes and cigars and telling lies. Those that had a mind to stole off into the woods for a little moonshine.

Even Reb Barnes had been there for a brief time. He told Billie he was glad to see her and glad that she had "fared well despite her circumstances." Since he was always saying things she did not understand, Billie smiled respectfully and politely ignored him.

As nightfall approached, Billie became apprehensive about spending the night, especially after her grandmother and Miss Laura walked down to the road to catch Mr. Pickett's wagon home. Grandma Gertie had kissed her on the cheek and told her she would be just fine.

Mother Hayes took Billie to the room she would sleep in and helped her draw her bath. She also told her she would be right outside the bathroom door if she needed anything.

Billie quickly bathed and went to the designated spare bedroom. It was a small room with two windows, a small bed, dresser, and a table with a wicker chair. Mother Hayes turned down the bed and asked her if she usually said evening prayers. Billie lied and said she did and was about to say she would, when her father stepped into the room. Mother Hayes went back into the hall and stood outside the door like a hovering angel.

Her father smiled down at her. "Hope you had fun today."

"Yes, sir, I did," Billie said, nervously returning his smile.

"There's a full moon out tonight, and it comes right in those windows. Lights up the room like daylight if you don't close the shutters. And Billie, see that skeleton key in the door? Lets you lock the door from the inside if you have a mind to."

Billie instantly felt better, and she replied, "Yes sir."

"Oh, and another thing. I think you have to call me something beside sir, don't you think?"

"Yes, sir—I mean, yes, sir."

James grinned and asked, "What do you call Mr. Brown?"

"Herb? Herb."

"Herb? You call him Herb?"

"No, sir—I mean, yes, sir. I call Mr. Brown, Herb."

"Hmm, that's not very respectful," her father said, trying to hide his obvious pleasure. "He doesn't seem like the kind of man to cotton to that."

"No, sir. I didn't want to call him Daddy, and they didn't want me to call him Mr. Herb. They said I was too stubborn and gave up trying to make me call him Daddy."

"Still not very respectful, and you didn't get a whipping, huh? Well, I certainly don't want you callin' me James, or Mr. James either, so what will it be?"

"Maybe I could call you Real."

"Excuse me? Real? What kind of name is that?"

"I just made it up. Maybe I could just call you ..." Billie hesitated. "Daddy."

"Sounds good to me. Good night, daughter. Sleep tight."

With that, he closed the door behind him and left the room. With her ear to the door, Billie tried to minimize the clank of the tumbler as she slowly and carefully turned the skeleton key in the lock.

* * *

Morning's early dawning bathed the room in soft light and amber warmth. Billie got up, walked over to one of the windows and looked out beyond the fence that enclosed the backyard onto a lush, verdant meadow dotted with dandelions and buttercups.

With some effort, she raised the window, stuck her head out, and was assailed by the smell of grass, hay, and wildflowers. In the distance, near the end of the meadow, which was also fenced, she saw a dozen or so well-fed cattle grazing. On the west side of the meadow's dark wooden fence was a matrix of white fencing, and she saw a lone rider putting a horse through its paces.

This was a different world, and she never knew it existed not far from the shack where she had lived. Her father never once brought her here. It was wonderful! It was certainly different from the view from Aunt Wilma's kitchen and the apartment. Actually, the apartment had no view at all. *Maybe,* she thought, *Grandma Gertie would let me stay another night in Daddy's house.*

She pondered her other possibilities. It seemed with every good thing came a bad thing. Living on the Hayes' farm would mean being close to Grandma Gertie, but away from her mother. She was not so much in love with Baltimore—it had not yet taken up full residence in her heart—but she would miss school, which she dearly loved, and Carletha and Tom. Though of late, Tom was preoccupied with hanging out with older boys.

A soft knock at the door startled her, and she bumped her head as she backed out of the window.

"Billie," James softly called. "Are you up yet?"

"Yes sir," she answered, struggling to get the window down.

"How did you sleep?"

"I slept good."

"Well."

"Sir?"

"You slept well."

"Oh, yes sir, I slept well."

"Good!"

"Good? I thought you said well."

At this, she heard her father burst into laughter, and she could hear the smile in his voice. "Never mind, never mind. Mother Hayes is about to gather eggs for breakfast. You can go with her if you hurry and have a mind to."

"Yes sir! Tell her please don't leave me!"

20

Herb gazed up at the ceiling with his hands folded behind his head and a shock of his conked hair in his face. He was naked.

"I been lookin' for Red for a week, and ain't nobody seen him," he said. "He ain't been to work, and his boss owes him money, so I guess Red is history. Hey, you listenin' to me?" he asked the naked woman laying next to him as he put out his cigarette. He slapped her voluptuous, dark chocolate butt.

"Of course I'm listenin' to you, baby," his lover whispered.

Since it seemed as if Red had vanished and skipped town, Herb dismissed him as a threat to him or his family for the time being.

"Anyway, I gotta get outta here and go home. We still got boxes to unpack, and Billie will be back in a coupla days. She's in for a surprise."

"Yeah, baby. Well, you better go."

"Uh uh. Not 'til you roll over here one mo' time."

* * *

Two weeks to the day, Billie returned to Baltimore. South Carolina had been a dream come true. Actually, she could never have dreamed of such a trip in her wildest imagination. Grandma Gertie, and her new grandmother and real father, had seen her off with kisses and hugs.

Her father had promised to call often and to see her soon. When he picked her up and kissed her goodbye, she thought she was on top of the world. The one sour note to the trip was that they sent her home on the train alone, albeit in the care of a kindly porter who saw that she was safe and fed.

When the train pulled into Mount Royal Station, there was no throng of excited kinfolk waiting for Billie when the porter took her suitcase and escorted her from the train. But she was just as thrilled to see her mother running toward her.

"Momma, oh Momma! I had such a time!"

Her mother embraced her and said, "I'm so glad you home. You can tell me all about it, but we have a surprise for you!"

Herb walked up to them and grabbed Billie's suitcase. "Little girl, you finally decided to come home! Did they treat you right down the country?"

"Yes sir! Better than right!"

Billie had vowed to herself not to share any of her experiences with Herb. And she knew for certain that she would keep calling him Herb.

As they made their way home, the streets were unfamiliar to Billie, and, to her surprise, the family had moved to Lanvale Street in Upton. She knew the family had planned to move because she had packed her own room before she went to South Carolina, and carefully hid her money boxes. But she had no idea that they would move into a neighborhood so entirely different from the old one before she got back.

The new house—and it was a house, with two floors and a basement—was huge in comparison to the apartment. The new house would mean a new school and new friends, but she hoped not new taunts.

Billie was in a tizzy. The world was moving too fast.

* * *

As the family settled in and got acclimated to the new neighborhood, Herb and Lilly Ann began to argue more about his comings and goings. But to Herb's delight, Lilly Ann became preoccupied with decorating the house and becoming part of the new social scene.

It was not too many months before Herb believed he had stretched himself too thin. With the rent on the house, new furnishings, the place on Carey Street, the upkeep on the car, and the upkeep on Lilly Ann, he was struggling to keep his head above water. Of course, he never considered his own extravagances: stylish clothes, frequent visits to the best clubs, flashy jewelry, and free spending on liquor and women.

He had even threatened to call James about support money for Billie. He had lit into Lilly Ann, saying if James was some big shot in *South Cakalakey*, he ought to support his daughter. Lilly Ann had hurled back at him his claim that Billie was *his* daughter, and the pride he took in saying he fed and clothed her.

To make matters worse, profits from the grocery story were down because he did not give it his full attention, and because Leon was in failing health, they had to pay for extra help. Lilly Ann refused to go back there to work.

Their short marriage was starting to unravel, but giving attention to it was last thing on Herb's list of priorities. One thing he believed he had learned about a beautiful woman, or at least his wife, was that she believed she could get any man she wanted and, therefore, did not feel beholden to any one man. Hence, one source of their friction. On the other hand, a less attractive woman, like his dark chocolate Carey Street honey, would do anything he wanted because she was so happy to have a man, especially him.

His ego loved that his wife was beautiful, and he was still drawn to her sensuality, but their passions had waned. She was young and inexperienced and too conventional, so he sought other outlets.

Then there was Brownies, which was holding its own, but because they could no longer afford to keep him employed, they let Tom Sr. go. Besides, when he was drinking, which was all the time, Tom Sr. became a lightening rod and instigated a lot of fists fights in the club.

Tom Sr. fell on hard times, but he only had himself to blame. He squandered his salary from the docks and continued to bully his wife and kids. At last refusing to take it any longer, Mrs. McNeal packed up the kids and moved in with relatives in Sykesville, Maryland.

Finally, there was the numbers racket. Herb could not break into the action in Upton. It was already covered.

On top of his financial and marital worries, Herb was shocked to discover that the burning doorknob curse had followed them to the new house. It angered and frightened him, but he managed to assuage himself with the voluptuous paramour he kept in his love nest on Carey Street.

Except for risqué remarks and accidental brushes against her out of earshot and sight of Lilly Ann, Herb spared Billie further abuse for the next few years.

Come Rain or Come Shine

I'm gonna love you like nobody's loved you come rain or come shine
High as a mountain and deep as a river come rain or come shine
I guess when you met me it was just one of those things
But don't ever bet me cause I'm gonna be true if you let me

You're gonna love me like nobody's loved me come rain or come shine
Happy together unhappy together and won't it be fine?
Days may be cloudy or sunny
We're in or we're out of the money

But I'm with you always, I'm with you rain or shine

I'm gonna love you like nobody's loved you come rain or come shine
High as a mountain deep as a river come rain or come shine
I guess when you met me it was just one of those things
But don't ever bet me cause I'm gonna be true if you let me

You're gonna love me like nobody's loved me come rain or come shine
Happy together unhappy together and won't it be fine?
Days may be cloudy or sunny
We're in or we're out of the money.

But I'll love you always, I'm with you rain or shine

21

1955

They found the body of Thomas McNeal, Sr. discarded like yesterday's newspaper. He had been shot to death, and his body thrown under a pile of garbage in the alley behind a neighborhood bar in East Baltimore.

Not too many people were surprised. It was inevitable that Tom Sr. would bully the wrong person and get himself killed. For a few days, he had been unaccounted for, but nobody actively looked for him. But after he did not report to work for the second day and could not be reached at home, his supervisor had called the police.

The police interviewed patrons of the bar and the neighbors, but nobody saw or heard anything. After a few weeks of no leads, the murder of a troublesome colored man was relegated to the bottom of the district commander's priority list.

The homecoming service for Tom Sr. was held at Phillips Funeral Home on Monroe Street. Since funerals are for the living, friends and neighbors—even those with no love lost for Tom Sr.—packed the modest parlor in support of Mrs. McNeal and her sons.

At the start of the funeral, the family filed down the aisle toward the casket as Phillips' in-house organist played, "What A Friend We Have in Jesus." The in-house preacher read from the Scripture.

"Jesus said, I am the resurrection and the life: he that believeth in me, though he were dead, yet shall he live: and whosoever liveth and believeth in me shall never die. I know that my redeemer liveth, and that he shall stand at the latter day upon the earth: and I shall see God: whom I shall see for myself, and mine eyes shall behold, and not another. We brought nothing into this world, and it is certain we can carry nothing out. The Lord gave, and the Lord hath taken away; blessed be the name of the Lord."

One could hear softly spoken "hallelujahs" and "amens" as the family took their seats. Tom caught a glimpse of Billie and Carletha as he passed their row, and his somber countenance lightened. He smiled a half-smile and nodded in acknowledgment of their presence.

This was only the third time that Billie and Tom had seen each other since the McNeals had moved to Sykesville. Billie felt like those old people she used to talk about, because she expected Tom to be the same size as when she last saw him. But, almost eighteen, Tom had physically matured into a man.

Like his late father, Tom was six feet two inches tall. He was lean and muscular from lifting boxes and stacking shelves in supermarkets, and from the anger-managing workouts he put himself through in the makeshift gym in his basement. His skin was a hazelnut color, and his face, with its square, strong jaw, was as smooth as a baby's bottom. His features were strong—dark, deep-set eyes, heavy eyebrows, full lips—but not overpowering, and his thick black hair was just long enough to fall into its natural wave pattern. Tom was gorgeous.

He seemed like the same old Tom, but at the same time, different. Billie couldn't describe the feeling she felt after seeing him for the first time in a long time. Periodically during the service, she found her gaze transfixed on the back of his head.

The service was brief. The preacher wasted no words on Tom Sr., a man he did not know and had never met, and there was no eulogy to speak of, so he preached a generic sermon. After the family recessional, Billie and Carletha hurriedly shouldered their way through the crowd to get to the boys before they got into the limousine for the trip to the cemetery.

Tom stood next to the hearse, and as Billie approached, he couldn't help noticing that she had curves where she once had angles.

"Tom, oh Tom. I'm so sorry about your father," Billie said, standing on tiptoes to hug his neck.

"Yeah, well … Thanks. That's okay," Tom replied uncertainly, stiffening at her embrace. Then he bent down to allow a shorter Carletha to hug him too, while Billie greeted David and John.

"Me too, Tom," said Carletha. "I'm sorry that your father—"

"Thanks, Carletha," Tom interrupted. "But he was David and John's father. He was my tormenter." And before Tom could say more, the funeral director ushered the three boys into the limo.

* * *

After the interment, the traditional repast was held at Mrs. Dorothy Black's house since the McNeal house was in disarray after so much time without a woman's touch. Billie hoped to say more to Tom there, even though she didn't know what she would say. At any rate, she did not get much of a chance because of the throng that had gathered.

Inching her way through the crowded house, she found Tom in a corner seated next to his mother and stroking her arm. While she was trying to decide whether to interrupt, Tom saw her and stood up.

"Hey, Billie. Glad you came back. Where's your partner in crime?"

"Lookin' for food, no doubt." They laughed.

"Look, Billie, I have to sort of look out for my mom, but maybe we can talk later, okay?"

"Sure, sure, I understand," Billie nodded as she looked through the crowd for Carletha or any familiar face. "Sure, but take care of yourself, too," she added.

"Got to do that. Nobody else will. Oh yeah, and guess what? I think we may be moving back into the house."

Just then, a couple interrupted. The wife patted Tom on the back, and the husband took his hand and pumped it.

With her mouth open and just a little put out from being bumped from her spot with Tom, Billie left and searched for Carletha to find out if she had the inside scoop on the McNeals' possible move back to Clayton Street.

* * *

Fortunately for Tom Sr.'s estranged family, his insurance policy paid off the house on Clayton Street, which he had managed to keep, and his pension and social security were enough for Mrs. McNeal to eke out a meager living for herself and the boys. By February, they moved back to the house. The boys got odd jobs, such as bagging groceries at the local A&P, caddying at the Carroll Park Golf Course, and running errands for neighbors to help their mother make ends meet.

Moving back to Baltimore meant that Tom had to transfer to Langston Hughes High School to complete his senior year. But transferring was no big deal for him, because even though he had excelled as an athlete in Sykesville and had many admirers, he was still a lone wolf.

Unfortunately, his athletic prowess did not save him from being kept back a year. The turmoil in his life had left him with little interest, energy, or patience for schoolwork, causing his grades to suffer. While academics were an inconvenience, football, wrestling, and track provided an outlet for the anger that always teemed just below the surface.

As fate would have it, Billie was a junior at Langston Hughes. Because she was so bright, her elementary school had skipped her from the fourth to the sixth grade, making her a year younger than the eleventh graders with whom she shared classes. But the age difference was not too obvious, because she was physically and emotionally mature.

Tom and Billie were two weeks into the school year before they actually ran into each. As Billie left her English class and rounded the corner, she ran into Tom, who was at his locker.

"Hey, Tom," Billie squealed, punching him on the arm.

"Little Sis," Tom grinned while rubbing his arm. "You need to pull that punch a little."

"How the hell are you, big man?"

"What did you say? You're not as grown as you'd like to think. Don't talk to me like that!"

"Good to see you, McNeal. Gotta go. Late for math." And she strolled off, leaving Tom smiling and shaking his head.

* * *

Billie and Tom naturally gravitated to different crowds, which meant their social lives intersected very little. Billie already had friends from the previous year, and Tom, the loner, was self-conscious about being a year older and, on average, bigger than his classmates. So when he hung out, it was usually with his football teammates. But even though they traveled in different circles, Tom had no problem giving Billie unsolicited advice on her choice of friends—especially if they were boys.

22

Fall 1955

It was Saturday, and Billie was in the basement doing her ironing for the upcoming school week. To catch the natural light, she stood with her back to the basement window and door, both of which opened into the small backyard.

Herb was in the alley washing his three-year-old Cadillac with the ever-present Camel dangling from his lips in defiance of a hacking cough. Her mother was in the kitchen humming and busying herself with the creation of a sweet potato pie for Sunday's dinner.

Traditionally, certain activities were forbidden on Sunday—no ironing, sewing, or housework of any kind, no card-playing, dancing, or listening to secular music, and no television or the like—and, in a lot of Baptist homes, Sunday dinner was prepared on Saturday. Her mother kept to the tradition, whether she went to church or not.

Billie heard Herb shut off the water, reel in the hose, and start walking toward the basement door. As he entered, she steeled herself. He walked up behind her and stood close enough for her to feel his breath on her neck.

"So you goin' to that prom, huh? What'cha gonna do after the prom?"

Without turning around, Billie said, through clenched teeth, "We're going out to dinner at Wilson's."

"Yeah, but what'cha gonna do after that?"

"I don't know. Go to a party … Come home. I don't know."

"I know what'cha gonna do. Think I'll tell your momma that you need to come home directly after the prom so you won't be givin' up nothin.'"

Billie quickly whirled around to face Herb with the iron in her hand, and as she did, her elbow caught him in the ribs. He recoiled just in time to avoid a face full of iron.

In a hot whisper, Billie hissed, "If you say one more disgusting, filthy thing to me, or come close enough for me to smell you, I promise I will scald you in your sleep. And if I were you, I'd be very careful when you ate my cooking, because I will poison your ass. If you think I'm playing, dare me!" She inched the iron closer to Herb's face, close enough for him to feel the heat.

Shocked, Herb threw his hands up as if to surrender, then backed away from the ironing board. He ran his hand through his hair as he quickly walked up the basement steps, muttering and hacking.

Billie was sure she could never do anything that would result in his death, despite how much she loathed him, but she was not above inflicting pain. The irony of it all was that when viewed from the outside, their relationship appeared to be perfectly normal.

Her mother, still busy cooking and humming, heard nothing.

* * *

The subject of the prom came up again when Tom and Billie were leaving their after school activities—he, track; she, student council— before they headed for their respective destinations.

"So, you're going to the prom with Butch Duvall?" Tom asked.

"Yeah," Billie said, knowing more was to follow.

"He's a senior, you know."

"Yeah, it's a senior prom, dummy."

"How well do you know Butch?"

"Oh please, Tom. What do you mean, 'how well do you know Butch?' I know him well enough. He's taken me to the movies a couple of times, and we saw a show at the Royal, but then that's nunna your business."

"Like I said, he's a senior. Senior cats prey on you freshman girls. You're putty in their hands."

"You forget I'm not a freshman, and Butch is a nice guy."

"You're barely fifteen! Technically, you *are a freshman*. I don't care what class you're in. Look, Butch is a jock, and I know jocks."

"What does that mean? You sound like Herb. You don't know me."

"What do you mean, I sound like Herb?"

"Never mind. Why aren't you going to your own prom?"

"Look, I'm asking the questions—"

"Why not? Can't get a girl?"

"I can always get a girl. Just can't get a tux. Actually, I don't care about going."

"Tom, I'm sorry. I—"

"Look, Little Sis, I just don't like the guy much. You know, guys talk."

"And?"

"And, nothing. Forget it. Gotta get to my bus stop. See you Monday."

Tom punched Billie on the arm and headed down the street before she could respond.

23

May 1956

The big night arrived, and Billie's mother helped her dress for the prom. Billie had enjoyed a rare bonding moment with her when they shopped for her dress, and they had picked out a pale blue taffeta gown with a princess-style fitted bodice and a gathered skirt. The full skirt was covered with a dotted nylon overskirt, and the modestly low neckline was halter-style.

"Billie, you are so beautiful in that dress!"

"Thank you, Momma. Can you get the Polaroid and take a picture?"

"Sure, let's take it in the front room. Come on downstairs. Don't forget yo' gloves."

Herb, who was on the sofa in the living room, pretended not to see Billie as she descended the stairs.

"Herb, Herb, go get the Polaroid so we can take some pictures. Don't she look nice?"

"Yes, very nice, very nice," Herb said as he got up to find the camera. The doorbell rang before he could return.

"Momma, I'm going back upstairs. You get the door." Billie gathered her gown, flew back up the steps, and waited at the top.

Billie's mother laughed and waited for Herb to return from the dining room with the camera. By this time, Butch had rung the bell again.

"Hold yo' horses, hold yo' horses," Herb said as he entered the living room.

"I'll get it, Herb," Billie's mother called.

"No, I'll get it myself. Jest hold yo' horses too," Herb said. "Little anxious, ain't you?" he muttered.

"Good evening, Mr. Brown, Miz Brown. Is Billie ready?"

"Good evening to you too, Butch. Is Billie ready for what?" Herb chided.

"Come on in, Butch. Don't let Mr. Brown tease you. Billie be down in a minute. Billie," her mother called up the steps. "Butch is here, and lookin' pretty handsome too!"

"Thank you, ma'am," Butch replied, nervously fingering the corsage box. He was keenly aware of Herb's steady gaze.

Billie finally descended the stairs, Loretta Young-style, to her mother's applause. Butch, with his five foot eleven height, broad shoulders, and narrow hips, was the perfect frame for a tuxedo. He was dark brown, with a perfectly round head that was accented by his close-cropped hair. His features were small and nondescript. He was average-looking, but his military bearing made him stand out.

After they had taken pictures and were about to leave, Herb dropped a bombshell. "Butch, have her home by midnight," he emphatically stated through a haze of cigarette smoke.

"Twelve? Twelve o'clock, sir?"

"Yep, twelve."

"But Herb, the prom's not over until eleven," Billie said. "We won't have a chance to go to dinner if I have to be home at midnight."

"I'm sorry 'bout that, but midnight it is. You got that, Butch?"

All Butch could do was put his hands to the side of his head in disbelief and turn toward the window, mad as a wet hen. "But Mr. Brown, this is my senior prom," he said, turning back to face Herb.

"Sorry 'bout that. May you shoulda' took an older girl."

Billie's mother said, "Herb, that's –"

"What kind of thing is that to say?" Billie yelled. She cast pleading eyes at her mother, who gave a defeated shrug of her shoulders, as if she could not do or say anything.

"Midnight, or don't go at all. Now I said my piece. You better go before I change my mind all together."

A fuming Billie snatched up her shawl and gloves, while a crest-fallen Butch shoved the corsage box in her hand and went out of the front door ahead of her. A limo driver opened the door for them as they approached, and a shocked Billie overheard Butch mutter, "Why that god-dammed son-of-a-bitch," as they climbed in.

"I'm sorry, Butch," Billie quietly said as she took his hand.

Butch snatched it away and replied, "Yeah, me too!"

* * *

The gymnasium was decorated with balloons and streamers in black and gold, the prom colors. By the time Billie and Butch arrived, the festivities were in full swing. The energy was high and charged with raging teenage hormones.

Upon entering, the heavy air assaulted Billie with the odor of cheap perfume, Old Spice, and sweat. The dance floor was a kaleidoscope of nylon, chiffon, silk, satin, and taffeta cotton candy gowns, swinging, swishing, and swaying to the beat of the band. Faculty chaperones kept a watchful eye out for bumpin' and grindin', and the girls—even a few boys with conks—worried about their hair "going back." Some of the boys snuck off to add Thunderbird or vodka to their punch.

Billie and Butch had barely stepped foot into the gym when Butch walked off to join a group of football players huddled at the opposite end of the floor. Already upset, Billie felt utterly foolish standing alone. She realized that the majority of the girls were seniors, and she didn't really know any of them. While contemplating her next course of action, Butch returned and asked her to dance.

"Thanks for just leaving me standing here," Billie said.

"I'm sorry. I was just mad at your father."

"Stepfather."

"Stepfather, same thing. This is one of the most important nights of my life, and I gotta take my date home at midnight. What's he gonna do if you don't come home when he said?"

"Look Butch, I'm sorry. I really am, but if Herb says I gotta be home at midnight, I gotta be home at midnight. You have to get me home on time."

"So you're gonna be a stick in the mud? Yeah, yeah, sure ruins my plans. The cats are already calling you Cinderella."

"Thanks a lot," Billie sarcastically replied. "Rub salt in the wound."

"Might as well try to make the most of a bad situation."

Butch pulled Billie close to him, and they danced to the band playing Ivory Joe Hunter's "Since I Met You Baby," the best bump and grinder of the night. After a few dances and a few more trips to talk with his boys, Butch grabbed Billie by the arm and pulled her toward the door.

"It's hot as hell in here. Let's go outside for awhile."

"Sure is ... Okay," Billie nodded in agreement.

She followed Butch to the gym doors that opened not far from the bleachers. When they got outside, Butch pulled out a pack of cigarettes and lit up.

"Feels a lot better out here," he said.

"Yeah, it does. I didn't know you smoked."

"Don't everybody?"

"No, I don't."

"Right, right, Cinderella. Goody-two shoes."

"Why are you being so mean, Butch?"

"Mean? I ain't being mean. I'm pissed, that's all. I guess you don't know me very well."

"You're right, I guess I don't." *Where have I heard that before?* Billie thought. "Come on, let's go back in."

"Naw, not yet. Let's take a walk."

"Take a walk? Walk where?"

"Just come on, would you?"

Butch took Billie by the hand and led her along the gym wall until he came to a door that ordinarily would not permit entrance from the outside. But it had a wedge of wood holding it slightly ajar. It was imperceptible in the dim light unless a person knew in advance that it was there. Butch opened the door, and said, "Go on, step inside."

Reluctant, but wanting to salvage what was left of the evening, Billie stepped into the pitch black room. "I can't see. Where am I? What's this room?"

"Take it easy. The equipment room."

"Equipment room?" Billie asked.

But before she could say more, Butch kissed her tenderly, but passionately. Billie responded in kind.

"Now that's more—"

"Butch, is that you?" someone whispered in the dark. Billie nearly jumped out of her skin.

"Skip, why you still here?" Butch asked, and an unseen girl giggled. "Come on man, get out! Times up!"

Billie heard the rustling of a crinoline and more giggling.

"Okay, okay. Come on baby, time to go," Skip said, and two shadowy figures, barely visible in the light of the exit sign, brushed past Butch and Billie and headed out the door.

"Don't move Billie," Butch cautioned. "Don't want you trippin' on nothing." He slowly walked along the wall until his foot hit something. "Okay," he said, taking Billie by the hand. "Now sit."

"Sit? Sit where?"

"On the floor. On the mat."

"I don't think so."

"Come on baby, it's clean. Cleaned it myself. Don't be a stick in the mud," Butch chided while kissing Billie on the neck.

"Okay, but only for a few minutes."

"Okay, the mat's right beside us. Just sit down."

Billie reached for the mat, and, finding it, got on all fours and crawled until she touched the wall. Then she sat with her back against it and stretched out her legs in front of her.

Butch followed suit until he faced Billie. He kissed her again, first on the lips, then along her neck and bosom. And again she responded, emboldening him. Butch sat back and slid closer, cupping Billie's breasts in his hands.

"Don't Butch, don't."

"Shh," Butch replied as he gently tried to push Billie over. "Lay down, Billie," he whispered.

"No … No, Butch!"

"Yes, Billie."

Butch pushed Billie harder, causing her to fall on her side. Butch stretched out beside her and began running his hand up her leg and under her dress.

"No, Butch!" Billie spat as she tried to get up, but she was pinned between Butch, a young athlete in top condition, and a cold and unyielding cinder block wall. But she pushed harder. "Stop Butch! Let me up!"

"Let you up? Come on, baby. You know I love you, and you know you want it. Besides, you owe me for ruining my prom night."

"Owe you? That's how you think? Get off of me!" Billie yelled, but to no avail.

Butch continued to grope her, more to exact pain than to elicit pleasure, but their awkward position prevented him from doing more. In one quick motion, he yanked the neckline of Billie's dress, pulling her onto her back, then rolled on top of her. But he could not navigate the dress, undo his own pants, and hold her down at the same time.

Billie squirmed, kicked, and pummeled Butch's back until he relented. As he rolled off of her, she elbowed him, unexpectedly catching him in the nose. As he cursed, Billie grabbed her shawl and stumbled her way to the door.

"You better think of a good story to tell you parents, 'cause I ain't takin' you home!" Butch yelled. But he instinctively knew that Billie would not tell her parents.

"Go to hell!" Billie said as she found the door and exited. She made her way to a spot under the bleachers and cried.

After taking several minutes to compose herself, Billie was glad she had the presence of mind to grab her shawl. When Butch yanked the neckline of her dress, the force snapped off the rhinestones buttons that held it together. She crisscrossed it across her exposed bra and tied it by the fringes in back. She was also glad her mother had insisted that she take money with her because, "A woman should always have her own money."

What do I do now? Billie thought as she aimlessly began to walk down Presstman Street. She shivered in the light rain that began to fall. When she got to the corner, she noticed a phone booth and went inside, seeking a temporary respite from the rain. She fished in her purse, found a dime, dropped it in the coin box, and reluctantly dialed a familiar number. *It's Friday night. Hope he's home.*

"Hello," said Tom.

"Tom, it's me. Can you meet me at Woodley Park?" Billie asked in a shaky, scared voice.

She naturally thought of the park because it was their special place. They met there at least one Sunday out of the month between Billie's eleven o'clock service and Baptist Training Union at six o'clock.

"Billie? Is that you? What's wrong? What's goin' on?" Tom asked in a panicked voice.

"Yeah, it's me. Can you meet me?"

"No—I mean, yeah, but not in the park. It's raining. Come to the house. Are you all right?"

"Yes, but are you sure about the house?"

"Of course. You know you can come, but how you gonna get here? Where are you?"

"I'm catching a cab."

"Hurry up then, and come in the basement way. Ma's gone to bed already."

Billie hung up and searched the street for a cab.

* * *

Tom went out into the backyard, nervously waiting for a cab to deposit Billie at the end of the street near the alley—and hopefully out of sight of the neighbors on the block, including the Taylors. He was not concerned about explaining anything to his family; he was the de facto man of the house. Besides, his mom had retired for the evening, David was listening to a fight on the radio, and John was working at the A&P.

After twenty minutes, Tom caught a glimpse of Billie running down the alley, her taffeta netted dress swinging from side-to-side. He dashed to meet her. "Billie, you're soaking wet! What happened?" he asked.

"I don't want to talk about it. Guess we can't go to the park, can we?" Billie said, in a feeble attempt to be funny.

Before she could say more, Tom threw her over his shoulder, John Wayne-style, and headed for the house. Once in the basement, he deposited her on top of a clothes hamper.

"Take off that wet shawl while I find you something dry."

"Can't."

"Can't? What do you mean, 'can't?'"

"Can't. Just find me something dry, please."

Tom dug through a neatly folded basket of clean clothes and came up with a shirt belonging to David, the smallest of the three brothers.

"Here, put this on."

Billie slid off the hamper and turned her back to Tom. "You turn around too, Tom."

"Huh? Sure."

After Tom turned his back, he heard Billie undress and slip into David's shirt. "Okay, you can turn back," she said as she handed him her wet shawl, which he threw over the sanitary tub.

Tom laughed at the sight of Billie in a rough-dry, plaid cotton shirt over a wet taffeta gown. "I'm sorry, but you do look funny. Maybe I can find you some pants or something."

"That's all right, this is fine," Billie said as Tom pulled out two folding chairs for them to sit on.

He gave her a few seconds to arrange herself and waited for her to say something, but her silence was longer than his patience and anxiety. Finally, he spoke up. "Okay now, what happened, and whose ass do I have to kick?"

"Nothing like that," Billie lied, and she started to shiver.

"Oh, nothing like that, huh? I guess your cheap ass dress just fell apart!"

Billie started to cry and blurted, "Why does this always happen to me?"

"What do you mean? What is 'this,' Billie?" Tom demanded.

"I don't know what I'm saying. I guess you were right about Butch. But please don't say I told you so."

Surprise! Tom thought. "Look, Billie, I'm a guy. I know how guys think. Did he, uh, did he ..."

"No, he didn't. He tried too, I guess, but no."

"You guess? If he coulda, he woulda."

Billie pleaded, "Tom, please let it go. Please. I need to figure out how to get home and what I'm going to say."

"Maybe ... Won't they be asleep when you get home?"

"I doubt it since I'm supposed to be home by midnight. They'll be up to be sure I made it on time."

"Midnight? Holy shit! It's quarter after eleven now!"

Billie sat and sobbed quietly as Tom paced back and forth. He finally went over to her, pulled her to her feet, and hugged her. All the tension and fear dissipated, and Billie felt strangely at peace.

"Don't worry, Little Sis. You're safe. Look, can you sew?"

"Sew? Yeah, a little."

"Okay, I'll find some thread—no, better idea. I'll just get a couple of pins, and you fix your dress. I'll call a cab, and you go home. Tell your parents it didn't look like Butch was going to leave on time, so you caught a cab and got wet waiting. Mr. Brown might be a little mad, but tell him you're through with Butch, and he doesn't have to bother himself chastising Butch about it."

"You're a genius! I think that might work. And I'm sure Herb will be happy about it." Billie's sarcasm escaped Tom.

"Get yourself together. I'll go get the pins and call a cab. I'll tell him to pick you up at the corner, but I'll wait with you. You got money?"

"Yeah. If it's not enough, I can always get more when I get home."

"No, the less you have to say the better."

Tom reached in his pocket, handed Billie two dollars, and gently punched her on the arm. He knew she didn't want to take money from him, but thanks to his various part-time jobs, he always had a few dollars in his pocket.

"You're right, thanks." And this time, she hugged him.

* * *

Miracle of all miracles. When the cab pulled up in front of Billie's house, there was only a dim light on in the living room. But there was a light on in the front bedroom, which meant that both Herb and her mother were probably upstairs.

As Billie unlocked the door and tiptoed up the steps, she heard her mother, who was apparently on the telephone, say, "Momma, what's wrong? What's wrong? Why you callin' this time of the night?"

"Momma, it's the same time up here in Ballamore as it is in Fairfield! Are you all right? What's the matter?"

Just then, Billie stuck her head around the bedroom door and said, "Hi y'all. Just a little wet, but I'm home. Talk to y'all in the morning. Night."

Herb, propped on two pillows with a magazine on his chest, had apparently dozed off. He stirred, but before he could gather himself or say anything, Billie left. She hurried down the hall to her room, closed the door, and breathed a sigh of relief.

Billie heard her mother call out, "Night, honey. You made it with a minute to spare!"

Her mother laughed and went back to her conversation. "Momma, are you sure you all right? Maybe you don't need to be in that house by yo'self."

With her door closed, Billie couldn't hear her mother's conversation with Grandma Gertie. But every time Billie thought of her, and her protective intervention, her heart smiled.

24

As soon as Tom had seen Billie off in the cab, he hotfooted it back home. Once in the basement, he locked the back door and searched for his barbells. Finding them, he furiously did curls for several minutes before he stopped and took a deep breath.

What am I going to do about Butch Duvall? he asked himself. *Can't go to Sandtown, 'cause that's his territory and his boys will get in it. A pick-up hoop game? I could clock him making a shot, but I don't know where he plays. I can't wait that long to wail on his ass. Butch don't know who he's foolin' with.*

Tom fished for his jump rope behind some boxes and began to jump like a boxer in training. *School? Naw. It's Senior week anyway. Won't be back in school. Besides, anything on the school grounds could get us pulled from graduation. Got to figure out a way to do this without getting the fellows in it. I don't want them to know what the beef's about anyway.*

But thinking about what Billie told him just rekindled his anger. Tom dropped the rope and started doing push-ups. *What, what, what—Baccalaureate! Yeah, Baccalaureate at Pennsylvania AME. No choice ... gotta take it to him ... Whatever happens, happens.*

"Tom, Tom? Whatcha doin' down there?" John called from the top of the steps.

"Hey John, just burning off some energy. You home? Good. There's a plate for you in the oven. I'll be up soon. 'Night."

"Solid. Talk to ya in the morning."

Tom kept tabs on his brothers' comings and goings, and, to his delight, they respected his new role.

Church tomorrow, that's a plan.

* * *

Tom got up early on Sunday morning and dressed in an old suit of his father's that his mother had pressed and laid out for him. He didn't particularly want to wear it—it was a little big—but he didn't have one of his own, and he had more important things to worry about that morning.

He caught the 51 bus, the first of two different buses, and headed for Pennsylvania AME Zion Church. The last bus got him to the church just in time to see members of the Langston Hughes Class of 1956 slowly file into the sanctuary to the majestic organ swells of "Land of Home and Glory" from the Pomp and Circumstances Military Marches.

Tom swiftly walked from the bus stop to get in line, all the while craning his neck and looking for Butch. Once seated, Tom ended up three rows behind Butch. He was so preoccupied with watching Butch's every move that he missed the rousing, fervent, but short on motivation homily.

Tom felt the heat of his anger slowly rise from the tip of his toes through his body, until he had to wipe sweat from his brow. He willed himself to think about something else so that his body temperature would return to normal. Fortunately for Tom, the church had a punch and cookie reception in the fellowship hall for the guests after service.

Tom milled around, making small talk with some of the guys as he kept an eye on Butch. He saw him head for the restroom, and without any real plan or knowledge of the restroom's layout, Tom followed Butch. He waited for Butch to go in, and since there was no clicking sound of a lock being turned, Tom assumed there was more than one stall. He waited a few seconds, and quietly went in too.

Once inside, Tom looked into the mirror on the wall opposite where he was standing, and saw Butch's head above one of the stalls. Tom was not visible to Butch, so he was unaware of Tom's presence. Just as Butch came out of the stall and walked the few shorts steps to the sink, Tom stepped toward him and called out his name.

"Butch!"

Startled, Butch jerked his head around at the sound of his name. "McNeal, man you scared me—"

And before Butch could say more, Tom delivered two quick jabs to Butch's jaw, followed by an uppercut that dropped Butch to his knees in pain and disbelief. Gasping, Butch tried to speak while throwing up his hands in a defensive move. Tom fought the urge to knee him in the Adam's apple while he was down, but something restrained him and he said, "That's for Billie!" He quickly slipped out of the restroom.

Instead of going back to the fellowship hall, Tom took the first set of steps he encountered. He reached the main level and found the nearest exit—a side entrance off the sanctuary—and rushed out. Once outside, he got his bearings and decided to walk to a bus stop a couple of blocks away from the church.

As his breathing returned to normal, Tom could not believe the euphoria he felt. The picture of Butch on his knees made him smile. *Bet he won't tell his boys about this one*, he thought. He was sure Billie would chastise him for his behavior while being secretly glad that Butch got his just desserts—that is, if he told her, which he had no intention of doing.

He had just enough time to get home and change out of what he called his monkey suit before meeting Billie at the park.

His right hand throbbed, but he was impervious to the pain. Until his father's untimely death, pain had been his constant friend. Without it, his anger—the anger that tore him apart inside and caused him to war with himself—had more room to grow. He discovered, however, and for some inexplicable reason, that the turmoil in his stomach settled, and the pulsing in his temple stopped whenever he was in Billie's company. He felt they were kindred spirits, but while she knew his demons, he did not know hers.

It was three o'clock, and Billie was waiting on the bench where they always met. The park was beginning to show its spring greening, but it was not as well-kept as it once was. There were lots of brown spots waiting to be seeded, and a dotting of dandelions poked through in places. The neighborhood kids still came to swing and see-saw and to ride their bikes, but the pedestrian traffic was light on Sundays.

Billie still had on her church dress, and seeing her caused Tom's heart to do flip-flops. It was not a feeling he had ever experienced before.

"Hi, Little Sis. How'd you make out last night?" he asked, punching her on the arm in their usual greeting. As he grew older, stronger, and more muscular, he was careful not to hit her too hard. Billie, on the other hand, demonstrated her need to exert her independence by giving him a stinging zinger every now and then. As he sat down, she punched him back.

"By the skin of my teeth," Billie said. "But my mother was on the phone with Grandma Gertie, so I went to my room without them really seeing me."

"Your grandmother must be your guardian angel. She's funny!"

"Don't talk about my grandmother," Billie playfully chided. "Tom, I'm so glad you're my friend. I don't know what I'd do without you."

"Don't go gettin' girly on me—"

"Okay, okay," Billie interrupted. "How was the Baccalaureate?'

"Better than you could imagine," Tom said with a sly grin.

"Whatta you mean? You met a girl or somethin'?"

"None that I didn't already know. Why are you always asking me about girls?"

"I dunno. All right, so what was the big deal?"

"Nothing, Billie. I was just pulling your leg."

"Yeah, okay. Did you see, uh, did you see …"

"Butch. Yeah, I saw him," said Tom, and he subconsciously rubbed his bruised right hand.

Billie jumped up, incredulous, and shouted, "You promised not to do anything! You lied to me! You lied!"

"Okay, I lied, but Billie, I just couldn't let him get away with it. I'm sorry. I had to do it. I had to!"

"You just can't pass up the opportunity to hit somebody, can you?"

"This was not an opportunity I wanted," Tom said angrily through clenched teeth. "I can't believe you're mad at me. Look Billie, the guy got what he deserved. Now drop it!"

"I'm sorry. I just don't want you to get in trouble because of me."

"You're too kind," Tom sarcastically responded.

They sat in strained silence for a couple of minutes, then Billie placed her right hand on Tom's back and rubbed it in a circular motion. His whole body tensed, and she immediately withdrew her hand. He knew that she probably thought it was his lingering anger that made his muscles tighten, but, in fact, it was his unfamiliarity with tender touch that caused the reaction.

"Don't you need some ice for your hand?" Billie asked.

"No, I *do not,* now let it go for Pete's sake!"

"Can't be concerned about you, can I? What … What did you actually do to Butch?"

"I tried to kill him. You satisfied? *Let it go!*"

"I can't let it go. Tell the truth," Billie stubbornly insisted. "What did you do?"

Tom jumped up from the bench, spun around, and bent down until his face was inches away from Billie's. "I just coldcocked him a coupla times. He'll survive, but he got the message. And if you ask me one more time, I'm outta here. Got that?"

"Yeah, I got it. Now get outta my face!"

Tom stood there for a second, glaring at Billie, but the sadness behind her eyes melted his heart. And for a split-second, just a split-second, he almost kissed her. Instead, heart racing and hands shaking, he walked toward the swings. He didn't know if anger or desire was causing the physiological reactions.

Tom sat in a swing with his head between his shoulders, brooding as he rocked back and forth without lifting his feet off the ground. When he heard Billie approach, he took a deep breath.

"Guess I owe you some money for the cab ride," she said.

"Naw, you don't ... owe me ... Forget it."

Billie hesitantly replied, "All right, thanks again. I'm gonna head back to the house. See ya."

"Yeah, later," Tom said, without raising his head.

He didn't see a crestfallen Billie shrug her shoulders and head up the hill to Clayton Street.

25

June 1956

As Billie packed her clothes for what had become her annual trip to South Carolina, she thought about Tom. It had been three weeks since the incident in the park, and she had not heard a word from him. They didn't talk every day, but in a three-week period, they would have connected at least a couple of times.

Billie rationalized that he didn't have time for her since he had started working full-time at the supermarket and went to summer school at Baltimore Junior College on Tuesday and Thursday nights. Why it bothered her so much, she wasn't sure, but she believed they left something unfinished or unsaid after their last meeting. She did not want to leave town without fixing it. Her reflections were interrupted by a shrill call from her mother.

"Billie! Billie! Telephone. Sounds like Tom."

Tom was one of only a few boys with permission to call her. Herb jealously monitored her phone calls and forbade her to receive calls from other boys. To Billie's relief, Herb believed Tom was harmless, even though he tried to listen in on her conversations with Tom whenever he could.

Hurrying down the steps, Billie took the phone from her mother. The extension in her mother's bedroom was closer, but she was not allowed to use it.

"Thanks, Momma." She hated that the telephone table was in close proximity to the living room, where Herb sat watching Saturday westerns. But at least she could see him and take comfort in knowing he was not listening on the extension. As she turned her back, she hoped Gene Autry, America's singing cowboy, would keep Herb engaged.

"Hello," she said breathlessly, as much from the excitement of having thought Tom up, as Grandma Gertie would say, as from the fast descent down the stairs.

"Hey, Little Sis," Tom responded.

"Hey yourself. I thought you got lost or something."

Since they were just friends, Billie didn't feel the need to be coy. If Tom had been a prospective suitor, however, she would have been less direct.

"Lost? Real funny. No, just busy. You going to South Carolina this year?"

"Yeah. In the middle of packing right now."

"Sorry, I'll make it quick."

"What you apologizing for—let me take that back. You do owe me an apology," Billie said emphatically.

"Apology? For what?"

"Don't play dumb, even though you're a blockhead boy."

"Will you stop it with the little girl dumb crap? I wanted to talk to you before you left for the summer, but—"

"Okay, okay. Packing can wait. Sorry I called you a blockhead. Come on by."

"Guess I could, but Mr. Brown gives me the heebie jeebies. Makes me nervous."

"You? Nervous? You gotta be kiddin'! Woodley Park doesn't work so well anymore. I mean, if I come over there, I'll have to stop by and say hello to Aunt Wilma and Uncle Larry. Not that I don't want to, but you know Carletha's not there."

"How's she liking Brooklyn?"

"Last time I talked to her, she was loving it. New York is a long way to go just for secretarial school, but you know Car's always looking for a new adventure. Her aunt never had any kids of her own, so she's spoiling an already rotten kid!"

Tom laughed in agreement. "*Her* aunt? Ain't she your aunt, too?"

"No, Uncle Larry's side of the family. Why can't you just come by?"

"Told you, I don't want to … Okay, how about this? Meet me at the Hot Shoppes on Route 40. You're almost sixteen. You think your momma and old Herb would let you do it?"

"*What*! No problem. You're cool with old Herb," Billie said with less assurance than she felt. "You sound like this is a date or something."

"How you figure?"

"Like a nigger!"

"Dumb girl crap again. Can you go or not?"

"I said, yes."

"I know you said yes, but what will your parents say? Come on Billie, get serious."

"When? What time? I have to catch the bus."

"How 'bout one o'clock tomorrow? Go ask now while I'm on the phone."

"No, I may have to negotiate. I'll call you back. What's the reason? I mean, what's special? I know they're gonna ask."

"Tell 'em I'm going in the service."

There was dead silence on Billie's end. When she recovered, she could hardly speak. "The service? Tom, the service?" She was sure eavesdropping-Herb was straining to hear.

"I'm thinking about it. Don't know for sure, but they don't have to know that. So get with the program and go ask!"

"Gee, Tom, that's quite a major decision," Billie said loudly. Then, in a much lower voice, she said, "I said I'll call you back! Goodbye." She hung up before he could respond and walked to the living room. She did not see her mother.

"Herb, where's Momma?"

"Down the basement. What's Tom talkin' about?"

Billie wanted so badly to say, "None of your business," but she ignored the question and excused herself as she crossed in front of Herb and headed to the basement. She found her mother folding laundry.

"Momma, can I meet Tom at the Hot Shoppes on Route 40 tomorrow?"

"Meet Tom? Why? What for?"

"Lunch, and he just wants to see me before I leave for the summer. He may be going in the service, so he thought we could have lunch and—"

"Slow down," her mother said, smiling. "Goin' in the service? Guess it's that time. Far as I'm concerned, since it's Tom, it's okay, but we have to check with Herb."

"Why? Why can't you just say yes or no?"

Her mother dropped the shirt she was folding and put her hands on her hips. "You not backtalkin' are you, girl?"

"No ma'am, but you know Herb is going to say no. He always says no."

"That's because you ain't officially takin' company yet."

"Taking company? Momma! What's taking company got to do with it? I'm certainly not planning to take company with Tom. This is Tom McNeal for Pete's sake! You know we're just friends—good friends—but just friends."

"You know Herb don't believe boys and girls can be just friends. By the way, whatever happened to Butch?"

"Butch? Nothing ... Why are you just now asking me about Butch? What's Butch got to do with this?"

"Nothin' I guess. He just crossed my mind. He stopped coming around. You musta been a bad date!"

"Momma!" Billie rolled her eyes and shuffled her feet. *If I had really been a bad date, he'd still be sniffing around here,* she thought, just as she heard Herb coming down the steps.

"What's going on down here?" he asked in the haze of blue Camel smoke that was his constant companion.

"Nothin' really. Billie wants to have lunch with Tom McNeal tomorrow at the Hot Shoppes. The one on Route 40."

"Why not?" Herb surprisingly responded. "Billie, you tell your momma Tom may be goin' in the service?"

"Yes sir," Billie replied. "So I can go?"

Herb shrugged his shoulders and nodded matter-of-factly in stark contrast to how he normally reacted to her requests to go out.

"Seems like Herb thinks it's all right, so yeah, you can go," Billie's mother responded.

Billie was almost too shocked to speak, but she mumbled, "Thanks, Herb."

"Don't say I never did you a good turn," he replied, taking a long drag on his Camel as he retreated up the stairs.

26

*T*his is just Tom, Billie told the butterflies in her stomach as she got off the 23 bus on Edmondson Avenue. *Calm down.* But she could hardly contain her excitement. This was a new experience for her, and she felt a little giddy.

She saw Tom standing in front of Hot Shoppes with his gaze fixed on her as she crossed the street. She had carefully chosen a pair of orange and yellow petal pushers and a yellow wrap blouse, not because they clung to her slim, but curvy body, but because she loved the outfit. It never occurred to her, until she saw the look in Tom's eyes, that he would take notice and appreciate her choice. But she convinced herself that she was misreading him. *This is just Tom*, she thought again.

"Hi," Billie said, punching him on the arm. But instead of the usual counterpunch, Tom grabbed her hand.

"Come on, let's go in," he said.

The restaurant was moderately busy, but they had to wait at the hostess station for several minutes. Two white couples came in after them and were seated first. When they were finally taken to a booth near the rear of the restaurant, they endured frosty looks from some of the patrons.

"I told you not to come out with your two heads on, but no," Billie said, rolling her eyes as they took their seats.

"It's those yellow and orange petal pushers," Tom said, sitting across from her in the booth. They laughed uncomfortably.

After giving their burger and fry order to the sour-faced waitress, they stared at each other in an uneasy, unfamiliar silence. Tom broke the silence first. "When do you leave?"

"Six-forty, tomorrow evening. I'm ready to go, too! Momma and Herb are getting on my last nerve."

"Be glad you have a daddy, stepdaddy or not. Half a loaf is better than none."

"I'm sorry, I forgot. I have two halves, but they don't even equal a whole. Funny thing for you to say, anyway. I thought you hated your father." Billie remembered Tom's ambivalence about his father.

"It's complicated, I guess. You should talk. Thought you loved your father—you know, James."

Billie reflected on Tom's comment for a few seconds before she spoke. "He's a good man, as far as men go, and I think I love him. But I don't know if I love him because I should, or because I just do."

"And that's not complicated? What about Herb?"

"What about him?"

"What are we talking about, Billie? Do you like him or what?"

"I guess he's all right. My mother loves him, I think, so it's not for me to say."

"He seems like a nice guy, but there's something about him that bothers me. Can't put my finger on it …" Tom said, trailing off. "Anyway, I'm sorry about Butch. I didn't expect you to come down so hard on me for trying to defend your honor."

"I didn't mean too. Butch deserved what he got, but you scare me sometimes. Plus, you've been a little weird lately."

"Me? Weird? I try to look out for you, and this is the thanks I get?" Tom joked, lightening the mood. They both relaxed.

"What's this about going into the service?" Billie asked, changing the subject.

"I'm exempt. The eldest son of a widow. I just wanted to see you before you left for the summer, and to make up for being a little prickly."

"Prickly. That's a good word. I couldn't have picked a better one myself. Why are *you* so prickly?"

"I said I want to *make up* for it, not *explain* it. Besides I can't. What are you going to do next year when you graduate?"

"Funny you should mention the service. That's what I was thinking about if I can't go to college."

"Service? You gotta be kidding. You know what they call women that go into the service, don't you?"

"No, what?"

"Dykes."

"They do? You know I'm not a dyke."

"How would I know?"

"Are you being prickly now, or just mean?"

"Neither. Promise me you'll go to college."

"Promise you? Why? Since when did you get to be my father?"

"I don't want you to end up like my mother. She was so dependent on my father, that when he was killed, she couldn't support herself or us. Nobody should have to depend on the kindness of strangers. That's a little dramatic, but you know what I mean." Then Tom said, more to himself than to Billie, "Besides, I can't stand helpless females."

Billie saw his jaw muscles tighten and, for a split-second, she saw something flash in his eyes that she could not describe. She wasn't sure if it was sadness, anger, or a little bit of both.

Ignoring it, she simply said, "Or like my mother, too dependent on some man. Not me! I promise."

Their orders came, and for a few minutes they ate in silence, reflecting on the substance of what they had just shared.

* * *

As Tom walked to the library to study, he could not help thinking about lunch with Billie earlier that day. From the time he saw her get off the bus and walk, gazelle-like, across the street, he was enthralled. And unbeknownst to her, she wore his favorite outfit.

He was glad Billie had shed her country-bumpkin persona and kept up quite nicely with the styles of the day. He suspected her father and paternal grandmother had a lot to do with that. But then, she'd look good in a burlap bag. *Or maybe nothing.*

Billie, he thought. *Little Sis. Can't call her that anymore,* he chuckled to himself. Not because she stood five feet, seven inches tall, but because what he was beginning to feel for her was not at all brotherly.

He had dated a few girls, but not seriously. He simply did not have the time or money for much dating and socializing, with school, work, his mother, and his brothers. Besides, girls always wanted more than he was willing—or had—to give.

But Billie was different. He didn't see her as a helpless female, despite having rescued her from more than a few situations. She could hold her own. They had always been friends, and he had always cared about her. But lately, the caring had turned to an unexplained longing. She had caught him off-guard that day she put her hand on his back at the park, and her touch had caused his nerve endings to tingle. She was no *JET* centerfold, but the effect was the same.

Just thinking about her excited him and made him uneasy at the same time. He had always thought of her as a sister. What if he ruined a perfectly good friendship? *But nothing ventured, nothing gained,* he thought.

He had to figure out how Billie felt without making a fool of himself.

* * *

At six the next day, Herb and Lilly Ann dropped Billie off at the Mount Royal Station. An important social obligation prevented them from waiting with her, but it was not an issue for Billie. She had done it plenty of times before. They said their goodbyes, and Billie headed into the station with her luggage.

Once inside, she looked for a bench to sit on while she waited the half hour for her departure time. Someone tapped her on the shoulder, and she spun around.

"Tom!" Billie screamed with delight. "What are you doing here?" she asked, throwing her arms around his neck.

"I don't know ... Seeing you off, maybe," Tom said, a little awkwardly in her embrace.

"Help me find a bench. Can you grab my suitcase?"

"Yes ma'am. I'm following you."

"This is such a surprise. Why ... you didn't tell ..." Billie struggled for words.

"You only have one suitcase for the whole summer?" Tom asked, avoiding the obvious.

"That's all I need. I wash my stuff while I'm there, and Grandmother Hayes will take me shopping. She always does, or one of the aunts will. I come back with more than I take, but I won't be gone the *whole* summer."

"You want an RC while you wait?"

"Thanks, but no. I still can't get over you being—" Billie was interrupted by a glaring voice over the loud speaker announcing departures.

"Sounds like your train is boarding," Tom said, thankful for the distraction. "Come on, I'll walk you to the platform."

He grabbed her suitcase, and they walked to the loading platform. They stopped and faced each other, waiting for the signal to board. "Enjoy the summer. I'm gonna miss you," Tom said.

"I'm not going to be away forever, you know. I told you, you've gotten weird—"

Tom suddenly bent down and kissed Billie. But his lips had barely touched hers when she hauled off and slapped him.

"What you do that for?" they both said at the same time.

"Don't ever touch me without my permission!" Billie snapped through clenched teeth.

Tom threw up his hands and backed away. "Billie, I'm sorry. I'm sorry," he stammered. "I didn't mean to offend you ... I just ..."

"Save it!" Billie nodded to the porter, who took her luggage, and she boarded the train.

As the train pulled out of the station, she walked down the aisle to her car. When she glanced out of the window, she saw a forlorn Tom standing on the platform like a little kid whose helium balloon had just escaped into the clouds.

27

Summer 1956

"Ease up some on that gas petal, Billie!" her father said quietly, but firmly. "There's two hundred and ninety horses under there. Slow *down*, girl."

"Yes, sir. I'm trying."

"Tryin'? Try taking your foot off of that gas petal! Slow down! Billie, pull over in the clearing up ahead, and let me take it into town."

"Yes sir," Billie said, lurching and braking as she steered the car to a grassy spot on their side of the two-lane country road.

"My Lord!" her father said as he exited the car from the passenger side. He placed his hands on his knees, bent over at the waist, and let out a hearty laugh. "Now I know what Miz Cunningham must have felt like!"

Billie slid over as her father got behind the wheel. "I did good today, didn't I?" she proudly asked.

Her father smiled and nodded as he wheeled the car back on the road and into town for lunch at the local rib shack.

* * *

Between forkfuls of potato salad, Billie queried her father about the car. "Daddy, how much does a Packard cost? Think I might buy one someday." She thought about the money she still had squirreled away in her secret hiding place.

"Just about forty-two hundred dollars. But this is the last year that Packard plans to make the Patrician. Better think of buying somethin' else," her father winked. "Mr. Brown still driving an Impala?"

"No, sir. Herb is a Cadillac man."

"Shoulda guessed that. Anyway, Billie, I have something I want to tell you." Her father deliberately wiped his barbeque-stained hands on his napkin and took a sip of his sweet tea.

Billie put down the rib bone she was holding and licked her fingers, expectantly.

"Billie, I'll be getting married next spring. I just wanted to tell you before we made an official announcement."

So kind of you, she thought. *But what difference does that make to my life?*

But she said, "I guess I'm supposed to say congratulations or something. I mean, that is really nice, Daddy. I guess I never thought of you as having a girlfriend or anything."

"You've met Margaret before. You remember?"

"Oh, Miss Margaret. Yes sir, I remember her. Nice lady, pretty lady … Yes sir." *Okay, so where do I fit into this picture?* Billie wondered.

"Great! This time you'll get to see a little more of her before you leave."

"That'll be nice. After I pick up some post cards, can I drive the Packard back home?"

"You cannot and you may not!" her father laughed.

* * *

Learning to drive her father's brand new Packard was the one saving grace of the summer of 1956, the worst one she had ever spent in

South Carolina. In part, because of the way she and Tom left each other—he had occupied too much time in her head—and because the routine had gotten old.

She had grown closer to her father and her paternal grandparents, but farm life was not for her. Going uptown on Saturday was not the thrill for her that it was for the locals, and now her father was going to throw a wife into the mix.

But there was Grandma Gertie. Billie loved being with her, and she loved the upgrades her father had made to the shack. But it lacked the creature comforts to which she had become accustomed.

While brooding late one rainy afternoon after the trip to town, Billie sat down at the kitchen table to write Tom a note. At first she wrote: *Having a lousy time, wish you were here.* But she decided that sounded too disingenuous, so she ripped up the postcard.

Next, she wrote: *Miss you, can't wait to see you.* But that, she decided, was much too forward, though it was closer to a truth she had yet to admit to herself. She ripped up the second card, too. Finally, she decided on: *Hope all is well. Sorry I left the way I did. We can talk when I get home.* She started to sign it, "Little Sis," but realized that that time was gone.

Grandma Gertie, who had been watching her from her rocking chair, quietly asked, "Think you got it right now?"

"I hope," Billie replied.

"What's troublin' you, chile?"

"Nothing, Grandma. Just thinking."

"Somebody you left at home is troubled, too. You need to fix it, but don't git in no trouble puttin' it back together."

"Ma'am?" Billie asked, puzzled. Herb played word games, but Grandma Gertie talked in riddles.

"If you can't figure it now, you will. Let your heart speak, and don't let that small spot of pain birth more pain."

Billie nodded her head, pretending to understand.

* * *

The uneventful summer vacation finally came to an end, and Billie found herself back at Mount Royal Station trying to catch a cab home. She knew her parents wouldn't be there, but she was hoping, even though Tom didn't answer her postcard, that some twist of fate would bring him to meet her. No such luck.

She had half a mind to ask the cab to drive her to Clayton Street, but she had no idea if Tom would be home. A simple phone call would have solved the dilemma, but she didn't call. Instead, she went home.

As the cab approached her house, Billie's heart quickened at the silhouette on the steps. *Tom! It's Tom!*

"Tom!" Billie yelled, jumping out of the taxicab before it came to a complete stop.

"Miss, Miss, please wait. Be careful," the driver cautioned, but his warning fell on deaf ears.

Billie ran toward the steps, and Tom stood up to greet her. She flung herself into his waiting arms. "It's so good to see you. I'm so sorry."

They were interrupted by the taxi driver, who put her suitcase by the steps and stiffly waited for a tip. Tom gently pushed Billie away, took a dollar from his pocket, and handed it to the driver. The driver tipped his hat, got back into the cab, and drove away.

"I'm glad to see you too," Tom said as he sat back down on the steps. "Careful, this is a public street. We're in front of your house."

Billie nodded toward the house and asked, "Do they know you're out here?"

"Your momma does. Mr. Brown's not home, but I don't think your momma wants us hugging on a public street—or maybe not at all," Tom said as he patted the spot next to himself. "Sit. We need to talk."

"I know ..." Billie began.

"Me first. I don't know where to start, but Billie, I think I love you."

"What do you mean? I know that. I love you, too."

"Billie, I don't mean like brotherly love. I think I'm *in* love with you. I realized that right after the prom. That day at Woodley Park. I felt something different. I want to be more than a big brother to you. Something ... more."

"Tom, you mean so much to me. I care for you a lot, but not like that. I want us to keep on being good friends. I don't want anything to mess that up. I think something more might ... I'm sorry."

From the look on Tom's face, she could tell he was wounded. Had she been honest with herself, she would have seen this coming, but it was a truth she didn't want to face.

"Wow, did I misread this one, even though you did slap me," Tom said, hanging his head and attempting to kick some invisible debris from the sidewalk. "Nothing to be sorry about. I was wrong to think ... to bring it up."

"But I *am* sorry, and you should have brought it up. I felt like we needed to clear the air, but I didn't know that's where you were heading. Hope I didn't lead you on, or hurt your feelings. Tom, I'm so confused."

"Don't be. *I'm sorry.* I shoulda known better. Forget what I said, please." After an awkward silence, Tom shrugged his shoulders. "Let me take your suitcase in the house."

"Wait," Billie said, grabbing his arm. "Are we okay?"

"Sure we are," Tom said. He punched her on the arm and picked up her luggage.

28

Fall 1956

Billie was glad to get back to school to begin her senior year. The miserable summer of 1956 had finally come to an end, with Tom feigning a friendship that no longer existed. Billie could get very little of his time and, according to David and John, he had a girlfriend or two.

She, on the other hand, generally went out in crowds to avoid giving her time or attention to any one boy. Besides, dating one boy was hard to accomplish with Herb's strict oversight and perverted jealousy. She unwittingly advanced Herb's agenda, because whenever she found herself interested in a boy, and the feeling was mutual, she immediately gave him the cold shoulder.

This habit of hers earned her the reputation as being both a tease and an ice princess. Little did she know that the sexual abuse she had experienced as a young girl—which Herb stopped when she entered puberty—and buried in the recesses of her mind, would prevent her from fully committing to a healthy relationship.

On this particular Saturday, she didn't want to go bowling with the crowd, or grocery shopping with her mother. She preferred being by herself, and, stretching out on her bed, she contemplated her future.

She wanted to go to college, but if she didn't, what would she do when she graduated from high school? The girls at school were boy crazy. They daydreamed about their weddings, and hoped to get married as soon as they graduated. They even signed their names with the last name of the boy they hoped to marry.

But marriage was certainly not in her plans, and it was the furthest thing from her mind. And even if she did marry, she would wait until she was old, like maybe thirty. For now, she wanted to enjoy being sixteen.

She wanted out of her mother's house, and she wanted to see the world. When she considered the grown women in her life— her mother, Aunt Wilma, Mother Hayes, aunts—they were all kept women, dependent on a husband to make their existence worthwhile.

How absurd, Billie thought. There was too much world out there to explore, savor, and experience, and she would not be constrained by some man called a husband.

Billie came crashing back to the present when she heard the husband in her house urgently calling her name as if the house were on fire. "Billie! Billie!" Herb's muffled yell came from the hall bathroom. "Billie, come here quick!"

She slowly got off the bed and walked down to the bathroom. Herb was bent over the sink with a head full of his lye and potato conk concoction. "What is it, Herb?"

"Help! Git a cup! I need to rinse this shit out of my hair. Quick! It's burning the hell out me! I forgot a cup. Quick!"

Billie slowly turned on her heels, and with false urgency said, "Getting the cup, getting the cup." Smiling to herself, she took her time and went to the kitchen to fetch a mason jar.

When she returned, Herb was writhing in pain. "Rinse it, girl! Rinse it!"

"I'm not putting my hands in that stuff," Billie replied.

"Just pour some water over it. I'll work it through. Pour the water, damn it!"

Though she disliked Herb, her disdain was disassociated from the true pain he had inflicted on her, and she somehow tolerated him. What she consciously exhibited first resembled stepparent resentment, then teenage angst. Somehow, the trauma of abuse was compartmentalized and unbeknownst to her, but it shaped her view of the world rather than her relationship with Herb.

"Yes, sir," Billie said as she filled the jar and poured water over Herb's head.

With a gloved hand, Herb finally managed to remove all the glop from his hair under a steady stream of water supplied by Billie.

"Thanks, Billie. Could you hand me that towel on the hamper?"

She handed Herb the towel, and he wrapped it around his head before he raised it from the sink. "Whew! Glad you was home. I coulda been bald," he laughed.

"You ought to stop using that stuff."

The bathroom was small, and they stood almost eye-to-eye. When she turned on her heels to leave, he caught her by the arm.

"Wait a minute."

"Get off of me, Herb!"

"Just wait a minute, now," Herb said. He grabbed the front of her Peter Pan blouse, let go of her arm, and pulled her toward him. "I knew you would ripen up nicely," he said with a lewd grin.

Billie shoved him hard. He fell against the sink, still clutching her blouse, and the buttons popped off and skidded across the floor, leaving a gaping opening that exposed her bra.

Billie protectively clutched her chest, quickly exited the bathroom, and ran smack into her mother. In the heat of the encounter, neither Billie nor Herb had heard her come into the house.

Her mother blocked her path and yelled, "What's going on here?"

"Ask your husband!" Billie retorted, trying to push past her mother.

"I asked you!"

With a towel wrapped around his head, turban-style, Herb casually came out of the bathroom. "I told you to do something about that little fast gal! She's smelling herself. She too grown."

Billie shot Herb an angry look as he headed toward his bedroom with her mother in hot pursuit. She stood frozen in the hallway as Herb and her mother argued.

"I said, what the hell is going on here?" her mother screamed at the top of her voice.

Billie watched Herb as he nonchalantly preened and toweled his hair in front of the dresser. "And I said, your daughter is too grown."

"You're a damned liar!" her mother shouted directly in his ear. Then, in one swell swoop, she picked up a bell jar from the dresser and slammed it against Herb's temple. Unfortunately, most of the delicate glass embedded itself in the towel and did more damage to her mother's hand than to Herb's head.

Herb calmly and deliberately said, "Excuse me while I get dressed. I gotta get out of here and get a breath of fresh air before I say or do something we both will regret."

"I suggest you do just that," Billie's mother hissed. "And stay where you take that breath!"

"I suggest *you* remember who pays the rent here!"

Her mother grabbed Herb's silk handkerchief from the dresser and wrapped it around her bleeding hand. Stunned, Billie rushed to her room and slammed the door.

Seconds later, her mother banged on the door. "Billie, Billie, open the door," she shouted.

Billie reluctantly complied and let her mother in. She noticed the bloodstained hanky, but said nothing.

"Look, Billie. I don't know what's goin' on here, but you need to leave."

Stunned, Billie asked, "What? Momma, what are you talking about? I didn't do anything. I didn't do anything," she tearfully repeated.

Two grown women can't stay in a house with one man."

"Now, I'm grown?" Billie whispered? "But I didn't do nothing! Where am I supposed to go? How can you do this to me? Can't you see it's Herb, Momma? It's Herb!"

"I didn't mean tonight, or tomorrow, but the sooner you go off to Delmarva State College, the better. The better for everybody concerned. You too young to understand these things."

Billie, now crying hysterically, asked, "How can I be too grown and too young at the same time? Momma, please don't do this to me. *Please*, Momma! Can't you see what kind of man Herb is?"

"Herb's my husband, and he provides for us. Yeah, I believe he has strayed a time or two, but wid grown women, not a child. He knows what he's got."

What kind of perverted logic is that? Billie thought. "Momma, I hope you know it ain't about beauty or age. It's about the smell of pussy."

Her mother's bloody hand struck Billie across the face.

29

Billie slowly unfolded her cramped legs and got up from the corner where she had slumped after the altercation with her mother. She had lost all perception of time. Her arms ached from hugging her legs so tightly, and her sobs had given way to dry heaves. She had wiped her face on the sleeve of her blouse, leaving a blood stain that reminded her of the humiliating slap. The tears began again.

She was startled when the deadly silence of the house was interrupted by the jangling of the telephone. When it kept ringing, she realized she was home alone, and she woodenly walked toward the impatient instrument.

Before she could reach the phone, it stopped, but knowing it would ring again, she froze in her tracks and stared in its direction. After a couple of minutes, the phone's peal sounded again, urgent against the quiet. Hoping her voice sounded normal, she lifted the cradle. "Hello."

"Billie? That chu? How you baby?" Grandma Gertie yelled into the phone.

"Hello, Grandma," Billie replied, holding the phone away from her ear. She and her mother had never been able to convince Grandma Gertie to talk in conversational tones on the telephone. "Just fine, Grandma Gertie," Billie lied. "How are you?"

"I'm kicking, but not high. I 'spect I'm doin' better than you."

"Ma'am?"

"Guess you home alone, huh?"

"Yes, ma'am." She didn't bother to ask her grandmother how she knew. Billie knew she just knew.

"Have you talked to your daddy?"

"No ma'am, not for a couple of weeks. I guess he's busy with wedding plans."

"Don't reckon he be too concerned with that. That's not what men do, but I 'spect he'll be puttin' that wedding on hold for a spell."

"He will? Why do you say that?"

"He's in Ballamore. Guess you didn't know. Miss Margaret, you know, his intended, has female trouble, and she goin' to that Johns Hopkins Hospital for surgery. They say she'll be laid up for six or eight weeks. Your daddy can't stay in Ballamore that long. You got to go and stay with her. Keep her company and help out a little bit 'til she heals. Your daddy will pick you up tomorrow afternoon, so pack your bags tonight."

"Grandma, wait a minute. Not so fast. I don't understand. Daddy and Miss Margaret are here, and I have to stay with her? Stay where?"

"James will explain in the mornin'. They renting one of them apartments on Broadway for a couple of months."

Billie was so perplexed, she didn't know what questions to ask. "How will I get to school? Have you talked to—"

"Gettin' to school is the least of your worries. You know I'll take care of your momma, and besides, you need to get out of there, don't you?"

Billie nodded her head, stunned into silence.

"Don't you?" Grandma Gertie repeated. "I think you do, before the roof caves in!"

Billie could swear she heard a smile in her grandmother's voice. *What in the world does she mean?* she wondered.

Before Billie could reply, Grandma Gertie barked her final order. "Be ready by noon tomorrow!" And, in her characteristic style, she said, "Goodbye," and hung up.

* * *

Gertie rummaged through the drawer of her chifforobe until she found a large brown envelope, the contents of which she dumped on her bed. Among the scraps of paper were letters, postcards, notes, and Polaroid pictures.

She carefully examined the photos until she found the ones she wanted: Lilly Ann in a blue shantung dress; Lilly Ann with Herb in a nicely tailored black suit; the whole family; Herb and Leon; Herb and Larry; and Herb alone. The wedding pictures.

She grabbed a pair of scissors from another drawer, carefully cut Herb's image from all of the pictures, and tucked them in the pocket of her apron. She went to her closet, and, standing on her tiptoes, tugged at a hat box that came crashing down on her head.

"Ouch," Gertie said as she kicked the lid and picked up the blue silkstraw that the box contained. She put the hat on and laughed at her reflection in the mirror. After she admired herself for a few seconds, she removed the hat, cut off a piece of the brim, and dropped it into her apron pocket with the pictures.

On crusty and hard, bare feet, she walked into the kitchen and took a small bowl from the shelf over the sink. She slowly and deliberately cut up the contents of her pocket and put them in the bowl. Next, she fetched a bow and arrow resting in the corner near the pot-bellied stove, and headed out the door and across the tobacco field.

As daylight started to fade in the early fall day, Gertie quickened her steps. From somewhere in the distance, came the "caw, caw," of a murder of crows taking flight at the sound of the intruder.

Gertie paused for a brief time and strained her ears and eyes, listening and looking for the crows. She stood motionless as some of them resettled in the bush at the end of the field. Slowly, and with precision, she took aim with her arrow and pierced one of the birds in the breast.

The crow fell from the tree with a faint thud, causing the rest to scatter again. Gertie retrieved it, removed the arrow from the bird's still quivering breast, and put it in the small sack she had brought with her.

Gertie plodded her way back home. When she reached the porch, she flopped down on her rocking chair, grabbed her corn-cob pipe from the table next to the chair, stuffed a pinch of tobacco in it, and lit it. Rocking contentedly, she threw her head back and blew smoke into the air. *This will just have to do 'til I can git to Ballamore again,* she thought.

After a bit, Gertie went into the kitchen and laid the crow on the counter. It was still warm, and its heart still beat faintly. She picked up a sharp butcher knife, slit open the chest of the hapless creature, and immediately drained some of its blood into the bowl containing Herb's picture and pieces of the hat. *No self-respecting potion is ever complete without feathers of some sort,* Gertie thought, so she plucked a few from the crow and put them in the bowl as well.

She walked out to the end of the porch, removed five smooth white stones from a clay pot, and picked up the can of kerosene sitting next to it. She arranged the stones in a small circle in the yard, placed the bowl in the middle, and poured a little of the flammable liquor on top of all of it. After setting the mixture ablaze, Gertie howled like a wolf and flung the bird across the road. She swore she saw it flap its wings and take flight.

* * *

Shortly after her grandmother's phone call, Billie sat cross-legged on her bed in a daze. *Pack or not pack. Pack what? What about my books*

and my typewriter? Does Momma know? When will they get home?
There goes my world spinning out of control again.

Billie got up and dropped a forty-five, "My Prayer" by the Platters, on her record player. She paused suddenly, thinking she heard something, and she poked her head out of her bedroom door. She listened for a few seconds, but heard nothing. Her room overlooked the backyard, and she peered out of the window to see if Herb's caddy was in the alley. To her relief, it wasn't.

Billie walked to the front bedroom and looked out of the front window, but she didn't see the car on the street either. "Momma, is that you?" she called as she went back into the hall. No response. She shrugged. *Must have imagined it.*

She started to check the doors and turn on some lights. Her mother and Herb, like a lot of their neighbors, often left their doors unlocked. But she went back to her room and shut the door.

The record player kept her occupied for a time as she pulled clothes out of her closet, but it wasn't long before she felt uncomfortable. She peeked out of her door again and called, "Who's there?"

Still, no response. She remembered the last thing Grandma Gertie had said and wondered if she should get out of the house. *Grandma would have told me if I needed to leave.* She contented herself with that knowledge, but turned down the record player.

She heard what sounded like someone coming in the front door. "Who is it?" she yelled from a crack in the door, and she was relieved to hear her mother respond.

"It's me, Billie."

Billie closed her door, not wanting to actually see her mother or let her know that she was relieved she was home. She was still hurt and unforgiving, but she didn't want to be alone in the house any longer.

Billie heard her mother come up the stairs, braced herself against her door, and closed her eyes, praying her mother would not knock or attempt to enter her room. To her delight, her mother went into her own bedroom and slammed the door.

After standing with her back against the door for a few minutes, Billie walked over to the window again and looked out. She noticed a misty rain had begun to fall, and she saw a lanky, fair-skinned man quickly making his way up the alley. His physique and gait seemed vaguely familiar, but she couldn't really place him.

Then, a strange thing happened. She wasn't sure if she had actually seen it, or if it was a vision in her mind's eye, but she saw his freckled face and kinky red hair. He looked like Red, the shoemaker's helper from the old neighbor. *What is Red doing here?* she wondered.

30

A fter Herb left the house in a huff, he stopped by Brownies to chug a couple of beers and a couple of shots of Johnnie Walker before he headed for Carey Street. He eased the Caddy to the curb and sat for a moment, arguing with himself.

You shoulda known better. Sixteen-year-olds talk and fight back. But couldn't keep your hands off, could you? Unrepentant, Herb thought, *Missed my chance. Shoulda popped that cherry for real befo' she turned twelve. Guess I'll just stay here a couple of days. Maybe a week, who knows? Hope Beatrice is here.*

Herb slid out of the Caddy and walked up the steps on wobbly legs, fumbling for his keys. When he turned the key in the lock, he was met by a deafening blast and an explosion of white hot pain that knocked him off his feet. He landed half-in, and half-out of the door.

Herb clutched his bleeding right shoulder, vaguely aware of a shadowy figure standing over him for a brief second, then fleeing. His brain called Beatrice, but his lips failed to obey.

* * *

Lilly Ann jumped out of the taxi cab in front of Provident Hospital and rushed to the emergency room, leaving Billie to pay the driver. As she entered the ER, a semi-circle of policemen were questioning a woman with a black eye and a fat lip in one corner of the waiting room.

Despite the disfigurement, Lilly Ann believed it was a hussy named Beatrice, with whom she was sure Herb had been messing around. Whenever Lilly Ann observed the two of them at Brownies, she could sense the connection between them. She suspected Beatrice's presence and Herb's condition were somehow related, though the hospital had not given her any details when they called other than to say it was urgent that she get there.

She inquired at the reception desk about Herb's location and motioned for Billie to go to the waiting room. She scurried to Herb's side and found him being tended to by doctors and questioned by the police. The doctors chastised him for driving himself to the hospital and exacerbating the blood loss, which could have been fatal. They decided to keep him overnight.

Herb, passing in and out of consciousness, could not provide any information on the assailant or the reason for the assault. Lilly Ann was equally unsuccessful in getting any clarity on the situation, and she eventually retreated to the waiting room while the doctors finished patching him up.

* * *

While her mother tended to Herb, Billie took a seat not far from Beatrice, hoping to catch the woman's conversation with the police. Apparently, she had come to the door when she heard Herb's key turning in the lock and found him wounded in the doorway.

Key in the lock? Billie wondered. *What's he doing with a key? Does Momma know? Has to! Why that dirty bastard—oops, sorry Lord. And she wants me out? Wake up Momma!*

Billie suddenly saw her visibly upset and shaken mother march over to the corner where Beatrice sat and push past the policemen. Her mother stood over Beatrice with her hands on her hips and venom on her lips. "Hussy, did he beat you up and you shot him?"

In pain and knowing she was on shaky ground, Beatrice reluctantly mumbled, "Hell no! I didn't shoot him, and he didn't lay a hand on me." Beatrice cast a pleading eye at one of the policemen, who grabbed Billie's mother by the arm.

"Okay, Miss. Move it along. We ask the questions. You're disturbing Mrs. Brown," the officer said.

Billie's mother indignantly wrenched her arm from the officer and spat, "*I'm* Mrs. Brown." She pointed an accusatory finger at Beatrice and said, "And that's a two-dollar whore!" She turned on her heels and left the waiting room with a wide-eyed Billie trailing her.

Billie caught up to her and tugged at her arm. "Momma, where are the car keys?"

"What?" her mother responded with a raised eyebrow.

"Car keys, car keys. Where are they? Go get them."

"Why? For what? Why you askin' about car keys?"

"Momma, are they in Herb's pants?" Billie spoke slowly and deliberately as she said, "Go get them, now."

When Billie couldn't make her mother move, she turned and headed down the hall to Herb's room. She politely smiled at the policeman who stood outside of the door and said, "I'm getting my dad's things."

The policeman returned the smile and nodded. Billie found the plastic bag with Herb's bloody clothes and fished the Caddy's keys from the pocket of his pants.

She started to leave but realized she'd better keep up the lie. She pushed the pants back into the plastic bag and took the whole thing with her.

Billie found her mother outside, fuming and cursing under her breath. Her mother's anguish had turned to unbridled anger.

"Let's go, Momma."

"Go where? No, I'm waiting for the cops to leave so I can beat Beatrice's ass."

"Momma, don't forget you're a Christian lady," Billie said, a little sarcastically. "Beatrice will get what's coming to her. Herb already got his. Come on. Let's go."

Billie took her mother by the shoulders and aimed her towards the parking lot.

"Where are we goin'?" her mother asked.

"To the parking lot and home."

"What are you talking about, chile?"

"Just come on, please. *Please!*"

* * *

Confident in her newly acquired driving skills, Billie approached the Caddy like a prospective buyer, walking around it and kicking the tires. Her mother watched in stunned silence as Billie ceremoniously unlocked the driver's side and climbed behind the wheel. She cranked up the V-8 engine and calmly told her mother to get in.

Her mother complied and asked, "When did you learn to drive?"

"Don't you remember? I told you my father taught me. You know, James?"

"Don't be sassy. I didn't think you could *really* drive," her mother stammered.

Billie eased the Caddy off the hospital grounds and slowly headed down Division Street. "Yes, Momma. I can really drive," she grinned.

As they approached their block, Billie noticed a police car parked in front of the house.

"Oops. Momma, look. A cop car." Billie made a quick right turn and went up the alley. "Hope he didn't see me. I'll give you the keys. If it comes up, you were driving. Okay?"

"Okay. Hope there ain't no cop in the backyard."

Luckily there wasn't, but as soon as they entered the house and turned on the lights, the police rang the doorbell.

"Comin,'" her mother called as she went to answer the door.

Two policemen stood on the porch. "Good evening, Mrs. Brown," said the older of the two officers. "I'm Sergeant Riley. May I come in?"

"Certainly," her mother said, stepping aside to let them in.

"I'm sorry to hear about your husband," Sergeant Riley continued. "Under these mysterious circumstances, we need to ask you a few questions. You and your daughter may not be safe."

Billie's mother ushered the policemen into the living room. The younger officer immediately went to the basement.

"You think Billie and me are in some kinda danger?" her mother asked.

"Yes, ma'am. Possibly. Sorry to ask this, but do you and Mr. Brown have separate residences?"

"If you had'a asked me that question yesterday, I woulda said no. But today I guess that's not true."

"So you're saying as far as you knew, everything was fine between you."

"No, I ain't saying that. In fact, I invited him out this morning, but I didn't know he actually had a 'separate residence' as you say."

"Mrs. Brown, what is your husband's relationship to Miss Beatrice King?"

"Look officer, your guess is as good as mine. You have to ask him that question."

"Fine, but I'll need a detailed account of your activities today, Mrs. Brown."

"What?" her mother asked, incredulously. "You think I shot him? I should have, but I didn't. And I could'a put a good whipping on Beatrice's ass, but I didn't do that either."

"No ma'am. We don't think you did, but we have to rule out everybody. The other thing is, if somebody has something against your husband, they may come here and take it out on you and your daughter. We know some of your husband's activities make him a target."

"Excuse me?"

"Mrs. Brown, we know Herbert Brown, and the two of you could be targets. We'll be stationed outside tonight, but we recommend you move some place for the next couple of days or so. By the way, may I speak with your daughter?" The policeman nodded toward the doorway, where Billie had been standing motionless and silent the entire time.

"Sure," her mother said, motioning with her hand. "Billie, come over here and sit down so the officer can talk to you."

"Yes, ma'am," Billie said, taking a seat on the edge of the sofa.

The officer flipped to a new page in his notebook. "Did you see or hear anything unusual tonight?" he asked.

"Unusual?"

"Yes. Strange. Different—"

"I know what unusual means," Billie said as her mother clamped a strong hand on her shoulder. "I'm just thinking." *I guess I'll have to tell him about the redheaded man.* "I thought I heard somebody in the house, but it was my mother." Billie shifted uncomfortably on the sofa and bit her lip. "When I looked out of the back window, I think I saw a tall and skinny, light-skinned colored man with red hair."

"You think you saw?"

"Well, yes."

"A tall and skinny, light-skinned colored man with red hair," Sergeant Riley repeated. "Hmm."

Just then, the younger officer emerged from the basement, walked into the living room, and said, "No sign of forced entry, Sarge."

Sergeant Riley closed his notebook and stared at Billie. "Billie, that is your name, right?" he asked. "How old are you?"

"Sixteen. Why do you want to—" Her mother squeezed her shoulder again.

Sergeant Riley ignored Billie's response and stood up. "Mrs. Brown, that's all for now. Like I said earlier, I strongly suggest that you and your daughter stay some place else for a few days. We'll be in touch."

"Thank you. Yes, sir," she said as she walked the two policemen to the door.

After seeing the two of them out, her mother walked back to the living room and stood in front of Billie with her hands on her hips. "It ain't enough for you to be freshing around with Herb, but you got to make up a lie about a red-headed man?"

Billie steeled herself for another attack from her mother, but the telephone rang. *Thank you, Jesus,* she mumbled, putting her hand on her chest as if to still her rapid heartbeat.

Her mother angrily snatched the phone from its cradle. "Hello," she curtly answered. "Momma, you sure do know when to call ..."

Although Billie could only hear one side of the conversation, she could guess what her grandmother was saying on the other end.

"No ma'am. She didn't tell me you called, but I can understand why she didn't ... Yes ma'am. We've been through a lot today. Herb's been shot ... No ma'am. He's not dead ... I know you don't like him, but he could'a been killed ... Yes ma'am, he'll be in the hospital for a while ..."

Billie waited for the explosion that would happen when Grandma Gertie dropped the bomb about her staying with Miss Margaret. She was disappointed.

"I guess that's a blessing in disguise," her mother said. "The police said me and Billie need to leave for awhile ... No, there ain't no other reason. Why you say that? ... Yes ma'am she'll be packed ..."

Like most calls from her Grandma Gertie, this one ended with the hum of the dial tone and her mother staring blankly at the receiver.

31

B illie was exhausted. The traumatic events of Saturday had left her emotionally drained. It was the wee hours of Sunday morning before her brain shut down and allowed her to sleep.

But despite the fatigue, she had gotten up early to pack for her stint as a nurse maid to her father's fiancée. For the life of her, Billie couldn't figure out how, but she knew Grandma Gertie had a hand in the situation. It couldn't be coincidence that after her mother had told her to get out, her grandmother had a solution to her problem.

Billie was pretty sure her mother had acquiesced to the arrangement with her father without protest in light of their confrontation. She also knew her mother would not apologize or even talk about what happened between them. But what she didn't know was why women were so forgiving of the actions of no-good men like Herb. He had managed to widen the invisible wall between her and her mother from the day her mother married him.

She had never been first on her mother's to-do-list, and no matter what the issue—clothes, make-up, curfews, dating, friends—

her mother sided with Herb against her. He criticized and belittled everything Billie did, and her mother never protested.

Billie had little respect for her mother because she accepted Herb's sleazy behavior. She was too easily bought off with trinkets and clothes and the night life. *Surely*, Billie thought, *Momma had to know about the other women.* But more importantly and more painful, she believed her mother had to know what Herb did to her. How insignificant could she be that her mother would ignore his actions?

Billie threw things in her suitcase while trying to figure out her ultimate fate. She had not thought much about her father getting married. At the time that he told her, she was sure it would be of little consequence to her, but she was learning that the twists and turns of life were strange. She was glad that Miss Margaret was a nice woman, or at least, appeared to be. Living with her would bear that out or not.

Her thoughts briefly shifted to Red. In thinking about her conversation with the police, Billie realized they were skeptical of her story. Admittedly, she had been a young girl when she first encountered Red, but it was an encounter she never forgot. She clearly remembered what he looked like. Her real concern was whether she did, in fact, see Red in the flesh, or whether her mind was playing tricks on her.

Days later, when Herb was presented with the possibility of his assailant being Red, he failed to corroborate the possibility. Billie considered the matter closed and an issue for grown folks, stupid though they may be. When the local policemen could not locate Red, they also considered the matter closed.

* * *

As James approached the Brown house at noon on Sunday, he was accosted by the policeman who had been the night sentry.

"Excuse me, sir," the burly white policeman said, getting out of his car. "Who are you, and what are you doing here? Let me see some ID."

James eyed the policeman, who was at least six inches shorter than he was, and he reached in his back pocket for his wallet. "James Hayes. I'm here to pick up my daughter, Billie," he said as he handed the officer his driver's license.

The policeman eyed the license suspiciously. "South Carolina? Billie your daughter? Who's Mr. Brown? Chopped liver?" the officer asked.

"Her stepfather."

"You came a long way to get her didn't you? How'd you get here so quick?" The officer put his hand on his holster and backed up to get a better look at James.

"I was already in town for business. My trip was planned before any of this—"

"How did you hear about 'any of this?'" the officer asked.

"Well, the short of it is that Billie's grandmother called my mother, and my mother called me. Bad news travels fast. Just one of those strange coincidences I guess." *If he only knew how strange,* James thought.

The officer handed James his license. "All right, Mr. Hayes. Go on in."

James walked the short distance to the door and rang the bell. A coquettish Lilly Ann answered it, and invited him in.

"Good Morning, Lilly Ann. How are you? I'm sorry to hear about your —"

"Morning, James. I'm *surprised* to hear you been in town for two weeks. 'Course, no reason why I have to know, I guess, except you and my momma been making plans about my child that I don't know nothing about."

James threw up his hands. "Whoa. I'm sorry, Lilly Ann, but Mrs. Cunningham assured me that the arrangement was fine with you."

"You take the word of a senile old woman? You could have, and *should* have called me. Billie's my daughter. And at the last minute? You had to know about this before yesterday," Lilly Ann angrily hissed.

"I said I'm sorry," James said, contritely. "I'm not going to argue that point, but Billie is my daughter, too. I've learned over the years—and you know better than me—that you don't buck Mrs. Cunningham. No. No. No. You just go along with the program." James abruptly changed the subject. "Herb, how is he?"

Lilly Ann took a deep breath before answering. "The hospital said this mornin' that he rested well overnight. They think he may have some nerve damage in his left shoulder, but I'll find out more when I go to hospital."

"Sorry to hear that. Is all that Billie's?" he asked, frowning and nodding toward the collection of suitcases in the corner of the living room.

"No, they're mine. Followin' orders. The police said I should leave for a couple of days or so, but not stay with family. I'll be stayin' with a friend across town."

"Why is that?" James asked.

Lillie Ann shrugged her shoulders. "They said we're not safe here. I dunno why."

Gertie had only hinted at Herb's unsavory character, but James had taken an instant dislike to him when they first met at the train station.

"I guess that's best under the circumstances," he said hesitantly, as if thinking over the situation. Getting back to the matter at hand, he said, "Good thing I'm here for Billie. It works out for everybody."

"Seems like circumstances named Gertie helped that along," Lilly Ann blurted.

James dropped his head to hide a smile and replied, "Seems so. Nevertheless, thank you for understanding and letting Billie come to stay with Margaret. Where is she?" He was anxious to be on his way.

"She's comin'." Lilly Ann turned and yelled up the steps, "Billie, your father's here. Come on down."

"Daddy, can you help me with some of this stuff?" Billie called.

"Sure, sure," James said, and before Lilly Ann could utter another word, he took the stairs two at a time. "Here I come."

After James lugged Billie's suitcases down the stairs, Lilly Ann walked them to the door and bid them farewell under the watchful eye of the cop on duty.

"I'll talk to you later, Momma. Take care," Billie said.

"You too, honey. I'll be right behind you as soon as I call a cab."

"I hope all goes well for you, Lilly Ann," James chimed in, a suitcase in each hand and one under his arm. "We'll be in touch, and thanks again."

As James loaded Billie's belongings in his car, he chastised her good-naturedly. "You're not leaving the country, you know. You can always come across town and get what you need. In fact, I figured you'd spend some time at home on the weekends."

"To tell you the truth, it all happened so fast. Grandma Gertie calling to tell me to pack, Herb getting shot, and somebody trying to break into the house. I haven't had time to think about it," Billie said as she handed him a garment bag. "And as far as coming home on the weekends, I dunno. When is Miss Margaret's surgery?"

"Surgery? What surgery?"

"I'm sorry if you don't want to talk about it."

"I would talk about it, if I knew what it was I didn't want to talk about. As far as I know, there is no surgery involved in the training."

"What training? Grandma Gertie said Miss Margaret had some uh, uh, female problems and had to have surgery."

Hearing this, James stopped what he was doing, slapped his thighs and threw his head back in a hearty, side-splitting laugh. He laughed so much that he could hardly speak.

"Your grandmother is an amazing woman. Margaret is enrolled in a six-month Lay Midwife apprenticeship at Johns Hopkins. As far as I know, that's all the female trouble she has!"

"You're telling me Miss Margaret is not sick? I'm glad about that, and it's six *months*, not six *weeks*? Tell me again, why am I going to stay with her?"

"For the first thing, I can't be in Baltimore for six months. The second thing, Margaret doesn't know anybody here, and I don't want her alone. And the third thing, your grandmother decreed it!"

This time, Billie joined James in the laughter. He always loved when she laughed, because he didn't hear it very often. But just as easily as she laughed, James noticed a sudden reticence as she slowly climbed into the car and waved goodbye to her mother, who quietly watched them from the door.

"What's the matter?" James asked. "Don't worry, honey, things have a way of working themselves out," he said reassuringly.

"Yes, sir," Billie replied. Then she mumbled to herself, "That's what y'all always say."

"Excuse me?"

"Nothing, just talking to myself."

James got into the driver's seat, nodded to the policeman, and headed for Broadway, happy to have his daughter in tow. As he wheeled the Packard to the apartment he had rented for six months, he didn't talk and left Billie alone with her thoughts.

When Gertie had called him and volunteered Billie as a companion for his fiancée, he had readily complied. Over the years, he had learned not to question Gertie's direct *suggestions.* They always seemed to work for the good of the parties involved. He couldn't wait to get to the apartment, where he had a surprise in store for Billie.

James was glad he had finally come to his senses and owned up to his responsibilities to his daughter. She was a delightful girl, and he loved her very much. She had inherited her mother's beauty, but was unaware of it.

Oddly, he was never quite sure of her relationship with her mother because she never really talked about it. In fact, she rarely talked about her feelings at all.

As far as her stepfather was concerned, he knew that Billie disliked Herb, but he didn't specifically know why. That was the lot of stepparents, he surmised, but he made a note to explore those feelings with her. Better yet, he vowed to have a chat with Herb to get an inkling of the substance of the man.

Gertie had once hinted at having Billie move to South Carolina to live with him, but at the time, he didn't give it much thought. Now that Billie was turning into such a fine young woman, he prayed that she had better control of her hormones than her mother had at her age. Yet, those wild, ungodly moments had created a precious gift for him and his family. Life was a paradox.

It occurred to him—though he didn't want to overstep his bounds—that it was better to be safe than sorry. He made another mental note to ask Margaret to talk to Billie about the birds and bees. *Of course*, he thought, *country girls usually have a pretty good idea about those things.*

James eased the car onto Broadway, a wide street with a tree-lined median. Some of the three-story houses had been converted to apartments to accommodate the spreading colored population of Baltimore City.

James had rented a first floor apartment, with the basement being shared with the tenants on the other two floors. The furnishings, which had been left to the landlord by the former tenant, were bare-boned, but it suited James' purpose just fine.

The living room had a sofa bed, which would be Billie's, and what was once a dining room would be Margaret's bedroom. French doors separated the two rooms, giving the occupants a modicum of privacy. The apartment was within walking distance of the hospital, but Billie would have to take a couple of buses to get to school.

James took a quick glance at Billie and realized she was deep in her own thoughts and oblivious to her surroundings.

* * *

During the ride to the apartment, Billie desperately tried to process the last several hours of her life. She wondered what her father knew about Herb.

Would he do anything if he knew? Doesn't he think the stuff going on here is kind of strange? Should I tell him about Herb? Maybe he already knows something, what with him and Grandma Gertie so close now. Did he shoot Herb or have him shot? No. Not my father.

She snapped back to the present when she heard her father call her name and announce that they had arrived. She sighed heavily and slowly glanced toward the apartment. In a flash, she was out of the car, squealing with delight.

"Tom? Tom McNeal! What are you doing here?"

Tom got off the step where he was perched, and he walked to greet Billie, smiling like a Cheshire cat. As he approached, Billie noticed he was sporting a pair of cool shades and a sexy mustache that made him seem older. His lightweight fall jacket was unbuttoned, and Billie could see that he had bulked up a little more since she saw him last. She rushed toward him and flung herself in his arms, catching him off-guard.

"Happy to see you, too!" Tom grinned. He released his embrace, but he slid his hand down her arm and grasped her hand.

"How did you get here? How did you know to come here?" Billie asked, ignoring the amused look on her father's face as he walked by, carrying luggage under both arms.

"Heard about Mr. Brown through the grapevine, so I walked up to your Aunt Wilma's to get details. And, to my surprise, your dad was there because he thought *you* were there. He filled me in on the details and invited me to meet you here. Here I am!"

Surprised, Billie asked, "He invited you to come?"

"Yes, invited."

"Tom, it's been so long since we've even talked!" Billie hugged his neck.

"Too long," Tom said, taking her hand again and leading her to the steps. "What have you been up to?"

"Not much. Rushing senior year so I can get the hell out of Dodge."

"I guess no matter how good you have it, you always want to leave home," he mused.

"How do you know whether I have it good or not? Don't get caught up on the hypocrisy of normalcy."

"Down girl! Besides, I don't even know what that means. You've been reading too many books. It looks like you have it good. Anyway, can we talk about something else, like how much I've missed you?"

"Sorry, but whose fault is that? And I missed you too. How's your mother, David, and Thomas?"

"Fine, but I'm sure you know that. Your aunt and uncle keep you filled in."

Billie nodded, and after a short pause, Tom raised her hand to his lips and kissed it. She smiled and held his gaze until Margaret came to the door and called them in for lunch.

32

Billie, Tom, Margaret, and James sat around the table in the small but cheery kitchen, eating tuna fish sandwiches and drinking sweet tea as if it were the natural order of things.

This all looks and feels so normal, Billie thought. *Yet there's nothing normal about it—not that I know what normal feels like.*

As Billie continued to nibble on her sandwich, she observed a calm and quiet chemistry between her father and Margaret that seemed a little dull. It was unlike the chaotic, drama-filled, and electric-charged atmosphere between her mother and Herb. She wondered which one she would prefer if she actually got married.

But how did you know what kind of man you would get? Billie thought. *Surely there was some middle ground.*

Oblivious to her father's discussion on the plan for the next few months, Billie turned her attention to Tom. *When did he get to be so fine?* Her arm and hand still tingled from his touch.

"Earth to Billie. Earth to Billie," her father said, interrupting her reverie. "How does that sound to you?"

"Sir? Sounds fine," Billie, said not knowing what she was agreeing to.

Tom smiled and stood up. "Thanks for the great lunch, Miss Margaret. Glad to meet you. And Mr. Hayes, good seeing you again. I gotta be going."

"Glad I caught up with you, Tom. The Lord works in mysterious ways. I'm counting on you to keep in touch with the ladies like we talked about. The neighbors need to see a man around the house."

A man. Yes he is! Billie swooned to herself.

Tom replied, "Yes sir. I'll stop by as often as I can."

Billie's father shook Tom's hand and said, "I'd drive you home, but I have some things to attend to here."

"That's all right. I planned to catch a cab—or a hack anyway. Can Billie walk me out?"

"I think she can, and she has my permission," her father said with that ever-present smile in his voice.

"Come on, Billie," Tom said, extending his hand to her.

When Billie stood, she was surprised to find that her knees were just a little wobbly. *Maybe I can't walk,* she thought to herself with a smile.

Once outside, Billie and Tom walked to the middle of the street and stood on the grassy median. Tom gently punched her on the arm while peering up and down the street, craning for a taxi. "Don't forget to call me anytime, but I'll be stopping by often like I promised your dad."

"I'll call, but my experience has been that the line's busy or you're not there."

"Yeah, my schedule has been a little tight with school, and work, and—"

"Girls," Billie said, cutting him off.

"I'm trying to transfer to Morgan next semester," Tom continued, ignoring her. "I should have enough credits to be a junior if Morgan accepts all of them. Momma's taking in children now. The money she earns babysitting helps us out a lot, so I don't have to give her as much. I just quit one of my part-times, which frees up a lot of my time."

"More time for girls," Billie persisted.

"Yeah, all work and no play, you know. Your dad wanted to pay me for keeping an eye on you and Miss Margaret. You know I refused his money."

"Offered you money! You better had refused."

"Like I was saying, I'll have more time, so I can come by."

"More time for your lady friends."

"What's with you, me, and girls? I like girls. I'm a red-blooded, all-American boy."

"I dunno. I hear you're quite a man about town."

"So? You believe everything you hear? I heard you don't like boys."

Billie, indignant, took a deep breath, which alerted Tom to her next move. He caught her raised hand in midair and tightly held her wrist. "Naw, naw. You've slapped me one time too many, but you'll be glad to know I did learn my lesson." Then he cleared his throat, and asked, "Miss Cunningham, may I kiss you?"

Unable to speak, Billie simply nodded and closed her eyes. In broad daylight on Broad Street, Tom met her quivering lips with a gentle kiss that made her feel hope and promise.

Billie hoped her father didn't see it.

33

October 1956

Six months was a long time, and it would keep Billie away from home until April, about two months from graduation. But over the course of her sixteen years, she had spent a fair amount of time away from her mother, and this was just another one of those times. So, she simply rolled with the punches, and she was thrilled that she did not have to be a nursemaid to Margaret. And to her great joy, recent events had brought Tom McNeal back into her life.

She found living with Margaret to be delightful. Margaret was part-mother, part-confidant, and part-friend. When she wasn't studying herself or otherwise busy, she helped Billie study for her finals, gave her tips on dealing with men, corrected erroneous high school girl beliefs about sexuality and morality, and gave her pointers on how a young woman should conduct herself in college. As was her custom, Billie took it all in, filtered it, and came up with her own conclusions. Other times, they chatted like old friends who had known each other for years.

Her relationship with her mother was still strained. Even though she had never offered Billie an apology or attempted to find out the truth about the incident that widened the breach between them, Billie went home on weekends and other occasions to see her, wash clothes, and get other things she needed.

She planned those visits when she was sure Herb would not be there.

* * *

True to his word, Tom made regular trips to the Broadway Street apartment to check on his charges and to perform small tasks, such as sitting the garbage cans out in the alley for trash collection and bringing them in, fixing a window shade, sweeping the front so neighbors could see him, or hanging a picture on the wall of the spartan apartment. Only Margaret's penchant for fresh flowers and plants saved the place from its uninviting pall, but he gladly went.

What he didn't do, as expected, was ask Billie out despite his strong desire to do so. When he had entered the agreement with her father to look out for her safety, Tom had also asked permission to take Billie out occasionally. Tom knew what James would hear was a request to court Billie, and he thought the act of seeking permission would impress the genteel southern gentleman.

James insisted, however, that Tom talk with Lilly Ann and Herb, a conversation for which Tom had not bargained. His other experiences required no such civility. Most of the girls he dated were usually eighteen, and their families did not adhere to such old-fashioned courtesies. Or, the girls themselves ignored the house rules and sneaked out for their rendezvous with him.

His ladies' man barometer had soared when his promotion at the A&P from stock boy to cashier spotlighted him at register two. He was a handsome addition to the front of the store, and women of all ages flirted with him, some good-naturedly, others with lust and forethought.

One attractive thirty-year old was particularly persistent, giving him her phone number more than once. After Tom had been convinced that there was no husband or boyfriend in the equation, he gave her a call and was instantly invited to come calling for dinner. He had gladly accepted the invitation, enticed by the idea of what would be served.

He knew full well the lady's expectations, and the experience had taught him more than he knew existed to be learned. But it was gratuitous sex, satisfying only his impulsive, irrational, and detached libido. His mother's words often echoed in his head: *Keep sowing wild oats, and you'll get a harvest you don't want to cultivate.*

When the gray matter kicked in, he was ashamed and disappointed with himself, and he feared he'd have a difficult time extricating himself from the woman. But he did not, because the nature of her liaisons were illicit and short-lived.

What he really wanted—needed, in fact—was someone with whom he could intimately converse. Someone with whom he could bear his soul and share his dreams. Someone to nurture the little boy whose childhood was stolen from him, to encourage his nineteen-year-old self into the man he was struggling to be, and to just hold him on the nights when the nightmares came.

When he finally got up the nerve to call Lilly Ann to set up a time to talk with her and Herb, he had breathed a huge sigh of relief when Lilly Ann responded, "Tom, you know you can take Billie to a movie anytime. You're like her brother. I know it's fine with Mr. Brown. No need to bother him about it. Just check in with Miss Margaret."

After crossing that hurdle, he still had to actually ask Billie. He desperately wanted to do so, yet he could not. Whenever he visited the apartment, he saw the questioning look in her eyes, but she never raised the issue—or the kiss. It wasn't that his ardor had cooled, but Billie was so different from the girls he dated. She was Billie. Special.

On the rare occasion when he couldn't get by the apartment, he sent David or John, both of whom went reluctantly. Billie let him know that compared to him, Miss Margaret thought the brothers to be a little rough around the edges.

In fact, David and John were the subject of several conversations between Billie and Tom, and she had the audacity to criticize his "parenting" style. On more than one occasion, she had chastised him for being too strict and confrontational with them. She intimated that David and John might beat him to a bloody pulp like the three of them should have done to their father. And she predicted that if he didn't get a grip on his anger, he would end up just like his father: feared and despised by his loved ones, and left lifeless on a garbage heap.

During their last conversation on the subject, Tom became infuriated by Billie's stinging, and uncharacteristically mean-spirited comments, and he had stormed out of the apartment, vowing never to return. He couldn't understand how he could be so angry with Billie one minute, and long to embrace her the next. But he reluctantly admitted that she was right, and that he needed to find a way to stop warring with himself.

34

January 1957

After a few months, the investigation of the attempted murder of Herbert Brown was relegated to the cold case file, and the family was cleared to move back into the house. As it turned out, Herb did not have any nerve damage, but his arm was mangled enough for extensive rehabilitation.

He had spent his recovery time with his brother, Leon, and it often occurred to him that he could have been dead. Why the assailant did not kill him when he stood over him was a mystery. Maybe he only wanted to maim him, but the experience was scary enough to make him rethink some of his behavior. Like Carey Street and his Carey Street honey, who was gone by the time he got out of the hospital.

But despite his other interests, Herb was still attracted to his wife. He figured he needed to make peace with Lilly Ann for the time being, and to get his piece from her, and her only. He amused himself with the thought.

* * *

Thinking similarly, but for her own economic well-being, Lilly Ann decided to recommit herself to her marriage. She had slowly begun to reinvolve herself in church and church activities, which led her to the decision to not leave Herb. But despite the atmosphere of reconciliation in the house, albeit tenuous, and his narrow escape from a meeting with his Maker, Herb refused to join Lilly Ann in anything spiritual unless it came from a bottle.

She continued to work and squirrel away most of her money, while demanding that Herb keep her in the style to which she had become accustomed. Although he had changed somewhat, she suspected Herb of an occasional dalliance. Her rediscovered religion made her turn her head and accept them, but she did not always acquiesce quietly.

There were times when they argued vigorously, and Lilly Ann threw things and slammed them down in her anger and disapproval. Ultimately, Herb would storm out of the house, and soothe her ruffled dignity the next day. Then, Lilly Ann would spend a small fortune on some trinket or Sunday-go-to-meeting outfit.

Neither of them mentioned Herb's near-death experience, and the iron curtain of silence regarding Billie was never breached.

35

March 1957

It was nearly April, and the time had swiftly flown for Billie. She had been occupied with going between home and the Broadway Street apartment, getting through her senior year and making plans for college in the fall, and trying to minimize the drama and tension with her mother.

But then there was Tom. He showed up to check on her and Miss Margaret, and to do routine chores, but he did so mechanically. He never attempted to engage Billie in any substantive conversation, and she felt foolish following him around the apartment as he worked. He even seemed uncomfortable when he made small talk with Miss Margaret. Billie had long grown weary of the elephant in the room when they were together—rather, when she was in his presence—and she vowed to bring the matter to a head.

She found the perfect excuse to call him, albeit on a Friday night. She was surprised to find that his phone was not busy, and she was even more surprised to hear him answer.

"Hello," Tom groggily answered.

"Hi, Tom. It's me. Did I wake you?" Billie asked.

"Wake me? Give me a minute … I think so. Guess I fell asleep over my textbook. Everything all right?"

"'Cause I called you?" Billie blurted out before remembering not to be a smart aleck. "Yes, everything is fine, but I did want to ask you something."

"Shoot."

"How about taking me to the Spring Fling? It's in three weeks, but no formal required. Just dress-up. That is, if you don't have to work or something." She thought she heard Tom take a deep breath.

"How did I get to be so lucky? I don't think I have to 'work or something.'"

"Look, Tom, I don't need the snide remarks. You've been avoiding me, and you know it. I don't know why, but I'd like you to take me to the Spring Fling."

"You don't know why you want me to take you to the Fling?"

"No, smart ass! You know what I meant. I don't know why you've been avoiding me."

"I haven't been avoiding you. I see you at least once almost every week—"

"You know exactly what I mean, and I'm not having this conversation over the phone. I'd rather we have it in person. So what about the dance?"

"You're right, as usual. We do need to talk, but I don't need a dance venue to do it. Besides, you know I don't like those things. And missy, I told you about cussing at me!"

"You can drop the big brother act. We're a little past that, I think."

"You're right, Billie. I'm sorry. Let's not wait three weeks to talk though."

Billie wasn't sure if she heard another sigh on Tom's end, but she was sure of the change in the tone and texture of his voice. He was almost melancholy.

"Just so happens, I'm not working tomorrow," Tom continued. "How about an early evening movie at the Boulevard, then we come back here to talk?"

"Sounds fine. I'll tell Miss Margaret so you don't have to bother. Did you say back to your house?"

"Yeah. I don't think we can talk very well in the movie."

Billie's hands inexplicably started to shake. "Sounds like a plan."

This is what she wanted, but her deepening feelings for Tom scared her too. She normally took pride in being able to control her emotions, but around Tom, she was defenseless.

36

Billie stretched, catlike, as the rhythmic beating of the shade against the windowsill woke her. She snuggled deeper into her chenille spread, shielding herself against the chilly late March air that came through the barely raised window. A few rays of sun managed to slip in under the shade and bounce off the trinkets on her makeshift dresser, sending shards of light dancing on the walls and ceiling.

Butterflies danced in her stomach, but her thoughts were warm like her bed as she mulled over the plans for the day. She allowed herself to be excited about going out with Tom. This was, after all, a real date, and they had shared a real kiss.

She recalled slapping him the first time he attempted to do so. At the time, she was taken aback because she never thought of him in such a way, but now it seemed so different, almost a natural evolution. She was thrilled, nervous, and a little afraid.

Billie reluctantly slid her long, slim legs from under the cozy covers, grateful for the shag throw rug she squished between her toes. She grabbed her terry cloth robe and heard the distant ringing of the phone just as she headed for the bathroom. Not wanting to wake up Margaret, she scurried to get it.

"Hello," she whispered.

"Billie, hello."

It was Tom. She inhaled with anticipation, but she was also a little apprehensive. Since the developing relationship was new, she wondered how she should react. Would it be appropriate to show her excitement at hearing his voice, or to play it coy?

No need playing games, she thought. *Tom knows me too well, anyway.* She decided to be herself and not over-think the situation.

"Sorry to call so early," Tom continued. "I got bad news."

Billie felt the butterflies fold their wings and die. "It's not too early. What's the matter, Tom?"

"I got called to work this afternoon. Since I'm the junior cashier, I get called first to fill in if somebody calls off. That's what happened this morning. Thought I'd call as early as I could. Didn't want to wait until the last minute."

Billie hesitated before responding, not wanting to show her disappointment. "You can't help it if you have to work. I am a little disappointed though, but I'll give you a chance to make it up to me."

"That's a relief! I thought you'd be really mad."

Oh, I am, she thought.

"I'll plan to spend a little more time at the apartment next week, and we can just talk there," said Tom.

"Dunno," Billie responded. "I have a lot of after school things to do next week. Senior Week is coming up, and I have committee stuff I have to take care of."

"Let's play it by ear then. Maybe I can meet you after school. Billie, I am so sorry."

"Don't worry about it. Call me later if you can. Bye," she said, and she quickly hung up.

* * *

The next week did not bode any better for their talk. Billie half-expected Tom to show up at school, but he did not. Coincidentally, David ended up being the male presence at the apartment for that week.

For the life of her, Billie could not figure out what the problem was, or what she could do to fix it. Even more baffling was why they even needed to go through some formal process to discuss their feelings.

The situation was indicative of their discomfort and uncertainty over how to traverse the uncharted landscape of a new relationship. It was true that at one time, romantic interest in Tom had been far from her mind. But that had all changed over time. She was glad she had taken a proactive stance and invited him to the Spring Fling. Even if nothing came of it, they would at least have fun.

In the meantime, she had to focus, not only on the activities related to graduation and her duties as a senior class officer, but to help Margaret close the apartment. Fortunately for the both of them, their graduations were during the same week in June. This meant that her father would only have to make one trip to Baltimore, and Grandma Gertie, now his favorite road partner, would be coming with him.

* * *

By the end of March, James had decided, and Margaret had concurred, that there was little need for Tom or his brothers to continue to drop by the apartment to check on the occupants because the neighborhood was safe. It had probably been overkill from the beginning, but Billie knew her father rested easy because of his initial decision. He wanted to be sure his fiancée and daughter were secure.

* * *

As April rapidly came to an end, Billie spent more and more time at home, until she was rarely at the apartment at all. She knew she was going to miss it terribly: the independence it gave her, the security, and Miss Margaret's friendship. She hoped and prayed that her mother would see things differently and that their relationship would be better.

And maybe she would listen to what she had to say about Herb.

Stormy Weather

Don't know why there's no sun up in the sky
Stormy weather
Since my man and I ain't together,
Keeps rainin' all the time
Life is bare, gloom and mis'ry everywhere
Stormy weather
Just can't get my poorself together ...

37

As the driving rain relentlessly beat against Billie's bedroom window, the ugly gray day infused itself in her spirit, making her miserable and near tears. She had a hacking cough that continued despite the vapor rub her mother insisted she put on her chest and the nasty onion concoction she made her eat. Her mother had cut up an onion, added sugar to it, and left it to marinate overnight. The result was a syrupy, onion mixture that made her gag as she tried to get it down.

She felt awful. Her chest hurt from endless coughing, and worst yet, the sleek aqua cocktail dress, with its spaghetti-straps and draped bodice, mocked her from where it hung on the door of her closet. *No Spring Fling for you!* she could hear it say. *And no Thomas McNeal, Jr.*

Bronchitis had driven her home, and Dr. Miller had instructed her to stay in bed for a few days. It was embarrassing to still fit the criteria for being seen by a pediatrician, but the upside was that he made house calls. Fighting back tears, Billie shivered and pulled the covers up under her chin. She drifted off into a fitful sleep as she imagined herself dancing with Tom at the Spring Fling.

A light tapping on her door woke her a short time later. "Billie, Billie, I have some soup for you. You awake?"

The day's cloudy mantle bathed her room in a gray that obscured the time. Was it morning or night? She was so sure she was dreaming that she didn't respond until the phantom spoke again. "Billie, may I come in?"

"Tom, is that you?" she asked in a disbelieving, sick-induced trance.

"It's me. Your mother sent me up with some soup. May I come in?"

"No, you might catch something," Billie said with a hoarse voice.

"Don't worry, I don't get sick. This tray is getting heavy. May I come in?"

Without waiting for her answer, Tom opened the door and entered. "Hey, you look like something the cat drug in," he said. "I'm sure sorry you're so sick, but here's your dinner."

Billie attempted to sit up as Tom moved toward the bed and leaned down to rest the tray on her lap. He wiggled his nose and asked, "What's that smell?"

"Don't ask. Some down-home onion remedy that was supposed to sweat out whatever was ailing me. At least the sweating part worked," she said, nodding toward the corner of her room where she had flung two perspiration-soaked nighties. "Thank God they also believe in Western medicine and called a doctor!"

After situating the tray, Tom pulled Billie's desk chair up to the bed. "Poor baby. I was looking forward to cutting a rug with you," he said, kissing her on the forehead.

"Aren't you afraid of getting sick? How long have you been here? Does Herb know you're here?"

"Let's see. No. Maybe fifteen minutes. And yes. In fact, he was on his way out as I was on my way in. He barely spoke. Must be something important to go out in this weather."

Or somebody, Billie thought. "Let's see. I take that to mean I must be very important."

"Billie, must we verbally spar? You are very important, and I'm sorry you're sick and missing a milestone event in your life. Now eat your soup."

Trying to grasp the moment, Billie had paid little attention to the tray, which held a bowl of chicken soup, crackers, a cup of hot tea, and a small box that caught her eye as she reached for the spoon. "What's this?" she asked, picking up the box and opening it. Inside, was a beautiful white orchid attached to an elastic band.

"It's a wrist corsage. The one you would have worn tonight, you know ..." Tom trailed off. "Put it on."

"It's beautiful. I don't care what they say about you. You're a cool cat," Billie said, sliding the flower on her slender wrist.

"Can we get serious for a minute?" Tom asked.

"Sorry, just trying to make myself feel better."

Perturbed, Tom shot back, "I thought my being here would do that."

"I'm sorry," Billie muttered, barely audible. "You know, I'm glad you're here. My head's in a fog. Must be the medicine."

"Billie, I'm going to cut to the chase. I'm crazy about you and have been for a long time. Not like when we were kids, when I thought you were a good buddy even though you were a girl. I tried to tell you this before, but you weren't having it. I kinda think you feel differently now, but I don't know where to go from here."

"It does seem a little strange. We were like brother and sister, but I'm feeling the same way. Let's just take it slow, but there is one thing, Tom. You have a little bit of a reputation. I'm not like—"

Tom cut her off before she could finish. "Few people are equal to their reputations. Yeah, I've dated a lot, but don't compare yourself to what you *think* my other relationships have been. And don't think I'm going to do that either. Like you said, we'll just take it slow."

"I know it's way too soon to talk about love or anything like that," Billie said wearily. "Plus, I'm not sure I know what that means. But one thing for sure, I'm digging you a lot. But I will not, and I repeat, *will not*, take any shit from you. You got that?"

"I promise, Miss Potty Mouth. And to tell you the truth, nobody takes you serious when you cuss! It really doesn't become you," Tom laughed. Billie stuck out her tongue and wrinkled her nose. "When you're better, I'll make tonight up to you," he said. "We can go to Wilson's, the Junction, or to the Elgin Lounge. You can wear your dress."

The only response was the soft clink of Billie's spoon as it fell from her hand. She had nodded off.

* * *

As soon as Billie woke up on Saturday morning, she knew she was better. Not completely well, but better. She yawned and moved her head from side-to-side, trying to clear the fog that had settled on her brain the day before.

She suddenly sat up, squealing with delight as she grabbed her right wrist. *Where is it?* she thought. *Must have come off in my sleep.* She rummaged through the covers, searching for the orchid. *That's funny. Where did it go?*

The room still smelled of onion and perspiration. The night gowns were in the corner, but no orchid.

Billie slipped from the bed and into her slippers and robe and peeped out of her bedroom door. The smell of coffee wafted up the hallway, letting her know that her mother was up. The door to her mother's room was ajar, letting her know that Herb was not at home.

Billie made her way down the stairs and found her mother in the kitchen, eyes closed and gently blowing on a cup of steaming black liquid.

"Momma, I can't find the orchid Tom left."

Her mother jumped slightly and opened her eyes. "Child, did you have to scare me to death? And good mornin' to you. What orchid? When did he leave it?"

"Sorry, Momma. Morning. He left it yesterday."

"How did he do that? I ain't seen him, and he ain't been here."

Billie put her hands to her head and exclaimed, "What do you mean, he hasn't been here? He brought me soup and an orchid and we talked about—"

"Honey, won't do for you to be in love if it's driving you crazy already. Come here, let me feel your head. You had a fever yesterday. I think you musta been dreaming, or just outta your head. You didn't eat nothing on your tray. Tom did call to check on you, but he didn't come. Called twice, in fact. Once to say he was coming, and once to say he wasn't coming. Weather was too bad."

"Dreaming? Dreaming? Out of my head? That's not possible! Tom was here. I talked to him!"

"No, honey, you didn't, 'cause he wasn't here."

"I'm going back to bed." Dejected, Billie slowly walked out of the kitchen shouting, "Why are the gods conspiring against me?"

"Girl, you better stop blaspheming!" her mother called after her.

* * *

On her way to take a bath, Billie peeped into her mother's room and found that half the bed was still made, signaling that Herb had been absent overnight. She rushed to the bathroom, locked the door, and ran a tub. While it filled, she sat on the commode, trying to sort out the last two days and past six months.

Nothing's really changed with Tom. Ball's in his court now. Think I may just go back to South Carolina with Daddy and Margaret, though it depends on what kind of bored I want to be this summer or which way the drop falls. She chuckled to herself at remembering one of her grandmother's sayings.

After her bath, she searched her chifforobe drawer for a fresh pair of pajamas. She put them on and climbed back into bed to nurse a developing headache.

"Billie," her mother called from the hallway. "Comin' in." And before Billie could respond, her mother was in the room. "Phew," she said, holding her nose as she stooped to pick up Billie's dirty laundry.

"Tom called while you were in the tub. Do you feel like some company later today?"

"Is this for real or am I dreaming?"

"No sassy, you awake this time."

"I don't think I'll be up to it."

"I think you'll be just fine. It's not Tom's fault you got sick and couldn't go the dance. He's a good friend, and he wants to drop by. How about two o'clock?"

"Momma, you don't understand."

"What's there to understand? I told him two's fine. You shoulda stayed downstairs for breakfast, but I'll bring you up something. Okay?"

"Yes, ma'am."

Her mother left the room, dirty laundry and forgotten tray in tow.

* * *

Tom was nothing, if not prompt. At five after two, Billie heard heavy footsteps bolting up the stairs, and her mother yelled, "Billie, Tom's coming up. You decent?"

Kinda late to ask, but yeah, I'm decent, and I have clothes on, too!

"Yes ma'am," Billie called.

As soon as the words were out of her mouth, there was a sharp rap on the door and Tom waltzed into the room with a flourish. He walked over to the bed and kissed Billie on the forehead. "Hey, Billie. How you feeling?"

Before she replied, she patted Tom's arm up and down and felt his face the way a blind person would do. "Are you really here?"

"What? You trying to be funny again? Yes, I'm here. I didn't come yesterday because of the weather."

"No, I'm not trying to be funny," Billie said emphatically. "I really want to be sure it's you in the flesh. I was so sure you were here yesterday, but Momma told me I must have been dreaming."

"I was here in spirit. What you been smoking?" Tom laughed.

"Sit down. I'm okay, just disappointed."

"Me, too. Not just with yesterday, but that the spring didn't turn out quite like I expected. But we still have the summer before you go off to college."

"Maybe. I may spend the summer in South Carolina. Dunno yet. Depends on which way the drop falls," she said, smiling.

"What? You still high?" Tom chuckled. "What are you talking about? I didn't think you wanted to spend any more summers in South Cakalakey."

"No, I'm clear-headed. It's something my grandmother says. What difference does it make to you anyway?"

"Okay. Let's cut to the chase. I'm crazy about you, and you know it."

"You have a funny way of showing it."

"I know, I know. I'm scared, I guess."

"Scared of what? Me? Why?"

"It's complicated."

"Tom, everything about you is complicated. I've heard that from day one. What am I supposed to do while you figure it out?"

Tom, uncharacteristically lost for words, was silent for a few seconds and he looked down at the floor. "Guess I don't know."

"Well, I know. I'm going to South Carolina after graduation."

"I wish you wouldn't, but that's your choice."

"I don't need you telling me what my choice is."

"Sorry, Miss Independent," Tom said contritely, but a little miffed. "I guess I'd better be going. Glad you're doing better." He hesitated for a second. "I almost forgot," he said as he reached down to pick up a box from beside his chair. As he handed it to her, his lips brushed hers. "Talk to you later."

Tom quickly left the room before she could respond. When she opened the box and lifted the tissue, she found a beautiful white orchid on an elastic band. She brushed its silky petals against her cheek and, despite her attempt to do so, could not hold back the tears.

* * *

Tom hurried down the stairs. "See you, Mrs. Brown," he called to Lilly Ann as he headed for the door.

"You gone already?"

"Yes ma'am," Tom said as he closed the door.

He headed for the bus stop. *What the hell just happened in there?* he asked himself. *She didn't even give me a chance to finish what I had to say. Cut me off at the knees. Women, they're all alike. Ball breakers! Hope she has a date for her prom 'cause I sure as hell ain't taking her.*

* * *

When Billie considered the events of the last prom she attended, she was not pressed to find a date. She had two offers but begged off, claiming that her responsibilities as class president would take up so much of her time, she wouldn't be a good date. It seemed to satisfy her suitors. Besides, her crowd was a mixed one, and she could hang with them without feeling like a fifth wheel.

She expected one cat in particular, Henry, to become her de-facto date at the after-parties. She did not know if the rumors about his limp wrist were true, but she knew she would be safe with him.

She had adamantly refused to ask Tom, because she was convinced he was just playing games with her. It hurt, but she was accustomed to pain. She buried it, and got on with her life.

The prom would be just a minor blimp on the radar of her unfolding life. There was graduation and parties, farewell dinners, and a dinner for Miss Margaret. Grandma Gertie, her father, and Carletha were coming to town, and then she'd have to pack for South Carolina, shop for her dorm room, and pack for college. It was all too exciting. Too exciting to worry about Tom McNeal.

38

1957

Gertie tapped her chin with her index finger as she faced the assorted jars and bottles on the shelf over the sink—her apothecary. She wondered which of the plants and herbs she wanted to take with her on her visit to see old lady Simms. Mrs. Simms' son had asked Gertie to visit because his mother was in failing health.

Reckon I'll make this a social call, rather than a spiritual one, she thought as she fingered the small cross she wore around her neck. *Somethin's prickin' my heart, and I think I need to go another way with this thing. I'll just sit and talk with her for a bit, with no spells or potions, and come on back home.*

The Simms' place was an hour's walk in the opposite direction from town, back in the country. Over the years, Gertie had made the trip many times for a variety of reasons. During those times, she deftly picked her way through the thorny vines that overgrew in places where the path was narrow, always on the lookout for reptiles and amphibians that sometimes made their way out in the open.

Even though it was spring, she prepared herself for a path that would grow hot as she traveled. The sojourn would take about two hours round-trip, and by the time she added an hour or so to visit and account for the possible delays on the way, she might be hungry. And she didn't want to depend on old lady Simms' ability to be hospitable. *Better safe than sorry*, she thought.

With her pick, she chiseled chunks of ice from the block in the ice box and dropped them in a mason jar that she half-filled with water. She also wrapped two biscuits and a slice of leftover slab bacon in a piece of cheese cloth.

Gertie walked back into the bedroom, picked up a red bandana from the chifforobe, and tied it around her gray braids. As was her habit when she left the house, she swept the room with her eyes to remember just how she left it.

On the way out of the room, she grabbed her straw hat from the hook on the door jam and put it on her head, tapping the crown. Then she slung the knapsack with her provisions over her shoulder and headed out of the kitchen door and down the steps.

The trip was not an entirely solitary one. There were shacks and trailers along the way that sat off the road. As was the custom, the occupants would stop what they were doing to wave, speak, or even offer a cool drink as Gertie passed. Between homes, she sang to herself and thought about her upcoming trip to Baltimore.

The Simms' trailer was across a set of railroad tracks, and as she neared it, the homes grew farther and farther apart. When she was a few yards out from the tracks, Gertie took off her shoes and seemingly massaged the earth with her toes. After a few seconds, she closed her eyes and was still. She felt no vibrations, so she stooped and put her ear to the ground. Hearing nothing, she prepared to cross the tracks as fast as she could. She did not distrust the crossing signal, but she feared she would not have enough time to cross if it sounded while she was in the middle of the track.

The trailer was only a few hundred feet away from the crossing, and Gertie picked her way through the junk-strewn yard to get to the door. She found out that the elderly woman was more lonely than sick. They spent a couple of hours talking, with Gertie convincing Mrs. Simms that she needed neither poultice nor portion for her aliments. She'd be just fine if her son visited more often. Gertie decided to take her leave after she found herself nodding with Mrs. Simms in the late afternoon heat.

She gathered her belongs, content with her good deed, and headed home. She made her way back to the crossing and repeated her ritual.

After she had gone a few yards, she heard rustling in the bushes along the path. She approached cautiously, not knowing what kind of animal to expect. Then she heard low mumblings. "Who go there?" she shouted, but she was with met with silence. "Who go there, I say? I'm just an old woman. Don't mean nobody no harm."

There was more rustling. Then the bushes parted, and an unkempt man slowly emerged from the brush. Hatless, he used his forearm to shield his eyes from the late afternoon sun.

"Afternoon, ma'am. I don't mean nobody no harm neither. Just a hobo waiting to hop the train."

Gertie eyed him suspiciously and stared at him intently, causing him to take a step back. "I see. Well good afternoon to you, too. Kinda danger, hopping trains, ain't it?"

"When you down on your luck, you don't have much choice," the hobo replied.

Gertie nodded and repeated, "I see." She took a couple of steps toward the man and took a closer look. "Boy, don't I know you?"

"No, ma'am. Can't see how. I'm not from around here."

"Where you from then?"

"Up north. I been around a lot of places."

"Sounds like you on the lam."

"No, ma'am," he stammered. "Just had a spate of bad luck."

"Luck's in the Lord. Devil's in the people. I know you," Gertie continued.

"Don't see how. I don't know you. I never been to South Carolina—"

"No, you don't know me, but I know you. You been to Ballamore, ain't you?"

"No, never in Ballamore—"

"No need to lie to me. I ain't the police, but you been to Ballamore," Gertie insisted, pointing her finger. "Anyway, you look like you could use some food. I got a little ham in my icebox. Come on go home wid me. I stay just a piece down the road."

The hobo hesitated a moment. "Yes ma'am. I am a little hungry. If it's no trouble, I'll come with you."

"Come on then," Gertie said, leading the way.

By the time they reached the shack, the hobo was winded and sweaty. Gertie gave him a basin of water to freshen up in while she sliced cold ham and made him some of her special ice tea. She took a pinch of ground greenish brown herbs from one of her jars and put it in a small piece of cheese cloth. Then she dipped the cheese cloth several times in the mason jar of tea.

"Gone sit down and eat," she said, putting a plate of ham and cornbread in front of the man. "And that's some mighty good tea, too!" she chuckled.

Gertie stared at the hobo as he gobbled up the food. He squirmed occasionally when his gaze meet Gertie's. After a few mouthfuls, he gulped some tea. "This is mighty kind of you. This food hits the spot."

Gertie continued to stare and said nothing. Finally, the man started to sway back and forth. "It sure is hot in here," he said, wiping his forehead with the back of his sleeve.

"Just rest yo' head on the table for a minute, son," Gertie gently coached. "Then talk to me." She quickly moved his food before his head hit the table. After a few minutes, Gertie called his name. "Red, git up son. What happened in Ballamore?"

In a hypnotic state, Red raised his head and began talking in a monotone.

"I went to this invitation-only, high-stakes poker game that I heard about, but it was a set-up. When I got there, this nigger, Herbert Brown, who cheated me out of some money, was there. We got to arguing. I was packin.' Everybody who comes to these games, pack heat.

"The houseman told us to take our beef outside, and if we couldn't settle it, we had to leave the premises. He didn't need no trouble at his game. When we got down to the alley, Herb's flunky, his so-called bouncer, that big nigger, Thomas McNeal, jumped me. We struggled. My gun went off. Me and that coward, Herb, hauled ass. As far as I know, nobody came down to see what happened. It was a set-up. There was no game. I left town. I heard McNeal was dead, but I still had a score to settle.

"I went back and looked for Herb, first at his house, but there was nobody there but the girl. Sweet little thing. I started to snatch her, but I didn't. Then I went to Carey Street where I knew Herb kept a woman. I was waiting for him when he got there. I shot him once, and he fell. I was about to finish him off, when I thought I heard somebody coming. It was his old lady. I punched her in the face a couple of times and knocked her out.

"I went back to finish off Herb, but I was surprised. I just couldn't kill him in cold blood like that, even though he was a no-good son-of-a-bitch. I hauled ass. I left everything I had, started drinking more and more, and just lost it."

"Red, Red," Gertie gently called. "Finish your food."

Red blinked several times and shook his head. "Ma'am, you say something?"

"Yes, I said is the score even now?"

"Score? What score? I don't know what you're talkin' about. I'm grateful for the food, but I have to move on." Red continued to shake his head as if to clear it. "Feels good to have food in my belly. Thank you, ma'am. I don't even know your name."

"Don't matter, son," Gertie said as she directed him to the door. "You best be on your way 'fore it gets too dark. Be careful. Riding the rails is dangerous."

"Yes ma'am," he responded as he headed off the way they had come.

Gertie closed the door and bolted it, something she rarely did. "Two good deeds in one day. Good for me!"

39

June 1957

The last strains of the school song drifted upward, colliding with the barrage of mortarboards raining down to be caught by anybody in the cheering throng of royal blue robes. Billie snagged one, tucked it under her arm, unzipped her robe, and darted through the crowd in search of her family.

As she ran toward the bleachers, her robe billowed like a super hero's cape, while her long strides strained the seams of the form-fitting white sheath she wore beneath her academic attire. As she bumped her way through the throng of happy parents and graduates, she heard her name being called in the distance.

"Billie, Billie! Over here!"

"Carletha!" Billie shouted as she ran toward her cousin, embracing her and nearly knocking her down. "I am *so* glad to see you!"

"Girl, look at you!" Carletha exclaimed, holding Billie at arm's length. "Don't tell me you grew some more and I didn't. You look good! All filled out and stuff. Where did the country bumpkin go?"

"What can I say? Boy, I'm glad you made it down," Billie said, embracing her cousin again.

"Wouldn't have missed it for the world. I met your daddy's fiancée. Not bad, for a country girl."

"There you go. You started already!" Billie laughed. "I told you she was good people."

"Yeah, but Aunt Lilly Ann is prettier."

Billie wrinkled her nose, but their conversation was interrupted as the rest of the family approached. Carletha put her right hand over her eye and mockingly looked into the distance.

"Hot damn! Is that Tom McNeal I see? Girl, you been holding out on me. You didn't tell me he was Belafonte and Portier all rolled into one!"

"Shut up, Carletha! That's not even possible, but he *is* fine!" Billie called over her shoulder as she headed to greet her grandmother.

As always, Billie was overjoyed to see Grandma Gertie. After a long embrace, Grandma Gertie backed away and gave Billie a once over.

"My, my, you sure done growed into a fine specimen," Grandma Gertie said as Aunt Wilma, Uncle Larry, her mother, father, and Margaret caught up to them and laughed.

Herb was conspicuous by his absence, because he had long since given up any attempt to be a surrogate parent to Billie. Tom, suddenly shy, hung back until Carletha literally leaped into his unsuspecting arms.

"Tom McNeal. How the hell are you? How's your mom and brothers? I came straight here from the train, but I'll stop by and see them when I get to my parents."

"Carletha, you haven't changed one bit. Still the roughneck. You maybe grew an inch, that's all!" Tom laughed, shaking her from his neck and glancing sideways at Billie.

"All right, everybody," Uncle Larry interrupted. "Let's get to my house. Billie, I know you got parties to go to, so you young'uns don't have to stay long."

As the group headed for the parking lot, Tom walked over to Billie and took her hand. "Congrats, lady. I'm proud of you."

"Thanks! Me too!" Billie said. She turned to look Tom in the eye and held his gaze for a second. Then she dropped his hand and skipped off. "Hey everybody, wait up."

* * *

Aunt Wilma had prepared a sumptuous spread and invited some of the neighbors. After some of the well-wishers had hugged and kissed Billie, and welcomed Carletha home, Uncle Larry took control of the room.

"Brothers and sisters, your attention please. First, we are happy to have my daughter home from New York for a few days. And we are equally happy to congratulate my niece on graduatin' from Langston Hughes High School." There was cheering and applause as everyone looked from Carletha to Billie, who nodded her head and grinned from ear-to-ear. "Hold on, folks. I think her daddy, Brother James Hayes, has somethin' he wants to say."

"Yes sir, I do," said Billie's father. "First, I can't forget to mention that my fiancée just completed training as a midwife and received a certificate from Johns Hopkins Hospital on Wednesday. I'm real proud of her. Not many colored girls get that chance."

He acknowledged Margaret with his outstretched hand amidst the nodding and clapping. Billie noticed that her mother looked on with disinterest.

"Billie, come on over here, please," her father beckoned.

Billie made her way around the dinner room table and stood by her father. He placed his arm around her shoulder and said, "I'll be the first to admit that I was not—am not—the best father in the world. But I do love my daughter, and I am mighty proud of the young woman she is becoming.

"I came up short sometimes, you know, but my family—my mother, mainly—instilled education in my brothers and sisters. And I promised myself that my daughter would get an education." Billie's father reached into his shirt pocket and pulled out an envelope. "I'd like to present to my daughter a check for $2,500. I've been saving this since she was born."

The room filled with "oohs and aahs," and a speechless Billie threw her arms around her father as Margaret stood, beaming.

"If she spends it well," James continued, "with her scholarship and maybe a National Defense Education Loan, she should have enough for her entire four years at Delmarva State College!"

"I don't know what to say," Billie said. "Thank you, Daddy. Thank God for you."

* * *

After more pleasantries were exchanged and food consumed, Billie announced she was leaving for a party. She kissed her parents, waved goodbye, and headed outside with Carletha and the McNeal boys close behind.

"We'll catch you later, Billie," David said as he and John headed down the street.

"Bye. Thanks for stopping by," Billie said, blowing them kisses. "Carletha, what are you going to do?"

"Me? I just got in town, so I need to hang with the folks for a little while. I know where you'll be, so I may catch up with you later. If I don't, have fun. It's your night. Love you, cuz." Carletha kissed Billie on the cheek and went back into the house, leaving Billie and Tom on the porch.

"Love that white dress," Tom said.

"Oh, this old thing?" Billie said, parodying a Southern belle.

"Yeah, that old thing. Can I go with you to your party?"

"Sure you can. I don't see why not."

"Walk down to the house with me then. I need to change my shirt and get a jacket, if that's okay with you—Oops, did it again. Almost forgot." Tom fished a small box out of his pocket and handed it to Billie. "Here's something for you."

"Tom you shouldn't have," Billie said as she lifted the lid to find a delicate gold locket. "This is magnificent!" she whispered.

"Glad you like it. Let's go."

When they reached the house, Tom fumbled for his keys and opened the door to a dark house.

"I thought David and John would be here," Billie said.

Tom turned on the light in the living room. "Why did you think that? It's Saturday night. Their time to howl!" he laughed.

"Dunno. Guess I didn't expect the house to be dark. I know your mom's up the street."

"Since when have you been afraid of the dark?"

"Shut up, Tom, I'm not ... I'll wait in the living room while you change."

"Hope I don't have to press a shirt," Tom called over his shoulder as he ran up to his room.

"You can iron?" Billie yelled up the steps, laughing.

After a few minutes, Tom returned, but he wore no shirt. "You'll find I'm quite self-sufficient."

Billie inhaled. She was caught off-guard by Tom's chiseled, hazelnut-colored chest, and she closed her eyes. Tom, who didn't notice, asked her to join him in the basement while he looked for a shirt in the laundry basket.

"Do I remember this basement!" Billie said on the way down the steps. "And the laundry basket of un-ironed shirts. Don't you guys know how to iron more than one shirt at a time?"

"No. Why should we? Iron 'em as we need 'em."

"At least you've done a little decorating," Billie said, flopping on the secondhand sofa that had not been there the last time she had been in the basement. She removed her shoes and put her feet up on the small, well-worn coffee table.

Tom said, with a sweeping motion, "By all means. Make yourself comfortable, my lady, while I make like a valet."

They both laughed. Tom plugged in the heavy iron and sat next to Billie while he waited for it to heat up.

"I really love the locket. It's gorgeous." Billie said.

"Gorgeous for a gorgeous lady. I'm glad you like it. Why don't you put it on?"

"Good idea." Billie fished the box out of her small evening purse and handed the locket to Tom.

"Turn around. Let's see if my big hands can finesse this."

Billie turned her back to Tom, and he put the locket around her neck. He managed to secure the catch after fumbling with it for a few seconds.

"Voilà!" he said as he kissed her on her neck. But then he left a trail of feathery kisses down Billie's neck and shoulder.

As Tom pulled her closer, Billie tilted her head back until it rested on his shoulder. He kissed her throat and nibbled on her ear lobe. "Billie, why won't you be my girl?" Tom whispered in her ear.

The passion Billie was beginning to feel overrode her indignation, and she spoke quietly. "Don't blame that on me, Tom. You never really asked, or acted like you were serious, for that matter."

"I am serious, and I am sorry. Sorry, for whatever I did or didn't do," Tom replied, turning her to face him.

He kissed her deeply, teasing her with his tongue while she caressed his naked back.

"Tom," Billie said, slightly pulling away from him. "I think you're too mature … too experienced for me. You know …"

"No, I don't know, and if I am, that's not a bad thing."

Tom kissed her bosom and slowing began to unzip her dress. His touch was gentle and giving, and not rough and demanding like that of other guys she dated and always repelled.

Billie felt as if she was swirling in a warm, silky whirlpool of passion. Her arousal drowned out the voice in her head reciting the words to Hymn #364: *Yield Not to Temptation for yielding is sin*. But she was prepared to throw all caution to the wind. As she sank deeper into a vortex of desire, a barely audible voice called her name.

"Billie, Billie … We gotta go. We can't do this."

In her dreamlike state, she made little sense of what she was hearing.

"What, what?" she responded.

"I said, we can't do this. *I* can't do this."

"Please don't stop, Tom."

"Yes. Go freshen up while I give my shirt a lick and a promise ... We need to get out of here."

Billie hesitantly agreed. "You're right. Seems you always are. Zip my dress back."

Tom complied, and Billie headed up to the bathroom, feeling like she had an itch that she couldn't scratch.

40

Despite the events of the graduation weekend, Billie did not change her decision to go to South Carolina for the summer. Tom had finally said what she wanted to hear, but now she was afraid. Afraid their friendship would be ruined, and of the strong emotions the new phase of the relationship had already evoked. And afraid that Tom would turn out to be a wolf in sheep's clothing like all of the other boys—men—she had encountered during her life. She could not let herself be sucked in and used.

When she had dropped the news on Tom about her unchanged summer plans, he was not happy. Billie had sensed his repressed anger, with which she was all too familiar, though it had never been directed at her.

"I wish you wouldn't, but that's your decision," Tom had said, working his jaw muscles. Before she could respond, he said, "I know. Don't tell you what to decide. We had this conversation before." Then he had thrown up his hands and walked away.

Billie was saddened by their conversation, but determined not to be swayed by someone else's emotions. "See," she told herself. "When we were just friends, I didn't have to worry about this kinda crap."

* * *

After closing the apartment, Billie's father discovered that he had more stuff to take back to South Carolina than the Packard could hold, which meant that Billie would have to take the train. That actually worked better for her because it gave her more time to get organized for college in the fall.

On the Tuesday following Billie's graduation, Billie's father came to Upton to pick up her grandmother. Just before he arrived, Grandma Gertie gave her a folded page from the Columbia newspaper and instructed her to read it in her room later, with an emphasis on later.

After they left, she went to her room and read the article.

Sunday, June 8, 1958, Florence, South Carolina. On Thursday, June 5th, Sheriff's Deputies were called to the woods near the Chattum Road crossing where the body of an unidentified colored man was discovered by two hunters. Coroner Moses McCarthy has ruled the death an accident. The Coroner believes the man either fell or jumped from the train and hit his head in the fall. The deceased was a light-skinned colored man, approximately 6'1, weighting about 180 lbs, with freckles, kinky red hair and a full beard, also red. Anyone with information on the deceased should contact the Florence Sheriff's Department.

Billie sat on her bed and reread the article. She had no idea what to do with the information. She was certain the unidentified man was the illusive Red, and he had finally gotten his just desserts. But it was a justice she could not understand. Both Red and Herb had dabbled in unlawful enterprises, but they expected honor among thieves.

Was Red righteous in seeking to get what Herb owed him? Billie wondered. *Is it worth killing a man, even if that man was Herbert Brown? Did Red deserve to die? Or Tom McNeal, Senior?* She simply did not know, but apparently her grandmother knew or thought she did.

Billie carefully refolded the paper. She rifled through her desk drawer and found a long forgotten pale yellow envelope with a birthday card from her father. She removed the card and stuck the article in the envelope. Then she dug to the bottom of one of the boxes she had packed for school, pulled out her diary, unlocked it, and placed the envelope in it. She returned the diary to the place where it had been hidden.

Billie went downstairs to phone Carletha, still musing over the newspaper article. They had planned to go to a movie together on the last night before they went their separate ways. Billie to Fairfield, and Carletha back to Brooklyn.

* * *

There. It was done. Tom had asked Billie. It didn't happen exactly the way he wanted it to, but the unexpected circumstances had presented an opportune time. Now it was out in the open, and she was his girl.

But one of the very things he had feared about a relationship had already occurred: game-playing and arguments about stupid stuff. That had been his experience with other girls, but he didn't expect it to be so with Billie. Yet after he laid bare his soul, she had still decided to exercise her so-called independence and go to South Carolina.

He took some comfort in the extraordinary control he had demonstrated in the basement. He had constrained himself—not so much because it was too soon, immoral, or the wrong place and time—but because something he could not explain had made him ashamed.

Okay, McNeal, you're a psych major. What's going on? Is it the classic, Madonna-whore complex? Boy, I hope the hell not!

The thought gave way to a few seconds of a hearty belly laugh, but Tom abruptly stopped short as he pondered the question again. *Is there some truth to the notion? Do I place Billie on a pedestal and think she's too pure to be touched?*

Tom made a mental note to recheck some of his class notes on the subject.

* * *

It was a hard lesson, but Billie now knew the meaning of the old adage, "Cutting off your nose to spite your face." She wondered how she could have forgotten how boring Fairfield could be.

She acknowledged that she enjoyed the time with her father and most of the Hayes' clan, and she certainly cherished the time with her grandmother. But after a few weeks, she missed Baltimore. Not so much her friends or mother, but her room, and, to her surprise, Tom. It wasn't that she had not anticipated missing him, but she felt an unfamiliar longing. Still, she had come to South Carolina to prove a point, but now she wondered, *What point?*

Because of the cost of long-distance calling, she had only talked to Tom a few times, and neither of them had bothered to write. She took some solace in catching up on her reading by finishing some of the classics she thought an educated and well-rounded colored woman should read: *The Great Gatsby, East of Eden,* and *The Invisible Man.* She saved the poetry of Paul Lawrence Dunbar for the tedious train trip home, where she would only be for a week before turning around and heading for college.

One week. Billie vowed to see Tom as much as she could in that one week. She hoped he would not be as vindictive as she was by avoiding her as pay back for the summer. After all, when she went away to college, it would be months before they saw each other.

41

Fall 1958

A restless Billie shifted in her seat as the warm Autumn sun beamed in the window of the Greyhound bus. The summer in South Carolina had been too long, and her week with Tom too short. They had gone to movies, the bowling alley, and skating. But the best was their time spent in Woodley Park. She was going to miss Tom dearly, but she was excited about starting a new life away at college.

The Chesapeake Bay Bridge, the longest continuous overwater steel structure, loomed ahead, but Billie could barely see it from her seat in the rear of the bus. She held her breath as the bus approached the large bridge, and she caught sight of the Chesapeake's calm, blue, and gently undulating waters.

It was beautiful. She had been to Atlantic City a couple of times and seen a large body of water, but she had never ever crossed such a bridge. It was also the reason she was making the trip alone, because her mother had a paralyzing fear of bridges.

Maybe I'll never see Momma again because her phobia will keep her from visiting me, especially if I refuse to come home. She amused herself with the thought, glad to take her mind off her traveling companions.

The horrible accounts she had heard about colored people riding buses in the South made her extremely uncomfortable among the sea of white faces on the Greyhound. Despite those stories, and the protests of other family members, her mother and Herb had still sent her by bus to the Eastern Shore. At least her mother had had the presence of mind to ship most of her things so she wouldn't be too encumbered on the trip.

Billie had prayed for a safe trip, hoping her necking with Tom would not prevent her prayer from reaching God's ear. Thankfully, she made the trip without incident.

* * *

A small van waited at the Greyhound station to shuttle incoming students to the Delmarva State College campus in Princess Anne. Billie dragged the one suitcase she had stowed in the belly of the bus as she made her way to the van. The elderly driver tipped his hat, took the suitcase from her, and shoved it in the back of the van.

"Take a seat, Miss. I need to wait for two mo' people 'fore I can head back to campus."

"Yes, sir," Billie said as she dutifully climbed into the van. Tiny beads of perspiration formed on her forehead, and her blouse clung to her in the humid Eastern Shore climate.

The other two passengers, a boy and a girl, arrived one at a time. They nervously greeted and eyed each other as they stepped onto the van. After acknowledging the girl, Billie pretended to be fully absorbed in the scenery outside her window. Once they were settled, the van bumped and sputtered its way to Bagley Hall, the admissions building.

"So this is it," Billie said aloud as her eyes roamed the landscape.

The grass was still green, and summer flowers—Black-eyed Susans, Crape Myrtles, Magnolias, and Hydrangeas—were still in bloom. Off in the distance, she saw a red brick building with a portico supported by four massive Doric columns that reminded her of the colonial buildings she had seen in pictures.

A red brick pathway led to the building before it branched off into two diagonal paths to the right and left side of the building. At the apex of each path were several off-shoot paths that led to other parts of the campus. The rustic setting gave her the same feeling she had experienced the first time she looked out of the bedroom window of her father's farmhouse.

The driver deposited his three charges in front of Bagley Hall and helped them retrieve their belongings.

"Well," they all said at the same time. They laughed, breaking the nervous silence.

The boy, who was short and stocky, extended his hand to Billie and the other girl. "Hi, I'm Jeff from Delaware. Where you people from?" he asked.

"Billie. Billie Cunningham from Baltimore. Pleased to meet you," she said, shaking Jeff's hand.

The girl, who was dark brown with enormous brown eyes, said, "I'm Deborah from Salisbury. It's close by." She shook Billie's hand.

"Guess we need to go in and find out where we belong," Jeff said, heading up the steps.

The girls nodded and followed.

* * *

The campus was not very large, and Billie easily found her way to Somerset Hall. She took the stairs and found Room 307, her new home. The room was empty, but her missing roommate had already cluttered the bed by the window with personal items and strewn things on the other half of the room as well.

"This ain't gonna work," Billie said. She entered the room and flopped down on a desk chair just inside the door. The room was hardly bigger than her room at home, and they expected two people—two girls at that—to live in it.

"This ain't gonna work!" she repeated, sizing up the room. She got up, looked down the hall, and spotted a telephone on the wall. She fished coins from her pocket and started to walk down the hall, but she saw a dark brown girl, draped in a towel, walking toward her from the opposite end of the hall.

"Hey slim," the girl called. "I'm your roomie."

Billie sucked her teeth and slowly took a couple of steps toward the girl. When they were face to face, she extended her hand and said, "Billie. My *name* is Billie Cunningham."

As her roommate reached for Billie's hand, her towel fell, causing Billie to unconsciously raise an eyebrow.

"Ain't you ever seen a naked girl before?" the girl asked.

"That's hardly the point, is it?"

"Hardly the point? You talk like that all the time? Anyway, sorry. Didn't mean to offend your sensibilities. I grew up with two sisters sharing the same bedroom. Naked ain't a big deal to me."

"Yeah, well I'll try to remember that. What did you say your name was?"

"I didn't. Janet Irby, but you can call me Rita. I'll call you Holiday."

"What? My *name* is Billie!" Billie wondered what life was going to be like for the next few months.

"You heard of Billie Holiday, haven't you? I don't like Janet, so I call myself Rita, like Rita Hayworth. Sounds sexier, you know?"

"No, I don't know. But what I do know is that my name is Billie, and you can call me Billie!"

Janet gathered her towel and retreated to their room. Billie followed and removed a couple of Janet's things from her bed.

"Guess, you forgot I was coming, huh?" Billie asked as she put them by the window.

"Sorry, Holiday. Just taking advantage of the space for as long as I could."

Before Billie could respond, three girls came to the door and peeped in. "Hey y'all! Meet my roomie, Holiday," Janet loudly instructed.

The girls greeted Billie with "Hello," and a "Glad to me you, Holiday," and Billie momentarily resigned herself to being called that name. Billie smiled and left the room to continue her quest for a phone. She dialed home.

"Momma, my roommate is a looney tune," Billie laughed into the phone.

"You just met her. How you know that already?"

"Trust me, Momma. I know crazy when I see it and hear it. Anyway, I got here fine, and I'm all right."

"Okay, baby. Glad to hear it. Call us if you need something. I'll let everybody know you got there safe."

"Yes, ma'am. I'll tell you all about the trip later. Talk to you soon. Bye." As soon as Billie hung up, she dialed another number and spoke to the operator.

"One moment please," the operator replied. Then she said, "Person-to-person collect call for Thomas McNeal. Will you accept the call?"

"Yes, this is Tom McNeal."

"Go ahead, miss."

"Hey, Tom. I'm here! I'm a college student!"

"I was hanging around the house waiting to hear from you. Everything go all right?" Tom asked.

"Pretty much. The campus is pretty rural, but I think I'm going to like it."

"I don't believe you're talking about rural, Country Girl."

"I'm a long way from that country girl you once knew. Anyway, I just want to get on with it. I have a life to live."

"Know what you mean, but this working and going to school part-time is killing me. And if I don't want to be a social worker, I'll have to go to grad school to make any money with a psych degree. You're lucky you can go full-time without working."

"Luck's in the Lord, devil's in the people."

"Sounds like something your grandmother would say."

"It is. I guess I *am* blessed, but don't judge me 'til you've walked in my shoes."

"I think I know the shoes pretty well," Tom retorted.

"Don't be so sure. Anyway, hang in there, honey. You can do it. I'm proud of you."

"Thanks for the pep talk. I forget which one of us is the psych major," Tom laughed. "Meet your roommate yet?"

"Yep, and I'm not sure about her. A couple of screws loose or something, but we'll work it out. You know me. I can get along with anybody, but don't mess with me!"

"Whoa, girl! You just met her. Why can't women get along?" But after a slight pause, Tom said, "I miss you."

"I'm cool. I miss you, too. Behave yourself while I'm gone," Billie chided.

"Think about me tonight. I'll be there in November for Homecoming. Don't forget, you can call collect anytime, just make sure it's person-to-person."

"Homecoming is three months away. Hope the time goes fast."

"It will. Don't forget … Think about me."

"Ditto. Gotta go. Bye."

"Bye. You hang up first."

"No, you," Billie laughed.

"Billie, I love—" Tom said, but Billie had hung up.

* * *

As it turned out, Janet—Rita—was a lovable nut and a bit of an exhibitionist. She and Billie got along famously when they saw each other. They didn't have any classes together, and Rita was seldom in the room. She somehow managed to avoid getting caught by the RA whenever she violated curfew, which was often.

Despite having been in the top ten of her one hundred-and-fifty-member graduating class, Billie found the first semester of college torture. Unlike high school, which had come extremely easy to her, she had to apply herself rigorously.

Maybe it was the year that made the difference, she thought. She would turn seventeen in the fall, while the other freshmen were already eighteen or turning eighteen. But she pooh-poohed that idea, knowing she could hold her own. Billie didn't know how Rita got by, because she rarely saw her crack a book.

* * *

On the Friday before Homecoming, Billie finished cramming for a Saturday exam and headed back to the dorm to call Tom to confirm that he was coming the next week. When she stopped by her room to throw in her books and take off her jacket, she encountered Rita, who was sobbing hysterically and stuffing clothes into her suitcase.

"Janet—Rita. What's the matter? What's going on?" Billie asked, concerned. She dropped her belongings on the floor and grabbed Rita by the shoulders.

Between gut-wrenching sobs, Rita said, "I have to leave school."

"Leave school? But why?" Billie asked.

"I'm pregnant!" Rita blurted.

"Sweet Jesus. How did that happen?"

"Come on, Holiday. You're not that naïve, are you?" Rita tried to laugh.

"Janet—Rita, are you sure? I'm so sorry."

"Of course I'm sure," Rita responded, and she started sobbing again.

"How far along are you? As naïve as I am, I know it can go either way in the first couple of months."

"Just about three months," Rita said, flopping down on her bed.

"Wow … Happened soon after you got here. What's the daddy saying?"

"Don't ask. He's married."

"Holy shit! I'm not judging, but what are you going to do? What is he prepared to do?"

"Nothing. Absolutely nothing. He has other kids. He's not going to leave his wife."

"They never do. No matter what they say about the wife, they don't leave. Maybe you should tell her yourself."

"What good would that do? He'll be angry at me, and she may or may not kick him out. I'll have to do this on my own. My sisters will help … We have to find somebody …"

"Find somebody? Find somebody for what? You *cannot* have some back alley abortion, Janet. Do you hear me?"

Billie sat down on the bed and embraced her roommate. "Please don't do it. Don't even think about it. Just tell me who the son-of-a bitch is so I can kill him for you."

As the two of them lay back on the bed, Rita couldn't help but laugh. "It takes two to tango, Billie."

"I'll be sure to remember that."

* * *

Billie, caught up in the gravity of Rita's situation, completely forgot to telephone Tom until she heard yelling in the hallway.

"Holiday, Holiday! Phone call."

She extricated herself from a sleeping Rita and went to take the call. "Hello," she answered.

"Hi. What's up? You didn't call."

"I know. I'm sorry. I got a little busy, and the time slipped by."

"I'm on break, so I can't talk long. You sound funny. What's the matter? You don't want to talk to me?"

"Come on, Tom. You know better. It's been a rough day."

"Sorry to hear that. What happened?"

"I'll tell you about it later. I can't wait to see you. I'll be on the quad at eleven like we planned."

"Good. I can't wait either. Don't forget I'll have a couple of my boys with me looking to meet some college women."

"There'll be plenty around. They won't need my help."

"I know that's right! Take it light, Billie. Gotta go. See you Saturday. Love you," Tom said, and he hung up.

* * *

When Billie returned from her exam on Saturday, all vestiges of Rita's occupancy were gone. The two of them had vowed to keep in touch. But Billie knew it was not likely to happen, and that she had probably seen the last of Janet "Rita" Irby.

Her heart bled for Janet, who was possibly stuck with having to raise a baby without a father. *Another woman dependent on a man,* she thought.

She knew from overhearing adult conversation that, when faced with an "outside child," the wife, with no skills or job, often accepted the predicament and rarely put the husband out. If any good was to come out of this situation, Billie would have the room to herself for the rest of the semester.

42

The crisp autumn air was perfect football weather. Friday night's pep rally had sent the student body into a frenzy and buoyed the confidence of the DSC Hawks. They were going to trounce their longtime rival, the Morgan State College Bears. Buses rolled in carrying the football team, the MSC band, and excited, rowdy students ready to see battle on the gridiron. A few students even drove their own vehicles.

Tom hitched a ride with four of his potential fraternity brothers. In college, albeit it part-time, he had become less of a lone wolf than he had been in high school. Even though he constantly reminded them that he did not have the time or the money to pledge Kappa Alpha Psi, they continued to court him.

Off in the distance, the boom-boom of the band's drums reverberated in Billie's chest as she made her way to the quad. She caught a glimpse of Tom among a group of guys and quickened her pace.

She ignored the guys and jumped on Tom, wrapping her legs around his waist. Tom, momentarily forgetting his aversion to public displays of affection, embraced her, and spun her around while whispering in her ear, "You smell good. You feel good."

He regained his composure and planted Billie on her feet with a kiss on the forehead and a punch on the arm. "Fellas, this is Billie. Billie, these are the fellas."

As Billie smiled and acknowledged each one, her sensitive nose caught a whiff of the smell of alcohol. *Don't tell me they've started already.*

As the quad filled with students headed for the field, the canteen, or to hang out, Billie saw several of her friends and beckoned for them to join the throng. As she inched closer to Tom's side, she saw Will, one of Tom's friends from New York, elbow Tom in the side and comment out of the side of his mouth, "You been holding out on us, McNeal. Whew! I know you've been gettin' some of that!"

The words had barely left Will's lips before he found himself flat on his rear, felled by an explosive McNeal punch. He would have fallen flat if he had not landed against the legs of the guys standing close by. Tom bounced on his toes, dukes raised in perfect prize-fighter form as he waited for a dazed Will to get to his feet.

As he was helped to his feet, Will realized he was bleeding. "McNeal, you crazy nigger!" Will said as a few of the guys helped him to his feet. He touched his bloody lip. "Come on. It's about time somebody beat your ass anyway."

The guys immediately restrained Will and Tom, but the crowd, having none of it, yelled, "Fight! Fight!" The crowd, however, quickly dispersed as two campus policeman arrived on the scene.

Billie, mortified and angry, turned on her heels and started for Somerset Hall in a huff.

"Billie, wait! Please wait!" Tom called after her, but she ignored him and walked faster, reaching the building.

Tom caught up to her and grabbed her arm, but she shrugged off his grasp and quickly ran up the dorm steps to her room, with Tom on her heels. Billie unlocked her door and attempted to close it in Tom's face, but she was no match for his superior strength. He forced the door open, slamming it behind him.

"Billie, I'm sorry."

"You sure are! Don't you get tired of apologizing to me? I'm sick of you fighting all the time," she yelled.

"I *do not* fight all the time. I'm sorry, but Will said something I didn't like. I wasn't gonna let him get away it. It was disrespectful. Besides, I was just protecting your honor," Tom said, equally loud.

"Give it a rest, Tom. I don't need you to protect my honor. You are not my knight in shining armor. Can't you just ignore some things? I have told you time and time again, your fists are going to get you in more trouble than you can handle. I can't be with you if that's your response to every little slight. You don't have to prove your manhood to me. And drinking? It's not even noon! I'm on a mission here. I can't afford to let your antics get me kicked out of school."

"My 'antics'? You sure have a penchant for hyperbole, Country Girl," Tom said sarcastically.

"Those are pretty fancy words for a street thug!"

"I got news for you. You're not the only one who has a brain and can read. Maybe I care too much, but you can't see that."

"I can see you don't know how to control your emotions."

"You can't see my side, can you? I'm outta here," Tom said, but before he could open the door to leave, someone pounded on it.

"Holiday, this is Sandy!"

Tom gave Billie a quizzical look and mouthed, "Sandy?"

Billie nodded and pulled Tom away from the door, whispering, "RA!" She walked to the farthest part of the room and replied, "Yeah Sandy, what is it? I'm not dressed."

"There is somebody in the lobby looking for a Tom McNeal," Sandy firmly said from the other side of the door. "I have to go to my room for exactly ten minutes. When I get back to the lobby, there will be no Tom McNeal or anybody looking for him, and you will be well on your way to the football game. You got it?"

"Got it!" Billie yelled back.

Billie and Tom heard exaggerated footsteps and covered their mouths to hold back the laughter. Billie attempted to reach around Tom to open the door, but he encircled her waist and kissed her.

"Please forgive me, baby," he whispered.

Billie gave him her best, you-got-to-be-kidding look, and pulled him out the door.

* * *

When Tom saw Will waiting for him in front of the dorm, he threw his hands up in surrender. "Will, I'm sorry, man. I overreacted."

"They told me you had a hair-trigger temper, but I was out of line. I'm sorry too, man. You do pack a hell of a punch!" Will said, extending his hand.

"Does this mean I still have my seat and won't get jumped on the way home?"

"We're cool. Just be at the car by one in the morning. Anybody not there when the driver is ready to go, gets left. And we will leave your ass for sure," Will laughed.

Like men do, they shook hands and slapped each other on the back, incident forgotten.

* * *

The Hawk trouncing never materialized, and the Bears won the game, 27-3. The after-parties were a little less exuberant, but party they did.

Billie kept a watchful eye over Tom's alcohol consumption, all the while pondering what anyone got out of being drunk. She shook her head as she observed some of the young women, because she knew that by the end of the evening, they would have little control over themselves and what could possibly happen to them. She was too much of a control freak to let that happen to her.

In the weeks leading up to Homecoming, Billie had done reconnaissance to find a foolproof way of getting Tom into her dorm. But the unspoken rule of the house was that Sandy planned to bend the rules for Homecoming, as much for her own enjoyment as for the girls. The watch words were, "Be careful," and "Be discreet."

Around ten o'clock, Billie and Tom made their way to her room. Over the course of the day, Billie had filled Tom in on the details of Janet's situation. But his sympathy for her misfortune was second to his delight in the knowledge that Billie no longer had a roommate.

Once they were in the room, they gravitated to a different bed and looked at each other, relieved that they made it to the room unnoticed.

"Let's talk," Billie suggested.

"What? Let's not. We've talked all day," Tom responded.

Ignoring him, Billie said, "We spend so little time together these days, that I can't waste it on being mad at you. But you do make me mad. Seems like since I've become your main squeeze—"

"Only squeeze," Tom interrupted.

"Better be," Billie said, pointing her finger at him. "Seems we argue more."

"Thought we weren't talking."

Tom dropped to the floor on all fours and crawled across the scatter rug to the other bed, stopping at Billie's feet. He removed her shoes, then her stockings, and slowly planted kisses up her legs, moving methodically and torturously slow until he reached the essence of her femininity. When her moans signaled she had reached the pinnacle of her desire, he gathered her in his arms and whispered in her ear, "Lay with me, Billie."

And she did.

* * *

Waking up in Tom's arms was both delightful and a shock. For a few seconds, Billie watched him sleep, trying to match her breathing with the rise and fall of his chest, and her heartbeat with the gentle pulsing beneath her hand. She wanted to get closer to him, but the only way to do that, she concluded, was to crawl into his chest. She smiled at her own silliness and gently stroked his face. Tom stirred.

"Tom, you better get up. You don't want to miss your ride."

Tom kissed her, slid her off his chest, and sat up. "Morning …
This must be heaven …"

Tom was momentarily at a loss for words. He stretched his well-developed arms and finally said, "Billie, I didn't know … I guess I should have, but I didn't know for sure … I'm sorry. I shouldn't have … But thank you for the gift."

"There you go being sorry again. And I think I'm offended. You had to know I never … I was a … Anyway, it was a gift to myself, not to you."

"I think I like the sound of that. Can we not fight after … after all this?"

"No fight," Billie said, and she moved to let him out of the crowded bed.

When Tom got himself together, she walked him to the door, where they kissed one last time.

"Wish I didn't have to go," Tom said.

"That's called marriage, and this ain't it."

Exasperated, Tom shook his head and slipped out the door. "I'll call you tomorrow when I think you're back from church."

Billie nodded, blew him a kiss, and closed the door. She leaned against the door with her eyes closed, and wondered if anyone would be able to look at her and tell what she had done. If her mother saw her, would she know? In part, it had been all she imagined, but she also wondered, *Is that all there is?*

On her way down the hall to the shower, her subconscious mind suddenly registered the absence of any disgusting, sticky substance between her legs, and she disassociated what happened with Tom from the similar acts in her past. Herb had never penetrated her, but he always left his disgusting release behind and took pleasure in cleaning her up. These memories were seldom in her consciousness.

Although her introduction to sex had come early and against her will, she had not become promiscuous. Tom had been gentle, careful, and responsible, and she had easily given herself to him for reasons she was still trying to understand.

As Billie showered, she said to herself, "Grandma Gertie, *please* get out of my head."

* * *

The November air had chilled the house, causing Gertie to pull the quilt up tighter around her skinny frame. It was another sleepless night, but it didn't bother her. It came with the territory.

So, she simply murmured a prayer. "Lord, forgive her. She know not what she do."

Those words quieted her spirit.

She liked Tom, and believed he was going to be a good man, but the time for them to be together was too soon. *Sometimes I can help, and sometimes I can't. Lord, forgive me, for I know what I do.*

* * *

Billie had no doubt that attendance at chapel would be sparse after such a riotous weekend. She intended to sleep in, nestled under her sheets with the lingering scent of Tom.

A knock on the door woke her from her blissful slumber. "Holiday! Holiday! Phone."

It was two o'clock. She had slept the morning away. Billie grabbed a robe and headed down the hall. "Hello," she answered with anticipation.

"Hi, it's me," said Tom in a soft, husky voice.

"Hi, yourself. I take it you made it home all right."

"Yeah, I'm lucky them Kappas didn't toss me off the Bay Bridge. I had to go to church to thank the Lord for that ... and other things."

"You went to church? Well, hallelujah! But I don't think you can thank the Lord for allowing you to partake in lewd and lascivious activities."

"Do you have to ruin everything? Please don't make light of it, Billie. I have enough inner conflict of my own without you dashing cold water on me."

"Now I'm the one who's sorry. Yesterday—last night—was wonderful," Billie whispered.

"Anyway, new subject," Tom replied. "I knew your mother could sing, but I didn't know she could *sang*! She had 'em falling out in the aisles."

"You went to Momma's church? And yeah, she slays 'em. She even gets called to sing at other churches"

"What's wrong with Mr. Brown? He looked bad."

"Herbert Brown was in church? Repent ye sinners for the Rapture is at hand! What do you mean? Bad as in, his do wasn't done, or his square didn't match his tie? What?"

"He looked thin. Gaunt."

"That nightlife catches up with you. That's the first I heard. Momma hasn't said anything to me. Wish you were here."

"Me too. Why did you go to Delmarva when you could have gone to Morgan?"

"Momma wanted me out of the house."

"Really? Didn't think she'd push her baby bird out of the nest so soon."

"It's more to it than that. Maybe I'll tell you about it sometime."

"Hope you do, because now I'm curious. This weekend wore me out. I called off from work so I can get some studying done, if I can concentrate."

"When will I see you again?" Billie asked.

"Dunno. With the holidays coming, won't you be coming home?"

"I guess. Sounds like not until Thanksgiving then. I miss you," Billie said again.

"Miss you too. Gotta go hit the books," Tom said reluctantly. "Think about me. Take care."

"I will. Bye."

* * *

Tom paced back and forth in his room. He had no idea that Billie would take up so much space in his head. From the time he left her room until this very minute, she was all he could think about.

Unbeknownst to Billie, he had jealously watched her at the game and parties they attended, and she had been totally unaware of the attention she commanded.

Was it her height? Her eyes, long legs, and sense of style? Or the genuine warmth she exuded despite her reserve? Her unassuming personality made her all the more appealing. Sometimes, the vestiges of the tomboy she once was would surface, especially when she had "to get somebody straight," and she would remind him of their childhood, which endeared her to him all the more.

But then there was the push-pull thing, the times when she seemed completely oblivious to his feelings, and she put up a wall and kept him at arm's length. Yet other times, she was affectionate and tender, wanting him near.

It didn't help his own inner turmoil to have her hot and cold. Perhaps he gave her more credit for being emotionally mature than she deserved. And the harangue about his temper twisted his gut into knots. She was right about it, but he didn't want her to be. And, to further complicate matters, he had done the very thing he said and thought he would not do. Did he regret it? Would she?

Tom was accustomed to partitioning his relationships from the rest of his life. No strings, no questions, and no regrets. In his other relationships, he simply pulled his shoes out from under the bed, laced them up, and left. But this was Billie. It was different. She was special.

He continued to pace, his thoughts rapid. *She thinks she's on a mission? Well, me too! I have to get out of undergrad and get to grad school. One year full-time would do the trick. Can't pull that off and work too, but I need to work. And I need a car. What was that the preacher said today? 'Whatsoever ye shall ask that will I do, that the Father may be glorified in the Son.' Can't be that simple. Can it?*

Tom wiped his sweaty palms on his pants, then bolted from his room and down the steps to the basement to lift some weighs. Intense physical exertion always helped him clear his head and work off frustrations. It occurred to him that Billie's being on the Eastern Shore was possibly a blessing in disguise.

43

1959

By the end of her freshman year, Billie had grown weary of crossing the bridge and desired a new adventure. She decided to go to summer school and work in a local crab factory, a decision she came to regret.

Crab picking was piece work, and after suffering from stiff fingers, cuts and abrasions, and substandard working conditions, she quit the job after three weeks. She concluded she would starve to death if she had to sustain herself by filling plastic containers with small slivers of smelly flesh pried from ugly crustaceans.

When she told Tom about the experience, he couldn't stop laughing. But she knew he was secretly glad that she had had a bad experience because he thought she should have come home for the summer.

The distance, and their respective, singular focus on graduating from college had brought their relationship full circle, and they had decided to become good friends again. And without the complication of romance or sex, Billie and Tom had given each other permission to explore other options.

* * *

Tom had fought his disdain of helpless woman and the urge to take advantage of their weakness, but Billie was a paradox. Even though she needed him at times, he didn't see her as helpless. She exerted her independence whenever she could, and she was strong-willed, stubborn, and always had to be in control. But what he most feared about Billie was her rejection, so he had agreed to just be friends.

He also believed himself unworthy of being loved. Why else would his father have brutalized him so? And why would his mother have allowed it?

* * *

Billie was still convinced that Tom was a lady's man, and she didn't want to burden herself with worrying about what he was up to when out of her sight. Besides, he had completely disarmed her and removed all of her inhibitions. She couldn't have that. She needed to be in control.

So, she dated a few guys, including Malcolm Beaumont. Billie had met Malcolm while home on spring break during her sophomore year. She had a paper to finish and had decided to use the facilities at Morgan State College. After spending the better part of the morning at the library, she had gone to the Student Union for a cup of coffee before heading home.

As she left the building, she had run smack into Malcolm and spilled her coffee all over his shirt. He was gracious about the ruined shirt and invited Billie to have a cup of coffee with him, and not on him. They had exchanged phone numbers, but it was several weeks before Malcolm called. After a few phone conversations, they went on their first date to a football game and dated seriously for about a year. Although Malcolm had no problem driving to the shore to see Billie a couple of times a month, the relationship had cooled.

Billie had remarked to Carletha during one of their regular phone conversations that although she was amazed to find such a variety of colored men at DSC, "they were all consumed with sex, money, and control, and not necessarily in that order."

Carletha had roared with laughter and asked Billie how she got to be so jaded at such a young age. *If only she knew*, Billie had thought.

44

1962

To Billie, time seemed to pass more quickly when one wasn't living in the moment, and always focused on next week, next month, or next year. Much to her delight, the spring of 1962 was rapidly approaching, and her four years at DSC had quickly passed without major incident. She would be graduating with a Bachelors of Arts Degree in Political Science, with honors.

Somewhere in the back of her mind, she contemplated law school. But for the present, she wanted to go to work and make some money. Despite all the financial help she had while in college—the bankroll her father had given her; money her mother sent; a scholarship; and her own secret stash—she ran short and had to apply for a National Defense Student Loan.

The loan required that she teach for two years if she did not want to repay the government, and she didn't. Although teaching would sidetrack her for a bit, she had taken all the requisite education courses and done student teaching in preparation for fulfilling the obligation. With high recommendations from one of her professors, she would be teaching at Lochearn Junior High School in Northwest

Baltimore County after graduation. She was leery, however, because she would be one of only three colored—now called black—teachers in the school.

* * *

The day finally came. With the euphoria of graduating, Billie couldn't help but feel a little melancholy at the thought of leaving the place that had been her home for four years. In that time, she had met a lot of people. Some would be friends for life, and she would miss them a great deal.

But mixed with her melancholy was anger and disappointment. On the most important day of her young life, her mother could not force herself to cross the Chesapeake Bay Bridge. Herb had not figured in the equation at all, but to make matters worse, her father and Margaret could not make the trip. After two failed attempts, they had just had their first child. Billie was ecstatic for them, but she just wished it could have happened at another time. As a consolation prize, one of her paternal uncles was scheduled to come in her father's stead.

The trip was also out of the question for Grandma Gertie, who was in declining health. That left Carletha, Uncle Larry, Aunt Wilma, maybe her uncle in New Jersey, and, of course, Tom. He had his very own car, a two-year-old Pontiac Catalina, and he would be her transport home on Monday after she tied up loose ends. The situation wasn't all doom and gloom.

Billie donned her burgundy cap and gown and looked at herself in the mirror. She pivoted on her toes, did a half-turn to see herself from the back, and left to take her place in line.

* * *

The burgundy robes were unbearable in the Princess Anne heat, and the keynote address was lost on most. Billie fanned herself with her program booklet and prayed for the proceedings to end. After it was finally done, the Class of 1962 filed past a throng of cheering, waving friends and relatives as the band played, "The Land of Hope and Glory," the standard processional.

The graduates shook hands, hugged, kissed, and patted each other on the back. Someone approached Billie from the back and threw an arm around her neck. She instantly got a whiff of Chanel No. 5 and knew who it was.

"Momma! Momma! You came, you came!" Billie shouted.

"Couldn't miss seeing my baby girl walk across that stage!" her mother said as she kissed Billie on the cheek. "Congratulations, honey."

"Thank you, Momma," Billie said, embracing her mother with tears in her eyes. "You don't know what this means to me."

"Thought I had breathed my last breath comin' across that bridge. I don't know how I'm gonna get home!" her mother quipped.

"Same way you came. On the floor in the back seat," Aunt Wilma chimed in, laughing as Carletha, Uncle Larry, and Tom approached.

After a couple of rounds of congratulatory hugs and kisses, Billie's mother announced their plans. "Why don't y'all go look around the campus? Me and Billie gonna go up to her room for a few minutes. We'll meet y'all back here, then get some dinner befo' we hit the road." Without waiting for an answer, she waved them on, took Billie by the arm, and started walking.

"Wrong way, Momma," Billie said, reversing their directions.

Billie and her mother held hands as they walked to Wicomico Hall, Billie's dormitory during her senior year. When they reached her room, Billie unlocked the door and let her mother in. "Sit anywhere, Momma. My roomie and I aren't finished packing and cleaning, but you can see that."

"Yes, I can, but you sit too."

Billie slid some linen and dirty clothes off the bed and sat down next to her mother. "Is there something wrong, Momma?"

"No, not at all. Just wanted to let you know that Herb is the reason I'm here. He insisted that I come no matter what I had to do to git across that bridge. So I did. I'm sure glad I did, too." She paused for a second, and Billie stared at her intently. "You need to know that Herb and me have an agreement. After three years of separation, I have no intention of taking him back, but no divorce. He won't be back. We have our own lives. And I want you to feel free to come home and stay as long as you want. I know you have a job lined up and will want to git your own place 'fore too long, but in the meantime, come on back home."

Billie was speechless. She hugged her mother, and they cried together, but neither addressed the real, long-standing issue.

After a bit, her mother regained her composure and said, "Now tell me 'bout the arrangements for the weekend. Where is Tom staying?"

Billie stammered, caught totally off-guard. "Off-campus housing. Some Kappas who still have their apartments are letting out-of-towners stay with them. Uh, Tom has his own bedroll in the car—at least he should. My roommate is going to sleep in one of the vacated rooms upstairs so Carletha can stay here with me—"

"Y'all got it all figured out, huh? You come too far to mess up now, if you know what I mean."

"For Pete's sake, Momma. Yes ma'am, I do."

"All right. Let's go find the rest of them so we can get some food and git on the road. Oh, Lawdy that bridge," her mother said, smacking herself on the forehead.

* * *

After the entourage left the campus, Billie, Carletha, and Tom joined a group at the Kappa house for final farewells and an impromptu party. Despite her usual position as a teetotaler, Billie had a cup or two of the vodka-laced punch. By evening's end, she was more giggly and silly than anyone had ever seen her.

"Don't think I can throw you over my shoulder like I did when we were kids," Tom laughed as the trio left to retire for the evening.

"Whoa, when did this happen? I don't know this story," Carletha protested.

"Another time, my dear. Another time," Tom said, supporting Billie as they entered the building.

"I can walk," Billie slurred.

The three of them headed up the stairs. When they reached Billie's floor, Tom waved to Carletha. "You okay, Carletha?" he asked as he took Billie's keys from her hand. The sleeping arrangements were not as Billie had reported to the adults.

"Yeah. See you guys in the morning," Carletha said as she took the steps to the fourth floor.

Tom opened Billie's door, and she flopped down on her bed.

"Do I have to tuck you in?" he asked a yawning Billie.

"Nope. I'm fine."

"God, I'm tired," Tom said, finding a space to sit on the bed.

"Come on, Tom. That line is lame. You can do better than that!"

"I *am* tired, and I *am not* trying to get an invitation to stay."

"Really? I'm certainly disappointed!" Billie laughed. "But I'm tired too. A long, but exciting day … A few surprises too."

"You mean your mom, looking like Dorothy Dandridge? That was great. Guess what? Got something for you," Tom said, handing her a small box.

"I'd be real mad if you didn't," Billie said as he moved to sit next to her on the bed.

Billie carefully lifted the lid and the square of cotton padding from the box. "Tom, you have such exquisite taste," she said as she examined a gold charm bracelet. Its single charm, a replica of a rolled sheepskin, dangled from the serpentine chain. "I'll put it away so it doesn't get lost in the shuffle," Billie said as she tiptoed through the mess strewn on the floor. She tripped as she came back to the bed and fell on Tom.

"Perfect landing," he said, smiling.

"Right. Time for you to head for the Kappa house."

"Without so much as a kiss?"

Without responding, Billie kissed him and got up. "Now go," she said, pointing to the door.

"Yes ma'am, but you need to know I'm twenty-four years old, and I'm too old for this cat and mouse game you've been playing with me all these years."

"*Me*? Playing cat and mouse with *you*? For Pete's sake, Tom. This is déjà vu, isn't it? One minute you're wooing me, then ignoring me the next. How do you think I felt after you got what you wanted, then retreated?"

"Whoa! That's not true. You don't think much of me do you? You just insult my character whenever you get ready. I told you I was scared. Still am … A little. And I thought you said it was a gift you gave yourself? What happened to that? Besides, you run off to South Carolina whenever I think we're making progress. What was I to think?"

"Scared? Scared of me? I thought I was another notch on your belt."

"Don't put me in that category. Truth be told, I put you on a pedestal of ultimate womanhood, not to be sullied," Tom said with dramatic flair.

"Yeah, right," Billie sarcastically remarked. "Anyway, you were too late for that. I was already sullied."

"What the hell are you talking about? You were a virgin."

"Nothing. Nothing. Forget it. It's the vodka talking."

Tom grabbed Billie's arm and pulled her back onto the bed. "What are you talking about?" he demanded. "You've hinted at this before. Talk to me."

Billie wrenched her arm free and tearfully said, "Nothing, I said. And do not manhandle me!"

Tom gently embraced her and said, "When you're ready, we'll talk."

He pulled her down beside him and stroked her hair until she fell asleep. After carefully removing her shoes and dress, he tucked her into bed, then frantically rummaged through a couple of the boxes in the room. Finding a towel, he quickly headed down the hall for a cold shower.

***

At midday on Monday, the trio hit the road, heading north on Route 13 and west on Route 50 to Baltimore. As they left the campus, Billie leaned out the window and yelled, "Goodbye, quad! Goodbye, Wicomico Hall! Goodbye, Somerset Hall! Goodbye, Hawks! Goodbye, Douglass Library! Goodbye, Delmarva State College—"

Carletha yanked Billie back into the car. They laughed, joked, and remembered their childhood as they made their way home.

45

The last thing Billie wanted to do was to live at home again. It didn't matter that Herb was out of the picture. She had gotten used to her independence and not having to deal with her ambivalence toward her mother. But with no money and just starting a new job, she had no choice.

The transition, however, went smoother than she anticipated, and surprisingly, her mother was easier to live with than she thought. But re-establishing her social network proved to be the bigger problem because her friends from college went back to their home states after graduation or stayed on the shore. A few acquaintances from Baltimore returned, but Billie had not been particularly close to them at DSC, and she did not expect to be in the same circle with them now that they were all back home. Some of her high schools friends had gone to local schools like Morgan, Bowie, or Coppin, but she had lost touch with most of them. Others had gone straight to work after graduating, and she rarely ran into any of them anywhere.

Of course, there was Tom. They communicated regularly and went out occasionally. But true to form, Tom was a busy man, and his focus was on interning and his doctoral thesis.

* * *

One Saturday after Billie and her mother had finished their chores, they sat down in the kitchen to eat lunch, and Billie got up enough nerve to attempt a heart-to-heart with her mother. She planned to broach two things that were weighing heavily on her mind.

She cleared her throat and plunged in. "Momma, I want to ask you something." Her mother looked at her expectantly. "I don't mean to pry, but how are you keeping this house on what you make? I know what I kick in for rent helps, but it can't be enough. I was wondering …"

Her mother put down her bologna sandwich and cocked her head to side, as if sizing her up. "Well, you are pryin,' but I manage."

"It seems like a lot of responsibility. You ever think about selling it?"

"No—yes. I will, but not for awhile. Besides, Momma told me not to sell it just yet."

"Grandma Gertie? What's she got to do with it?"

"Nothin' really, but she told me not to sell. She said the Lawd will provide. That's a funny thing comin' from Momma."

Billie laughed. "You got that right! She must have had a come to Jesus meeting with Rev. Barnes!"

"I don't know," her mother said, smiling. "But you and I both know we have to heed what that old lady says. Besides, Herb still gives me a little somethin' every month."

"Gives you a little something every month?" Billie repeated, incredulous.

"Yes, he gives me a little something every month. He is still my husband, you know."

"What does that mean, Momma? You're still his wife? What wifely duties do you have to do for a little something every month?"

"Who do you think you talkin' to, girl?" her mother asked, raising her voice. "That don't come before you. You ain't too big or too grown to get slapped!"

Billie pushed herself away from the table and threw up her hands. "Sorry, Momma. I was only thinking about you."

As she got up from the table, the phone rang. Billie was glad for an excuse to leave the kitchen, and went to get it. *Guess I screwed that up,* she thought. *Can't say anything about that Herbert Brown.*

"Hello," she said, still thinking about her mother's stinging words.

"Hey, sweetie," said a mildly familiar, husky male voice.

"Sweetie? Who is this?" Billie asked, momentarily unable to identify the voice.

"Who is this? You breakin' a brother's heart!"

"Malcolm? Malcolm Beaumont? Thought it was you, but I wasn't sure. And I don't think I'm your sweetie."

"How about, Malcolm, how are you? Glad to hear from you."

"Yeah, how are you and do I care? How did you get my mother's number?"

"Whoa, what did I do? It's listed."

"You mean besides not calling for months?"

"I think we both let the flames go out. I'm in the neighborhood. Can I stop by?"

"In the neighborhood? Who do you know in this neighborhood? You came from Cherry Hill on a humble, thinking I'd be home, didn't you?"

"No, I have a friend in the neighborhood. So can I come by or not?"

"Tell your friend in the neighborhood I said hello, and I'll see you when I invite you!"

"What's up with you? If I beg, can I come? I'm on my knees. Please, Miss Billie. Please, I won't take up much of your time!"

Billie laughed, but she knew she needed to check with her mother. "Hold it a minute, Malcolm." She returned to the kitchen, where her mother was dumping her lunch into the garbage pail.

Before she could ask, her mother waved her hand and said, "Go ahead." Then she brushed by Billie and went upstairs.

Billie shrugged and went back to the phone. "Malcolm, I'm not busy the rest of the afternoon. What time did you have in mind?"

"Social calendar free, huh? I'm a lucky man. About thirty minutes. What's the address?"

His snide remarks reminded her of how irritating he could be at times, but she held her tongue and gave him the address. "I'll see you when you get here. Bye."

Billie cradled the phone and went upstairs to freshen up. Now that she was home, and Malcolm had called, she wondered if she wanted to resurrect their relationship.

*　*　*

An hour after the phone call, Malcolm rang the doorbell. Billie was still bruised by the conversation with her mother, and Malcolm's lateness only added to her snit.

She opened the door and greeted him with a forced smile. "Well, look what the cat done drug in. Come on in."

She was both amused and annoyed when Malcolm gave her what she called, the roving eyeball reflex. Some men tried to be discreet about it, but others were just lewd.

Malcolm stepped into the vestibule and kissed Billie on the cheek. "Hey, sweetie. You're looking good as ever," he said with a crooked smile. Malcolm was barely six feet tall, with a medium build and Anglo features on a mahogany covered face.

"Thanks," she said, raising one eyebrow. "Come on in. Make yourself at home and meet my mother." Billie yelled up the steps, "Momma, could you come down and meet Malcolm?"

When her mother came into the living room, Malcolm got up to greet her. "I see where Billie gets her good looks," he said, extending his hand.

Billie made the introductions. "Momma, this is Malcolm Beaumont. Sorry the two of you haven't met before, but—"

"No need to explain," her mother interrupted. "Glad to meet you, Malcolm. Make yourself at home. Can I git you something to drink?"

"Since you asked, yes ma'am. How about a beer?"

Billie and her mother exchanged amused looks, and Billie said, "Sorry, Malcolm. We don't have any alcohol in the house. But how about some sweet tea?"

Malcolm sheepishly responded, "Sure that'll be fine." He made himself comfortable while Billie got the tea and her mother retreated upstairs.

Billie returned with the tea and put on some forty-fives. She and Malcolm chatted for a couple of hours, bringing each other up-to-date on their lives. But when Billie deflected Malcolm's attempts to play in her hair, nuzzle her neck, and kiss her, he got up from the sofa and held out his hand to pull Billie up. "Gotta go. Thanks for the afternoon, though I didn't expect the cold shoulder."

"I don't believe you said that," Billie snapped. "What did you expect? You ought to be glad I let you in at all. We just can't pick up where we left off, wherever that was."

"Sorry, you're right. You're right. Can we do this again sometime? Maybe take in a show at the Royal? Start over?"

"Anything's possible, Malcolm. Just call me."

Before he could respond, the doorbell rang. "Excuse me," Billie said, heading for the door. *Wonder who it could be?* she thought.

She was pleasantly surprised when she opened the door. "Hey, Tom. Come on in. What brings you to this neck of the woods?"

Tom punched her on the arm as he slipped by her and headed for the living room. "Hey yourself. I know I should have called, but I was in the neighborhood."

Billie chuckled. "A lot of that going around."

"What?" Tom remarked. He stopped dead in his tracks when he rounded the corner and saw Malcolm.

Both men stood frozen, facing each other like Bighorn sheep in heat, until an amused Billie broke the ice. She pulled Tom into the living room by his shirt sleeve. "Malcolm, this is Tom McNeal. I've mentioned Tom to you before."

"Oh?" Malcolm cockily said. "If you did, I don't remember." He looked stoned-faced at Tom and extended his hand. "Malcolm Beaumont. Glad to meet you."

Tom grabbed Malcolm's hand in a vice-like grip. "Tom McNeal. Likewise. I'm sure she never mentioned you to me either," he said flippantly.

The two men held gazes until Tom released his grip. "Billie," he said, "I should have called. I have a project I wanted to run by you, but we can do it another day."

"It's all right Tom," Billie responded. "Malcolm was just leaving anyway."

"Well, not exactly ..." Malcolm started.

"In that case, I'll go yell at your mother while you say goodbye to Malcolm," Tom said, and he left the room.

Malcolm glared at Tom's back and picked up his jacket from the wingchair. "Guess I know when I'm not wanted."

"For Pete's sake, Malcolm," Billie said. "You were leaving, and you don't have any right to have an attitude. I enjoyed your company, and you said you'd call. Be nice."

"You're right. I'm sorry, and I will call. Can I get a kiss now?"

Billie ignored him and walked him to the door. "Take care. See ya."

"Tell your mother goodbye for me. Talk to you later."

Billie nodded and closed the door. *Men! Wonder what kind of project Tom wants me to help him with.*

It didn't take Billie long to find out. Tom was sitting at the dining room table when she walked into the room. They made small talk for a few minutes, and then Tom told her about the project.

"Billie," he said, "I'd like you to be a case study for some research I'm doing."

Billie gave him a quizzical look. "Me? What kind of case study can I help you with?"

"I'm collecting data on women who have been raped or almost raped."

Billie gripped the end of the table and leaned forward to face Tom squarely in the eye. "Raped? I was never raped," she insisted.

"Okay, almost raped."

"I wasn't even almost raped!"

Tom stared at her for a second before he spoke. "What the hell do you call it then? Remember Butch Duvall?"

"Oh, Tom. You can't call that attempted … rape. It was a misunderstanding. I gave Butch mixed signals."

"Do you hear yourself? You're blaming yourself for Butch's behavior. This is textbook."

Billie stood up. "Textbook, my ass," she said, her voice growing louder. "I shouldn't have gone to the equipment room, that's all. I am *not* a candidate for a case study."

"Sit down, baby," Tom said softly. "Okay … Have you experienced unwanted sexual advances—"

"No, Tom. No. Hell no!"

"That makes you pretty rare. Why so defensive, Billie?"

"Defensive?" she practically shouted. "Why are you being so *offensive*? You just can't walk into a person's house and ask this kind of stuff. Have you lost it?"

"I haven't, but I'm not sure about you. Look, I'm sorry. I didn't mean to upset you. I got it wrong. Okay? I got it wrong."

Neither of them heard Billie's mother walk into the room. "What's going on in here?" she demanded. "Got what wrong?"

Tom was immediately apologetic. "I'm sorry, Mrs. Brown. We were just discussing a project I'm working on."

"Sounds like a fuss to me," her mother said, not sure whether to believe Tom.

"It's all right, Momma. No fuss. Tom was just asking me some questions for a survey. We're finished now. He has what he wants and is leaving," Billie said emphatically.

Tom got up from the table. "Yes ma'am. I have what I want all right. I can see myself out. Sorry for the ruckus, Mrs. Brown. Later, Billie."

Tom headed toward the door. Billie started in his direction, but she turned and went up the stairs.

"What's wrong with you, Billie?" her mother called after her, as she scurried to the door to catch Tom.

Billie paused at the top of the stairs to hear what her mother was saying to Tom.

"No fuss, huh?" her mother asked Tom.

"No ma'am," he replied. "See ya."

"Okay. I'll talk to you later. Bye, Tom."

Billie heard her mother close the door. She went to her bedroom, closed the door, and crawled into bed. When her mother knocked, she refused to let her in and said she was nursing a headache.

She buried her head in a pillow to muffle her heart-wrenching sobs. It had been a long time since the painful memories surfaced and scraped the scabs off her emotional wounds. She curled in the fetal position and took a fitful nap.

46

Two weeks went by, then three, and Billie didn't hear from Tom. She was in a funk, but she wasn't sure if it was because he didn't call or because he touched a nerve. What she knew for sure was that she did not want to broach the topic of Herb with her mother. She didn't think her mother would be the least bit convinced that she was telling the truth.

On Sunday, after the eight o'clock service, her mother invited her to breakfast at Double-T Diner on Route 40, a popular hangout for the early church crowd. Billie agreed, having nothing better to do. On the way, they chatted about the sermon, a couple of ugly hats, and a few sour notes song by a member of the choir.

Once in the restaurant, Billie and her mother had a short wait before the hostess led them to their booth. As they followed her, Billie saw Tom seated in a booth, and he appeared to be alone. *This town is too small,* she thought.

Her mother spied him too and said, "Billie, can you believe it? There's Tom McNeal up ahead."

"For Pete's sake, Momma," Billie retorted under her breath. "You act like he's Elvis or somebody!"

As they approached him, they were momentarily taken aback. Tom sat across from an oddly cute young woman who was too short to be seen over the booth.

Billie regained her composure and said, "Morning, Tom." She nodded at Tom's breakfast companion, said "Hey," and kept walking.

Her mother paused for a more cordial greeting, and Billie heard her remark, "Don't mind her, she's hungry. Enjoy."

As she sat, Billie was speechless, angry, hurt, and confused. She knew Tom had girlfriends, but she had never seen him with one of them. The young woman was petite and light-skinned, with the curly and sandy blond hair that biracial people often had. Her features were strong, but provocative. Billie felt betrayed and didn't know why. *How could he do this to me? She's the exact opposite of me. Is that what he likes?*

Her mother interrupted her thoughts. "Billie, Billie. Hey, the waitress wants your order." She hadn't noticed the waitress standing at their table.

"Sorry, I'm not ready yet. I'm not hungry. Could you come back in a minute?"

"Sure," the waitress said, and she went to the next table.

Her mother looked at Billie and shook her head. "It hurts when you see your man with another woman, don't it?"

"Tom's not my man!"

"Oh? Who you trying to fool? Me or yourself? What's wrong with you then?"

"Nothing. Nothing's wrong with me. I got a little light-headed. Guess I need to eat."

"Really? Hungry, not hungry, which is it? Listen, honey. You love Tom, and you need to stop running from it before he gets away. He's a good man."

"Momma, is there any such thing? A good man?"

"Before I answer that, let me tell you something. Down home, some of the women used to call me the fresh-tail gal. Not because I was in love with your daddy at fifteen and threw myself at him—

although that didn't help," she laughed. "But it was because some of their husbands and boyfriends were taken with me."

"Momma, you're making my case for me."

"Hush, Billie! Let me finish. You can't keep playing the field. A woman can't do what a man can do. You need to settle on one man and make a life, or people will call you names."

"I hear what you're saying, but I can't help what people say. That's their problem, not mine. And what has that got to do with whether men are good or not?"

"Maybe nothing, but you got a reputation to guard. And yes, you right. All men are dogs, but some are Chihuahuas, and some are Great Danes. Tom's a Chihuahua, and you can make him a good lap dog."

"Momma, your homespun wisdom is priceless," Billie laughed. "I don't think it helps me, but thanks anyway." *It didn't help you much either. Guess Herb wasn't trainable.*

The waitress came back to take their orders. Billie ordered the blueberry pancake special, even though her stomach was churning.

There is no way I'm going to be able to eat. Tom is sitting up there with another woman, having breakfast. When a man has breakfast with a woman, it means they spent the night together. I think I'm gonna be sick.

Their food arrived. Billie swirled her pancakes around on her plate as she sipped her coffee.

"Guess you lost your appetite, huh?" her mother asked.

"Guess so. Can you hurry up?"

"No. You just sit pretty 'til I finish, and you may want to take that heart off your sleeve."

Billie ignored her mother and signaled for the check.

* * *

Three days later, Billie was still smarting from the Double-T Diner incident. She was so distracted that she couldn't concentrate on the lesson plan she had spread out on the dining room table. The telephone rang, startling her, and it took her a couple of seconds to connect the noise to instrument. "Oh, the telephone," Billie said as she went to answer it.

"Hello."

"Hi, Billie. How you doing?" Tom said.

"Tom. What a surprise," Billie said, trying to control her emotions.

"Meant to call you before now. You got away so fast on Sunday, I didn't get a chance to say anything to you."

"Guess not. You were busy with Goldilocks."

Billie heard Tom take a deep breath. "God don't like ugly, Billie. You sound like a jealous girlfriend."

"Hardly," Billie responded.

"Girlfriend, no. Jealous, yes," Tom replied.

"Not to be rude, but why did you call?"

"It's like that, huh? I called to say hey. I was glad to see you. The last time I saw you, it didn't end so well. Speaking of the last time, who was that clown, Malcolm?"

"*You* sound like a jealous boyfriend," Billie shot back.

"You're half-right. Boyfriend, no. Jealous, yes."

"Tom, why do we do this?"

"Got me. My intentions were good. You started it. The fuss, your mother would call it."

"The road to hell is paved with good—"

"I'm going to hang up and call back," Tom said, exasperated.

"Wait, Tom. No. I'm sorry. I don't know what gets into me."

"I do, but that's beside the point. Back to my original question. How are you? What's been going on?"

"I'm fine. I found an apartment in the village, and I'll be moving out in about a month."

"How's your mother taking it?"

"She knew it was going to happen sooner or later. She's cramping my style. On second thought, I may be cramping her style. Why didn't you introduce me to your girlfriend?"

"Girlfriend?" Tom laughed. "If you must know, Peggy is not my girlfriend. She's one of the subjects for the research project you refused to help me with."

"You always interview subjects over breakfast?" Billie asked.

"I interview them when I can catch them. I don't owe you any explanation, because the last time I checked, you didn't have any papers on me. But since we're on the subject, who was Malcolm again?"

Billie couldn't help laughing. "Who's out of line now? *If you must know,* an ex."

"Creeping back, huh?"

Billie ignored Tom's question. "How have you been?" she asked.

"Actually, that's one of the reasons I called. I've been awarded a research fellowship at McHenry University in Atlanta. It's for a year."

Billie slowly sat down on the telephone bench and tried to sound nonchalant. "That's wonderful, Tom. A year? You'll be living in Atlanta, Georgia for a year?"

"Yeah. The fellowship covers room and board, with a small stipend to live on. I'm used to pinching pennies, but I'll find a part-time job for a little extra spending change."

"A whole year ... Congratulations," Billie said, with a lump in her throat.

"Thanks. I want to see you before I go. What about it? I'm leaving in a couple of weeks."

Billie took a moment to regain her composure. "Sure, you know it. How about Sunday? Come to dinner. I'll cook."

"Sounds good. What time?"

"After church. About three o'clock."

"Great. See you then."

"Tom ..."

"Yeah?"

"Never mind. See you Sunday," she said, and hung up the telephone.

She didn't know why she felt as if Tom had hit her in the stomach. After all, she rarely saw him, even though they both lived in Baltimore. What difference would it make if he lived in Atlanta? But at least she could visualize his location in Baltimore, and could find him if she needed to. She couldn't conceptualize Atlanta. It was not in her frame of reference. She knew where it was on a map, but it might as well have been the moon.

Before she got up to go back to her lesson plan, she yelled up the stairs. "Momma, Tom's coming for dinner on Sunday."

* * *

On Sunday, Billie prepared a sumptuous meal for her mother and Tom. She had promised herself not to be bitchy and to enjoy the moment. The afternoon went off without a hitch. Shortly after dinner, her mother excused herself to go to an afternoon church service. Tom stayed to help Billie clean up.

"Can I take a piece of pie home with me?" Tom asked, drying the last plate.

"Sure. You're not going to eat and run are you?"

"Naw. I'm staying for awhile. I'll wait for you in the front room," Tom said as he walked to the living room. When Billie joined him, they chatted until early evening.

After awhile, Tom stood up and stretched. "Gotta run, but I'll talk to you and try to see you again before I leave."

"I'll miss you," Billie said sadly.

"You sound as if I'm leaving the country."

"I know. Sentimental, I guess. Please keep in touch."

"You know I will. Seems we say goodbye a lot."

"Not goodbye. Say, so long."

"Hug?" Tom asked.

Billie nodded, and they embraced. Tom nuzzled her neck and abruptly let her go. He punched her on the arm. "Later, little girl," he said.

She took his hand and walked him to the door.

47

As was their custom, Billie and Tom touched base from time to time. Much to Billie's consternation, Tom loved Atlanta, and at the end of his fellowship, he committed to a one-year teaching assistant position.

Billie had offered him the perfunctory congratulations, and never gave in to the urge to ask Tom to come home. They had talked about Billie coming to Atlanta for a visit, but the trip never materialized. The time never seemed right. *Life goes on*, she had thought.

But just as Tom had arbitrarily chosen to stay in Atlanta, he unexpectedly turned down a contract for the following school year and headed back to Baltimore.

His mother, delighted to have her oldest son come home, hosted a small welcome home reception for him. Billie was equally excited, and now she carefully surveyed her closet for something eye-popping to wear. She decided on a pale blue, polished cotton sheath dress that accented her tiny waist and round hips. She couldn't decide whether to go early under the guise of wanting to help, or late to make a grand entrance. She opted for the latter.

When she arrived, she let herself in through the unlocked screen door. To her surprise, the crowded room was filled with unfamiliar faces. A couple of people glanced her way and went back to their conversations. A little deflated, Billie uncomfortably looked around the room.

Tom saw her, broke away from a guy he was talking to, and walked over to greet her with outstretched arms. Billie's knees buckled as she melted in his embrace.

"Billie! What took you so long?" Tom asked, holding her tightly. "I've been watching the door for you. You look great!"

"Tom, I am so glad you're home—to stay, I hope." For a moment, she forgot there were other people in the room.

Tom took her by the hand and led her around the room, making introductions. It was then that she realized that the two of them operated in completely different circles. That difference was what kept them apart so much.

At least he's home, she thought.

48

1965

Billie was grading papers when she looked up and saw a man with a mass of wavy, black hair peeping through her slightly opened classroom door.

"Hi!" the man said as he walked into the room. He was of average size and height, and Billie had seen him in the teacher's lounge on several occasions. But after mentally running down the list of possible names, she could not come up with his.

He pulled a chair close to her desk, swung it around backwards, and straddled it. He stretched out his hand and said, "Hi. I'm Vincente Ciantola. They call me Vince. Don't think we've been formally introduced."

Billie reached across the desk to shake his hand, straining the fabric of her blouse. The action diverted Vince's attention to her cleavage for an almost imperceptible millisecond.

Roving eyeball reflex! Should have walked around the damn desk, she thought. "No, we haven't. I'm Billie Cunningham. Glad to meet you."

"Same here. Looks like I'm going to be Mr. Lawson's permanent sub for the rest of the semester. Back surgery. Anyway, why aren't you in the lounge at the Christmas party?"

"I was there for awhile. I could ask you the same thing."

"Too many tight-assed Republicans and horny divorcées for me."

Billie could not help but laugh. *This man must be nuts! He doesn't know me.* "Are you always so forthright?"

"Hell, yeah! I don't have time to beat around the bush. How long have you been here?"

"I'm going into my fourth year. Teaching wasn't in my original plans, but I love it."

"Mine either, and I *don't* love it! At the end of the school year, I'm heading out to the west coast for a job with Northrop. Did you know you're gorgeous?"

"Excuse me? Yes—I mean, no," a flustered Billie replied, staring into the bluest eyes she had ever seen. "Look, Vince, it was nice to meet you, but I've got to finish up these papers so I can get home ahead of the weather."

"Excuse me. Sorry to hold you up. I have no manners, or so I've been told. I didn't mean to embarrass you, or myself for that matter. Great to finally meet you. Merry Christmas!" Vince unwound himself from the chair, gave a mock salute, and left the room.

Billie sat back in her chair and stretched out her legs as she threw her head back and laughed. *Wow! What was that about?*

* * *

Tom peacefully gazed out of his office window at the light snow that had begun to blanket the streets. As always, he was amazed at how the snow covered the landscape in a heavy white mantle without making the slightest sound. He loved it. Snowfall slowed him down and gave him an excuse to throttle back and downshift his engines without making him feel guilty for his idleness. The serenity of the moment was interrupted by a soft knock at his door.

"Come in," he called over his shoulder.

"Sorry to disturb you, Dr. McNeal, but I'm leaving now," his intern said.

"Not a problem, Ralph. Get on home, and Merry Christmas," Tom said.

"Thanks, doc. Some of us are heading to the Spinx Club for a drink. Want to join us?"

"Thanks, but no thanks," Tom replied. "Enjoy your holiday."

"Yes, sir. Take it light, doc," he said as he left.

Tom turned back to the window. Ralph, his intern, was only a few years younger than he was, but he called him sir in deference to his position.

Tom had been about Ralph's age when Dr. Marvin Kaufman had given him an internship in the psychiatric ward at Baltimore General Hospital. It was a requirement to be licensed as a counseling psychologist. Tom's ultimate goal was his own practice, but at twenty-seven, he was content to be on the staff of Trinity Hospital for now.

His nonstop plans had paid off. He often pinched himself at his good fortune, and how he and his brothers had turned out. David worked for the post office, and John taught high school physical education.

Early in his relationship with Dr. Kaufman, the good doctor had told him that any counselor worth his salt should go through therapy. Since Tom had resisted that urging, Dr. Kaufman, under the guise of mentoring, had dissected him and turned him inside out until he relented and entered therapy with an independent counselor.

Tom discovered, much to his surprise, that on some level, he did not respect women because of his mother's helplessness in the face of his father's abuse. He also came to realize his father's abuse, and ultimate fate, was not his fault.

Tom gave up drinking, and his anger was well-managed and kept at bay by weekly trips to a local gym that trained amateur boxers. For awhile, he was even a sparring partner, but he quit when he grew weary of the pain and explaining his occasional black eye and fat lip to his patients.

But for all his progress, nightmares still plagued him on occasion, and he'd wake up whimpering and in a cold sweat. And although he still loved Billie, he allowed their friendship to lapse into benign neglect. They only touched base from time to time.

Except for the small, nameless emptiness he sometimes felt, he was finally at peace with himself. Dr. Kaufman, a reformed Jew, had told him to examine his relationship with God, which was nonexistent at the time.

The peace of the present moment reminded him of the peace that he had eventually come to know by taking Dr. Kaufman's advice. Tom reluctantly closed the blinds and gathered his things to leave.

49

1966

The hustle and bustle of the holidays was over, and life was back to its mundane pace. Old Man Winter still had his icy fingers around the throat of the city, and from his burrow in Gobbler's Knob in Pennsylvania, Punxsutawney Phil saw his shadow, presaging six more weeks of winter.

Billie hated the cold, but she never let it interfere with any of her plans. As she braced herself to go out, she preened in front of the full-length mirror on the back of the bedroom door in her small, Edmondson Village apartment. Pleased with what she saw, she hummed while she waited for Carletha to pick up the phone.

"Hello," Carletha answered.

"Hey, Car. It's me."

"Hey, Holiday!" Carletha responded. Billie hated the sobriquet left from her college days as much as Carletha hated "Car." They did it to their mutual annoyance, which usually signaled that one of them was planning to rib the other about something.

"It's Friday night. What are you doing home?" Billie smugly asked.

"You don't really want to know. You just want to let me know *you* have a date. You ain't slick. Good for you, I think. Tell me it's not Vince."

"Yeah. I turned him down for as long as I could. I've been holding out on you, though. This is actually the fourth date, not counting when he stops by my office to lock lips."

"Have you lost your freaking mind? Those white folks will fire your ass in the blink of an eye."

"He's the best kisser I've ever met."

"Girl, I'm telling you. You're treading on dangerous ground."

"Lighten up, Carletha. It's 1966. Free love and all that."

"I repeat, you had better watch yourself!"

"Don't worry, I will. It's just a diversion for the both of us."

"A helluva diversion, but from what? You sure he's not slumming? And I thought I was the adventurous one. I can't feed you when you lose your job and your momma don't want you back home!"

Billie winced at the comment about her mother. "That's cold! And no, he is not slumming. I'm enjoying his company, and I feel special when I'm with him. He's quickly becoming my magnificent obsession!"

"Why? Because he's white? I don't believe you! Has he called you exotic yet?"

"We had that conversation, and the whole *National Geographic*-portrayal-of-native-people discussion. He was shocked at my reaction. I almost bit his head off."

"Poor choice of words ... I'm sure he'd like that."

"Get your mind out of the gutter! But speaking of him being white, kissing him is one thing, but if he takes off his shirt and the rest of him is white, I think I'll pass out."

Carletha laughed until she could hardly talk. "When do you think you'll find that out?"

"Probably tonight! I'm going to his house."

"What? You're moving too fast, and you don't know what you're getting yourself into!"

"Oh, but I do. You don't give me much credit."

"Maybe. I just know you have a poor relationship track record. You say he has a house? Hmm … An ex-army brat … Transient bachelor with a house. What's wrong with this picture?"

"Okay, so he's separated from his wife, and he'll be divorced in a couple of months, but that's got nothing to do with me."

"How you figure? Besides, that's one of the three biggest lies that men tell."

"I know. Number one is, 'Baby, I'm divorcing my wife.' Two is, 'I love you,' and three is, 'Baby, I'll pull out!'"

"So you know. Act like it. *It ain't funny!*"

"I'm not looking to be a wife, Carletha. I gotta go. Got to meet him—"

"Meet him? See what I mean? Can't he pick you up at your door? Are you naïve or stupid? Be careful, girl. You know you bruise easily."

"Give it a rest, Car! But you're right. I'll be careful. Bye." Billie hung up, knowing her cousin meant well.

She grabbed her purse and a small overnight bag from the sofa, turned off the lights, locked her door, and bounced down the apartment steps to her car. She headed west on Route 40 to the Edmondson Village Shopping Center and slowly drove to the back of the Hecht Company.

She spotted Vince's bright red Corvette and parked next to him. She collected her things, walked to the passenger side, and got in. She was barely in the car when Vince cradled her head and pulled her to meet his demanding tongue.

"For God's sake, Vince. At least let me get in the car!" Billie said, freeing herself.

"You know you make me crazy. I can't help myself," Vince said, releasing her and leaning back on the head rest. "There's been a slight change in plans."

"What, you're not going to fix me dinner?"

"No. I moved out today. My apartment's not ready for company, but we can go to a motel—"

"Excuse me? What do you mean you moved out today? What are you talking about? And motel? I don't think so!"

"I can't have an affair with you and live with my wife, so I moved out."

"Live with your wife?" Billie shouted. "I thought she was in Vermont, New Hampshire, or some damn where. You mean all this time, you had a wife at home? Why, you slimy bastard! And I don't say that lightly," Billie said, getting out of the car.

"Wait a minute, Billie, "Vince called. "I was going to tell you. She was in Maine, and we *are* getting a divorce …" His voice trailed off as Billie slammed the door and got into her own car.

"Go to hell!" Billie yelled. She gave him the finger as she put her key in the ignition.

With tires squealing, Billie backed out and sped east on Edmondson Avenue. Through hot, angry tears, she missed the Wildwood Parkway turn to her apartment, but she kept going anyway.

Carletha was right, again! I do bruise easily. Not because I'm so sensitive, but because I drop my dukes and get sucker-punched.

Not wanting to go home, she decided to head for the Elgin Lounge in Walbrook Junction. But she took a sharp turn way too fast and hit a patch of ice. Her car careened out of control. As Billie screamed and fought the steering wheel, her car jumped the curb, grazed a light pole, and came to rest on the grass.

Horn blaring, Billie slumped over the steering wheel.

* * *

Tom was about to leave for the evening when his private phone rang. It had to be his mother. He sighed and turned to answer it. "Hello, Mom. What is it?"

"Mom? No, no, Tom. It's me, Mrs. Brown. Your mother gave me this number. Sorry to have to call you on it, but I need you to do something for me. It's an emergency."

Tom caught the urgency in her voice. "What is it, Mrs. Brown? What's wrong?"

"Billie's been in an accident, and they took her to your hospital. Me and Wilma are on the way, but can you just go to the emergency room and see about her 'til we get there?"

"Yes, ma'am. On my way," Tom said, shocked.

He hung up the phone and dashed to the elevator, continually punching the call button until it stopped on his floor. When he reached the basement, he made a hasty exit and rushed to the reception desk.

"Excuse me," Tom said to the staffer on duty. She failed to acknowledge his presence. Tom cleared his throat and said, more loudly, "Excuse me, miss. Are you on duty or not?"

The woman looked up, and, seeing his work identification, immediately changed her demeanor. "Yes, sir. May I help you?"

Tom held his tongue about her behavior and said, "A Billie Cunningham came in by ambulance. What room is she in?"

The woman looked over her list of admissions and replied, "Room 12."

Tom headed down the hallway in a half-run. When he entered the room, he was met by the attending ER doctor, who put up his hand to stop him.

"Sorry sir, you can't come in—" He stopped in mid-sentence after seeing Tom's badge, and ushered Tom back into the hallway. "Dr. McNeal, is this somebody you know?"

"Yeah, an old family friend. What happened? How is she?"

"I really need to speak to her family, but she was conscious when they brought her in. She's in and out now. As I understand it, the accident wasn't nearly as bad as it could have been, and it looks like a mild concussion. I'm waiting for transport to come take her for X-rays, then I'll know for sure." The doctor patted Tom on the arm and said, "This is a little out of your league, but don't worry. We'll take good care of her. Find me when her family gets here." The doctor headed toward another room just as a nurse and orderly appeared with a gurney.

Tom waited in the hallway, biting his lip. A few minutes later, he saw Billie's mother and aunt running toward him just as the orderly eased the gurney out of the exam room and wheeled Billie down the hall.

"Is that Billie on the stretcher? Wait, please wait," Lilly Ann called after the orderly. The orderly stopped.

As they all crowded around the gurney, Billie slightly opened her eyes. "I'm okay, y'all. Just bumped … my head on something … Where am I? Mom, Aunt Wilma … Tom?"

The orderly cut in before anyone could speak. "Sorry folks, but I have to get her to X-ray. One of you can accompany her."

Billie's mother took her hand and walked alongside her as the orderly rolled the gurney down the hall.

* * *

After a nerve-racking five hours, the ER doctor came out to the waiting room to update the family.

"She has a mild concussion. We'll need to keep her overnight for observation, but I think she'll be fine. No broken bones, even though she has some nasty soft tissue bruising on her chest. She was lucky she didn't crack her ribs. The steering wheel did the most damage. Had she hit the light pole at another angle and with just a little more force, we would be having an entirely different conversation now. She is indeed a very lucky woman. Somebody will come out and give you her room number."

What's that she always says? Tom thought. *Luck's in the Lord, Devil's in the people.*

Everyone thanked the doctor and breathed a sigh of relief.

"Anybody know where she was going or what happened?" Tom asked.

"No telling, Tom. It's Friday night. You know how you young people do," Mrs. Brown responded. She patted his hand. "You sure are a blessing. Thanks for being here."

"You don't have to thank me, Mrs. Brown. You know I'd do anything for Billie."

"I hope she knows that too. Let's find out what room she's in so we can see her."

After getting Billie's new room number, they filed up to the third floor and found a drowsy Billie in a lot of pain. Mrs. Brown stood by the bedside and stroked Billie's forehead while Tom looked on from the foot of the bed.

"You all right? What happened, baby?" Mrs. Brown asked.

"I'm not sure … I was headed for the Junction … When I went around Hilton Parkway … The car skidded," Billie said with some difficulty. "That's all I remember …" Billie nodded off.

"Don't worry about details tonight, Lilly Ann. She's not up to talking. Just thank God it won't no worse. Let her rest," said Billie's aunt.

"You right. Might as well go on home. Nothing we can do here, and she do need to sleep. Probably won't even know we here anyway."

"If you don't mind, Mrs. Brown," Tom said. "I'll stay the night. I don't think they want her in a deep sleep anyway, so I'll just hang out here."

"I don't think that's necessary, but if you want to, I don't have no problem with it. Bless you."

Billie's mother and aunt kissed the sleeping Billie on the cheek, and Tom walked them to the elevator. On the way back to Billie's room, he stopped at the nurse's station to let them know he was staying the night.

He knew his actions would be grist for the rumor mill. Nobody had ever heard anything about him being associated with a woman.

* * *

Billie gingerly fluffed up her pillows and turned back to her telephone conversation. "I'll be home from work for the rest of the week, but I'll see how it goes. Thanks for not saying, I told you so."

"Being right is good enough," Carletha laughed. "God takes care of fools and babies. I hear your boy Tom was Johnny on-the spot. He's a great guy. I never understood the dynamics between you two."

"Me neither. And you're right. He is a sweetie. He stayed the night with me in the hospital, brought me home this morning, and he's going to bring me lunch today. But now that he's this Ph.D psychologist, I'm afraid to talk to him," Billie half-joked.

"Tom's the same old Tom, but better."

"How do you know? Didn't know you still talked to him that much."

"I don't ... How do you keep getting yourself into these fiascos?"

"I don't know. I must have a sign on my back: Abuse me, I'm easy."

"Please don't say that about yourself. The right guy will come along. Sometimes I think you don't love yourself. I know I love some me."

Billie forced a laugh. The truth hurt. "Don't go getting heavy on me, Car. I know I've made some bad choices."

"Some bad choices?" Carletha asked. "What about that cat before Vince? I know you called him a few choice names, but you never gave me the full story."

"Oh yeah. Old what's his name. At first, butter wouldn't melt in his mouth. Then he got possessive and bossy. Even tried to manhandle me a couple of times."

"I didn't know that. Holding out on me again. He didn't hit you, did he?"

"He tried to. He got mad—I don't even remember about what— and grabbed my arm. When I pulled away, I lost my balance and tripped over the coffee table. That was the first time. The second time, he didn't like something I had on and tried to shove me back into the bedroom to change. I quoted some Paul Laurence Dunbar on his ass. He didn't see the lamp coming."

Carletha, practically hysterical with laughter, could hardly speak. "Dunbar? You were quoting poetry as a prelude to a fight?"

"You know the poem, 'In the Morning?' There's a line that says, 'You done felt yo'se'f too strong an' you sholy got me wrong.' After that, I picked up the first thing I could get my hands on and threw it. Needless to say, he thought I'd lost my mind, but the relationship went downhill from there and, as they say, the rest is history."

"Girl! Why am I just finding out about this stuff? I need to be back in Baltimore! Seriously, though, Billie, you're almost thirty years old. You don't want to be an old maid, do you?"

Billie winced and shifted the headset to her other ear. "Twenty-five, Carletha. I'm only twenty-five. Anyway, I gotta go. My chest hurts. I've been talking too long," she said, in an attempt to avoid the rest of the conversation.

"Liar! But okay. Hurry and get well. You have got to get up here soon to help me and Momma finish up my wedding plans. It's already February—the wedding's at the end of June, you know—and you need to get here no later than early April. Momma's coming about that time, so call her. And when you come, I have somebody I want you to meet."

"No, Carletha. One minute you're telling me I need a relationship break, and the next you're trying to fix me up with somebody. No! No! I don't want—"

"Shut up, Holiday! You're in pain, and you need your rest. Feel better. Love you. Bye."

"Love you too, *Car!* Bye."

As soon as she hung up, Billie heard the apartment buzzer. Moving like a pregnant woman ready to deliver, she stiffly swung her legs over the side of the bed and labored to get up. She ambled to the living room and pushed the button on the intercom.

"Who is it?" she asked.

"It's me, Billie."

She sighed heavily before she spoke. "Why are you here, Herb?"

"I was in the area and thought I'd stop by to see how you doin.'"

"Thanks, Herb. I'm fine. You shouldn't have bothered. Momma could have told you how I am."

"You know your momma's not speaking to me most days. I just wanted to talk to you."

"Talk about what, Herb?"

"You know," he said hesitantly. "Things."

"No, I don't, and I'm not up to talking to you. Besides, I'm expecting Tom with my lunch any minute now."

"Tom, huh. I coulda brought you lunch."

"Yeah, well … Thanks anyway."

"Maybe some other time. Glad you doin' all right," Herb said.

"I am, but you need to leave," Billie said emphatically. She heard him wheeze, and mentally saw the Camel dangling from his lips.

"Okay, Miss Billie. I'm leavin.'"

Stomach churning, Billie released the intercom button and rested her now aching head on the unit. She began to pray.

"Lord, forgive me for wishing ill of Herbert Brown, and protect all little girls from men like him. Amen."

50

After school on Friday, Billie took the train to New York. She had arranged for a substitute on Monday just in case she was too exhausted to go to work. With the accident and Vince behind her, she was excited about Carletha's upcoming wedding and meeting her fiancé, but she was less enthused about the prospect of meeting a new man.

The high-energy, New York atmosphere made her heart race and her pulse quicken, and the crisp April air invigorated her. She loved New York's hustle and bustle, but only for a weekend. She had no idea how Carletha managed to live there without having a nervous breakdown from sensory overload.

Billie took a taxi to Carletha's brownstone and paid the driver. She nervously tugged at her miniskirt in a futile attempt to cover more of her legs than the designer had intended. She wore Courréges go-go boots and a short leather jacket, and as she headed up the steps of Carletha's building, she looked like a model on a go-see.

Carletha and her fiancé came to the door. She emitted squeals of delight, while he took Billie's luggage. After the hugs and kisses, Carletha introduced her intended.

"Billie, this is William, my future husband," she said, practically bursting with pride and happiness.

Carletha said she had met her fiancé at the deli in the building where they both worked, but Billie had the immediate feeling that she had seen him before. And, not knowing William, she didn't know how to read the odd expression on his face.

"I am so glad to finally meet you," William said, kissing Billie on the cheek.

"Me too," Billie said, hugging William. "You look so familiar to me. Have we met before?"

"I don't think so," William quickly said. "Think I would remember."

"Yeah, and I don't know where it would have been …" Billie trailed off.

"Come in, girl, and get settled," Carletha beamed, bear-hugging Billie again. "Let me show you where to park your stuff so you can freshen up for dinner."

"The sooner the better, 'cause I'm starved," Billie said, following Carletha up the steps.

"What do you think?" Carletha asked as she put Billie's overnight bag on the bed in the guest bedroom.

"Gimme a chance, would you? But I will say this: he looks good!"

"Billie, I am *so* happy, I don't know what to do with myself!"

"Couldn't happen to a nicer cousin!" Billie responded. But in the back of her mind, she was still trying to figure out what it was about William that seemed so familiar. *Maybe I don't want to remember,* Billie thought.

"Come on down when you're ready. The guy we want you to meet should be here in a little while." Carletha disappeared into the living room.

"Carletha!" Billie called after her in a loud whisper. "Couldn't you give me just one night? I thought it was tomorrow. Carletha, come back here!"

Not long after Billie came down the stairs, sans her boots, the doorbell rang. She made a beeline for the kitchen as William went to the door. She busied herself by pouring a glass of water as she heard male laughter and voices.

Carletha came into the kitchen and started to push Billie toward the living room.

"Come on. Act like a big girl. It's just an introduction, for crying out loud!"

When Billie entered the room, her mouth dropped open and she was speechless.

William made the introduction, looking like the cat who ate the canary. "Billie Cunningham, I'd like you to meet an old and dear friend of mine ... Tom McNeal."

Billie could have been knocked over with a feather as William continued, hardly able to contain himself. "Tom, meet Carletha's cousin, Billie Cunningham."

Still speechless, Billie stood frozen in place as Tom embraced her. "Glad to meet you, Billie," he said, quite seriously as Carletha and William roared.

After Billie regained her composure, she returned Tom's embrace. "Okay, what kind of game are you guys playing? Wait a minute ... Wait a minute! William, you're Will! Will on the quad, from freshman year! I thought I knew you!" Billie pointed her finger at Carletha, and, using her best Desi Arnez accent, said, "Lucy you got so 'splaining to do!'"

Carletha, William, and Tom laughed.

"William—aka Will—and I, had more in common with each other than with the other guys since we were a little bit older," Tom said. "We became very good friends after the DSC incident, and once we graduated, we kept in touch over the years. I guess I never mentioned he was a New Yorker. There were times when we didn't communicate for months, but when we did, we always picked up where we left off."

"When I asked Will for his guest list," Carletha continued, "I saw a Thomas McNeal from Baltimore. It's a pretty common name, but I thought, hmm ... Could it be *my* buddy, Tom McNeal? And sure enough, it was. I couldn't believe it! Small world, isn't? Anyway, the rest is history."

"I remembered you when Carletha told me," William added. "And when I saw you just now, I didn't want to ruin the surprise before Tom got here."

"That's wild!" Billie responded. "So the whole, help with wedding plans, was a ruse! Tom, were you in on it, too?"

Tom hesitantly replied, "Not entirely ... Yeah, sort of ..."

And the laughter began again. William grabbed two light jackets from the living room closet and handed one to Carletha. "You kids get acquainted," he said. "Carly and I are going to pick up some carry-out for dinner."

Billie wrinkled her nose. "Carly? That's so cute. Okay. Seems I'm the only mushroom in the group," she said, heading for the sofa as Carletha and William left.

Tom joined her and punched her on the arm. "Game over. Tonight—this weekend—we'll have all those talks we never had, and make a definitive decision about us."

"Talks? Definitive decision? Please don't play doctor with me."

"Actually, that's not a bad idea."

Billie hit him on the arm. "You know what I mean!"

"Yeah, I do. And the playing is over. This is me, Tom. Your buddy, your friend, and your part-time lover. Not your therapist. It may sound like psycho-babble, but I need closure. I need some questions answered. My head is finally clear about me, and I need to know the next step."

Billie was thoughtful before she spoke. "I know I always tried to make light of it—which I always accused you of doing—but you're right. We both need closure. I need to be honest with myself, as well as with you."

Tom nodded. "So, here's the plan. I've rented a cabin in the Poconos for tomorrow and Sunday night. You'll help *Carly* with whatever she needs help with, and we'll leave late afternoon. It's decision time."

"Presumptuous of you, isn't it?" Billie asked.

"Very, but I did it anyway, cheered on by your favorite cousin."

"Seems the cards are stacked against me. Looks like I don't have a choice."

"Baby, never think that. You always have options. You in, or out?"

"In, I guess, but I didn't bring clothes for the mountains."

"That miniskirt works for me," Tom said as he leaned away from her to avoid a punch on the arm. "Can't you borrow something of Carletha's?"

"Excuse me? Too short, and a little too big. I have a pair of dungarees."

"That'll work."

"But I can't wear dungarees if we go out to eat," Billie protested.

"Who said we were going out to eat?" Tom asked, and he leaped off the sofa, with Billie in hot pursuit.

51

For the better part of the scenic ride to the Poconos, Billie and Tom were silent. They were lost in their individual introspections while the soulful sounds of Motown played on the radio. When Tom went to check in and get keys to the cabin, Billie began to feel uneasy, but she said nothing when he returned to the car.

Tom followed the map in the welcome package and found the cabin, which was nestled in a small grove of trees. The scenery was breathtaking, and Billie started to relax. Tom parked his BMW and walked around the car to open her door. He popped the trunk, removed both pieces of luggage, handed Billie the bag of groceries they picked up on the way, and started up the short path to the door.

Billie, suddenly feeling trapped, walked two paces behind. She hoped Tom didn't sense the change in her mood. He unlocked the door and let her in ahead of himself.

The cabin was small, but inviting. To the left of the entrance was the living room, and it had an overstuffed green and yellow plaid sofa, flanked by two armchairs of the same fabric. Beyond it was the kitchen. To the right of the entrance were two bedrooms, each with its own bath. Billie's relief was palpable at seeing them, and Tom smiled.

"Take the one you want," he said, putting her overnight bag against the wall between the two rooms.

"Doesn't matter," Billie replied, walking into the first room.

"I'll get a fire started while you make some coffee," he called after her.

They both relaxed in front of a roaring fire. After a few minutes, Tom said, "I'm just going to talk, and it may sound like stream-of-consciousness—sorry for the jargon—but it fits the situation. You can stop me whenever you want to."

Tom took a deep breath and continued. "I think I've finally got myself together, but there's stuff I'm still working on. I think I've loved you since the day you were snatched off your bike. I've always wanted to take care of you, protect you. When I got older, I realized there was more than one kind of love, and it scared me. I didn't believe it was right to think certain things about you, even though I couldn't help myself. I was uncomfortable with intimacy, closeness. I didn't know what to do with the emotions, and I didn't want them. You were the good girl, and I messed that up, or so I thought. While I was lovin' and leavin' them, I hated what I thought you were doing with other guys. And, as you liked to remind me, I was angry most of the time. Keeping the temper in check took a lot of energy.

"The classes in my major helped, then I finally went into therapy myself. But the biggest change was I gave my life to Christ. It's given me peace and a measure of contentment with myself. I am still far from perfect, and I have a hell of a way to go." He stopped when Billie put her hand over her mouth and wagged her finger at him. "I know. I said it that way to prove a point. But the good thing is now I'm dealing with the spiritual old man—I can do all things through Christ—and not the psychological little boy who was so needy and clueless. The abuse my father inflicted on me has shaped my life. I'm still trying to handle it, but at least I know what I'm dealing with. Bottom line, I want you in my life."

Billie waited a few seconds before she spoke. "Wow ... I don't know what to say. I could sense a change of some kind in you. But you know, no matter what you did, I always wanted you around. I may not have expressed it, but I did. I'm happy for your confession of Christ. My walk isn't what it used to be ... have to work on that.

"Though I always accused you of playing games, I did a fair amount of it myself. I never had any trouble attracting men. For whatever reason, I get a lot of attention, most of it unwanted, though, and it was all so shallow. As soon as I found someone I thought I really liked, and he got too serious, I broke it off. Not that there have been a lot, but enough. I never trusted any of them. Never wanted to be beholden to any one of them."

Tom interrupted her. "Who hurt you so much that you don't trust any man?"

"I don't know," Billie lied. "Maybe because my father was not there in the beginning. I don't know."

"I'm baring my soul here. I need you to do the same thing," Tom said.

"I know. I am, too."

"I'm not so sure about that. But anyway, what about me? You pull me in, then push me away."

"I don't mean to do that. I'm just not that demonstrative—"

"Au contraire, my dear. Yes, you are. If you remember, most of your greetings were always like frontal assaults! But I get what you mean. Let's say, for the sake of argument, that you're not demonstrative, but you certainly are the most passionate woman I have ever met."

Not wanting to hear anymore, Billie got up from the sofa and went to refill her coffee cup.

"I know you have trust issues, but I've never lied in a relationship," said Tom. "The women I've dated—and there haven't been as many as you'd like to believe or accuse me of—they knew what to expect going in. If they could deal with it, they stayed. If not, they split. I'm waiting for that special one, but did you ever consider that we just may be the real deal? That we belong together?"

Biting her lip, Billie sipped her coffee. "Yes and no. I don't believe there's only one particular person for anybody. I think a person can be happy with a couple of different people. Their lives would be different, depending on the choice."

Tom tried to lighten the mood. "I hope these 'couple of people' are one at a time."

"Of course, stupid. But interesting thought," she teased. She returned to the sofa and put her head on Tom's shoulder.

"I used to think," he said pensively, "that I wasn't good enough for you. Then I realized I thought more of you than you thought of yourself."

"What?" Billie said. "How can you say that? I always depended on you and thought you were a great guy, taking care of your family and me the way you did. I don't think I ever considered what I thought of myself, at least not consciously."

"Exactly! You weren't aware. Your choice of boyfriends was my first clue. The second clue was your need to be in control of everything, especially your emotions. Then there was the invisible sign you always wore."

"What are you talking about?" Billie asked, raising her head and looking Tom squarely in the eye.

"The look-but-don't-touch sign," Tom responded, returning her gaze.

"I don't get it. A minute ago, you said I was the most passionate woman you know. Now I wear a hands-off sign," Billie said as she attempted to get up from the sofa.

"Hold it," Tom said, pulling her back down. "You're a beautiful woman. You just don't know it, which makes you all the more attractive. But most guys are scared of a beautiful woman, and you give off a not-available vibe."

Billie rolled her eyes.

"Don't roll your eyes. It's true. Lucky for me, though, I know what lies beneath that exterior. I know your buttons, and which ones to push. But I never did ... Well, maybe once, which left me guilt-ridden. Anyway, you don't have to protect yourself from me. I'll never hurt you like you've been hurt. And I've worked hard to become the man I know you deserve."

"Tom, you're trying to tell me that what you've done with your life to overcome your circumstances was for me? That all your self-improvement was to make you worthy of me? Come on, get real."

"Hold on before your head gets too big. But partially, yes."

"Wow! That's heavy. I don't know what to say."

"Say it was worth it. Say you love me."

They fell silent for a few moments. Tom attempted to kiss her, but she deflected it.

"Okay," he said, putting up his hands. "Don't forget I'm still working on the old man."

Billie yawned and got up from the sofa. "No harm, no foul," she said. "All this soul-baring is exhausting. I need to think. Thanks, but I think I'll turn in. Night, Tom."

She felt his eyes on her as she walked into bedroom and gently closed the door.

* * *

The aroma of coffee and bacon tickled Tom's nose and aroused him from a peaceful sleep. For a split-second, he forgot where he was.

He went to the bathroom to brush his teeth and splash water on his face, and he padded out to the kitchen. Billie was standing at the stove in a pink robe and slippers, her back to him.

He paused for a second, feasting on what he saw, and thought to himself, *I could get used to this.* He walked up behind her and got as close as he could without actually touching her.

"Good morning," he said softly, breathing ever so lightly on her neck. "Can I do something?"

"Good morning. No. I'm just doing bacon, eggs, and toast."

He sensed the small quiver of anticipation in her body, but he ignored it. "What, no grits?" Tom asked in his best southern accent as he moved to a stool at the breakfast bar.

"No grits," she grinned.

Billie finished cooking and fixed their plates. Tom said grace and they began to eat.

"How did you sleep?" he asked.

"A little fitful. Strange place."

"Too bad. I slept like a baby. Why didn't you wake me up to keep you company?"

Billie shrugged and got up to get more coffee. He grabbed her arm and patted his lap. "Sit," he said. Billie complied. "Look, I love you. Don't know how else to say it, or what else to do. I hope last night helped, but I know there's more to talk about."

Billie nodded in the affirmative. "It did, and I'm willing to give it a try. Truth be told, I don't want to lose you."

"That'll never happen. I was hoping for a little bit more of a ringing endorsement, but it depends on how you want to keep me. Friend or ..." Tom reached into the pocket of his robe and took out a small black velvet box, which he opened and handed to her. "Husband. Billie Cunningham, will you marry me?"

Tears streamed down Billie's face as the modest, one carat marquis-cut diamond twinkled at her. She was lost for words as Tom placed the ring on her finger. She held her hand up to admire it.

"Look," Tom said. "I know there'll be times when I'll be paying for the crap some other guy did to you. But as long as you own it, and acknowledge it for what it is, we can deal with it. Remember, I'm the guy who was always there for you. Say yes, and I'll cherish you forever. Say no, and I'll dump you on this kitchen floor!"

Crying and laughing at the same time, Billie took Tom's face in her hands and kissed him tenderly. "Cherish me forever," she whispered.

They sat quietly for a few seconds, savoring the moment and taking in the significance of what they had done.

"I love you, baby," Tom said softly as he passionately kissed Billie.

"I love you, too. Just remember your promise."

After a few seconds, a giddy Billie got up and starting pacing from the kitchen to the living room and back. "I gotta call Carletha, and my mother, and my father—"

"Down, girl," Tom said as he moved to the sofa. "If we're not back by this evening—and we won't be—Carletha will know the deal. I think we should tell your mother face-to-face. And, as far as your father is concerned, he already knows."

"Why you conniving—you had it all planned, didn't you?" Billie laughed. "Presumptuous of you."

"No. Better safe than sorry. I had to ask your father for his blessings first, and you should have heard him shouting over the phone. I could just see him slapping his side the way he does, but I still need to talk to him about some stuff—"

"What stuff? Don't forget, I'm my own woman."

"Yeah, I know. Man stuff. Now come sit down," Tom said, nodding his head toward his outstretched arm. "I'm cold." Billie sat back down, and Tom felt the heat from her body as she snuggled against him.

"What stuff?" Billie asked.

"I told you. Man stuff. But in the meantime, we need to talk about a few things, okay?"

Billie nodded. "I'd say that's an understatement."

"First, let's not put the wedding off for too long. It's not like we don't know each other."

"Yep. Even in the Biblical sense."

"Good knowledge to have," Tom said out of the side of his mouth like Groucho Marx. "I'm serious. I've been a student longer than I've been a practitioner, but I know things. I'm not the blockhead boy you used to call me—"

"For Pete's sake, Tom. I know that."

"Let me finish please," he said as he twisted his body to look her in the eye. "I saw things as a boy that didn't make sense to me until I was a man. I overheard things that I didn't understand until I was a student of human behavior. You even said some stuff as a kid that made me wonder. I'm not sure how to ask this, so I'll just say it: what did Mr. Brown do to you?"

"What? What do you mean?"

"Billie, I know you don't want to talk about it. Maybe you don't even remember half of it. Surprisingly, that's normal. But, baby, you gotta talk about what you do remember." Billie tried to get up, but Tom pulled her back. "Please, baby. You have to start dealing with it now, or sometime in the future, when you least expect it, it will surface and bite you—us—in the butt."

"There's nothing to tell," Billie insisted, with tears rolling down her face. "It wasn't me. I'm not damaged."

"No, you're not, but you've had damaging experiences. It did happen to you, but you'll be all right. Do you know you've never told me you loved me until tonight? I know that's hard for you to say for fear of being hurt. Don't you know you're precious? You're worthy to be loved. No more playing games, and bad relationships. I'm here."

Billie started crying loud, gut-wrenching sobs, and she buried her head in Tom's chest. He tried to be clinical and detached, but his stomach was in knots. He hurt for her, and with her. He mouthed a silent prayer.

The clock over the mantel ticked off an hour before Billie sat up and began to speak. She spoke nonstop, in a dispassionate, disjointed way, as if her recollections of her childhood abuse were somebody else's life.

Tom was right. Some things were vague memories. But when she finished, she paused and took a deep breath. "Tom, don't tell my father."

Tom shifted his position so that Billie could lay down and rest her head on his lap. He grabbed a throw from the back of the sofa and threw it over her. "Why not? He may even confront Herb."

"First, it's not your place, husband-to-be or not. Besides, what good would it do at this point?" Billie asked through dry heaves. "Daddy will only feel more guilt for not being there for me when he should have been. He's sorry for that. I don't see any reason to make it worse. And Herb ... He's not really an issue anymore."

"Maybe. You're a better person than me. I'd have to say something to the SOB. Beat his ass ... Something. He needs to suffer the consequences of his actions."

"Please, Tom. Don't get self-righteous. You haven't always been of clean hands and pure heart."

"You're right, and I've made a lot of progress. Right now, though, it's about you. What does your mother know?"

"I haven't the foggiest. I think she just buried her head in the sand. She didn't want to see. I don't want to talk *about* her, and I don't want to talk *to* her about it. In fact, I don't want to talk about any of it any more. I have a headache. I think I'll go back to bed," Billie said as she got up.

"Want some company—no, ignore that. No more Biblical knowing. Just trying to lighten the mood. Seriously, besides the headache, how do you feel? Mentally, that is?" Tom asked as he followed her.

"I feel like you've torn the scab off a puss-filled wound and its gaping hole is surrounded by stinging insects."

"Aw crap, Billie. That's not in my textbook." Tom put his arms around her. "But, it'll be all right. I promise you. You take a nap, and I'm going for a run." He walked her into her bedroom and tucked her in. "I'll be back in a little bit."

Tom rooted through his suitcase for something suitable, and quickly put it on, all the while working his jaw muscles. On the way out, he peeped in on Billie, blew her a kiss, and quietly closed the door.

When he stepped outside in the crisp, light mountain air, he took a deep breath that helped clear his head. *What do I do now, Lord?* he asked as he headed for the footpath.

* * *

Luckily, Tom finished his run a few seconds ahead of an April shower. When he returned to the cabin, Billie was still asleep. He quickly showered and dressed, grabbed the throw from the sofa, and went into Billie's room. Without turning the bed back, he lay beside her and covered himself with the throw. He smiled as he watched the bed covers rise and fall with Billie's breathing.

* * *

Lulled by the steady rain, Billie and Tom didn't get up from their naps until late afternoon. Tom decided to drop the subject of Herb for a while. He had opened Pandora's Box, and he had begun to doubt his ability to handle the situation. Maybe Billie was right, and it wasn't his place to expose it.

But despite the conflict, he was happier than he had been at any other time in his life. He was finding more and more comfort in Biblical truths. *Thou wilt keep him in perfect peace, whose mind is stayed on Thee.*

That evening, they had dinner in a quaint restaurant in the valley and made wedding plans. Tom was insistent on a very short engagement. They laughed and joked as if the morning had never happened. Tom knew the elephant was still in the room. *But at least,* he thought, *it's moving.*

The next morning, they gathered the few things that they had brought with them and threw them in the car for the trip home. Tom opened the passenger door for Billie and helped her in. He kissed her and gently punched her on the arm. "This would be a good place for a honeymoon," he said.

Billie's expression changed, and her eyes suddenly watered. "Maybe, but let's call it a wedding trip," she whispered.

"Whatever you say, baby," Tom said as he closed the door. He walked to the driver's side of the car and wondered, *Wow, what's that about?*

* * *

The drive back to Brooklyn was peaceful and uneventful. The spring flowers budding along the roadside were like signs of a new beginning. When Tom and Billie weren't talking or singing along with the radio, Tom stole glances at Billie to make sure she was all right. They were only going to be in Brooklyn long enough to pick up anything they had left behind, and to grab a quick lunch with Carletha, who took off from work to see them off to Baltimore.

When Tom maneuvered the BMW into a tight spot in front of Carletha's brownstone, Billie leaned across him and blew the horn. "Hey everybody in Brooklyn, I'm engaged!" she shouted. She knew the windows were up and nobody heard her, but she didn't care.

Tom walked around the car and opened her door. "*We're* engaged. Don't get us arrested for disturbing the peace," he smiled as he helped her out of the car. They walked up the steps, hand-in-hand.

Carletha was waiting at the door with arms wide open and a big grin on her face. "People, people," she said, embracing the both of them. "At last you're on the right track. Congratulations! Come on in."

They went into the house, and Billie waved her left hand in Carletha's face. "Isn't it gorgeous?" Billie asked.

"Don't know until I get my magnifying glass," Carletha joked. She took Billie's hand and examined the ring. "Oh girl, this is beautiful. I'm so happy for y'all. Tom McNeal, I'm proud of you, boy. You finally got up the nerve to do the right thing."

"Yeah, yeah, *Carly,*" Tom said, walking to the kitchen. "Where's the food?"

* * *

After lunch, Tom and Billie kissed Carletha and thanked her for everything. They got back on the road and headed down I-95 South to Baltimore.

"Why did we wait so long to come to this point?" Billie asked.

"Dunno. I guess we had to exorcise our demons," Tom responded.

"A week ago, I would have denied having any," Billie said. "I don't know which hurts more: the denial or the realization."

"You can't heal without acknowledging the pain. I have an idea. Let's not wait any longer. How about a Justice of the Peace?" Tom asked.

Billie laughed. "I want a wedding."

"Yeah, but I want a marriage."

"I know what you want, but you gotta wait," Billie said lightly, but then she turned serious. "I think that might be a problem for me sometimes ..."

"I suspected it would be, but I'm not worried about it. We'll work it out. All things are possible, if you only believe."

"Love you, Tom McNeal."

"Love you, Billie Cunningham."

* * *

When they got back to town, Billie and Tom shared the news with their mothers. Mrs. McNeal was thrilled, and Billie's mother said it was about time. Later, they headed for Billie's apartment.

"I'll stay a little while," Tom said, "then head on home. Tomorrow's a workday. For you too, right?"

"Yep, gotta show this ring off," Billie said, waving her hand.

Tom parked in front of Billie's apartment building, helped her out of the car, and grabbed her luggage. Once inside the apartment, he put the suitcase inside the door, went to the sofa, and stretched out on his side. He patted the space next to him. "Come here, little girl."

"No, not little girl," Billie said as she lay down beside him.

"Sorry," Tom said as he wrapped his arms around her. They lay that way until they both fell asleep and didn't wake up until the wee hours of the morning.

52

While Billie and Tom were basking in their newfound happiness, forces they knew nothing about were at work. Back in South Carolina, Gertie squinted at the telephone on the kitchen wall as she dialed a familiar number.

A pleasant male voice answered on the other end. "Hello."

"Hello, James?" Gertie shouted into the telephone.

"Yes, ma'am, Miz Cunningham. It's me. I can hear you."

"Your bags packed for Ballamore?" Gertie asked.

"Packed? No ma'am—"

"When you told me the other week that Tom was gwine to propose to Billie, I told you to pack yo' bag."

"Yes, ma'am. You did, but I didn't think you meant it liter—seriously. I thought you were joking about getting ready for the wedding."

"No, siree. When I say it's raining po' chops, you git out yo' fryin' pan."

"Why am I going to Ballamore now?" James asked. "They haven't even set a date. Besides, I can't just pick up and leave—"

"Yes, you kin. Margaret and little James will be jest fine for a coupla days. You got plenty of family 'round here to look out for her. When can you leave?"

"Miz Cunningham, please tell me why I'm going."

"You come by here, 'for you leave, and I'll tell you. When I tell you, you be glad to go. You ain't gotta go tomorrow, but in a few days. Call me and let me know when you comin.' Oh, and James, I hate to have you lie to your wife, but this between you and me. Figure somethin' out. It'll work."

James was about to respond when the phone went dead.

* * *

James had never been caught in Gertie Cunningham's crosshairs, and didn't want to be, but he was reluctant to go to Baltimore. When a week had passed and he hadn't responded, Gertie called back. Since she always yelled into the phone, it was difficult to tell whether or not she was angry, but James got the message and packed his bag for a quick trip. He simply told Margaret the truth: he had to go to Baltimore to take care of some business for Miz Cunningham, and she was not to mention the trip to anybody.

When James got to Gertie's house, he parked his Buick—he had given up his beloved Packard—along the dirt road in front of Gertie's shack. He reluctantly walked up the dirt path toward the door.

Gertie was standing on the porch, corn-cob pipe in her mouth and her hands on her bony hips. Her trademark gray braids, which hung over her shoulders, reached down to her waist.

"Morning, James," she said without removing the pipe. "Long trip from the Hayes farm, ain't it?"

"Ma'am? No ma'am. Mornin'," James said, cautiously.

"Must be. Took you two weeks to git here."

"Sorry, Miz Cunningham, but I'm here now." *No need arguing. I can't win*, he thought.

"Come on in. I got a package I need you to deliver."

As James started up the steps, Gertie's phone rang. While she scurried to answer it, James went in and sat down at the kitchen table.

"Hello," Gertie shouted in the telephone. "Lilly Ann, this you? ... How you been doin' with all that excitement goin' on in Ballamore? ... What you say? ... He is? ... What's the matter with him? ... Oh, they gotta run testes. Well, I'm sorry to hear that ... Yes I am. You know I don't mean Herb no harm. Let me know what them doctors say ... You do the same ... Bye."

James waited for Gertie to speak. He somehow knew that the call was related to his mission to Baltimore.

"Guess you could tell that was Lilly Ann," Gertie said. James just nodded. "Herb's sickness got worse, and she had to put him in the hospital the other day."

"Sorry to hear that," James responded without emotion. "Okay, Miz Cunningham, what do I need to do, and am I going to be able to live with it?"

"Son, you got me wrong. I wouldn't impose my burden on your soul. First, you need to brace yo'self. I got some ugly mess to tell you about."

Uncomfortable with talking to a man about taboo subjects, Gertie explained in euphemisms the nature of Herb's character and the harm he had done to Billie. James exploded. He banged on the table with closed fists and stomped around the kitchen, calling Herb names that would make a sailor cringe. When his anger was spent, he sobbed. Gertie looked on from her rocking chair, calmly smoking her pipe.

"Why didn't Billie tell me? Why didn't she tell her mother? Did Lilly Ann know about it? How could she have stood by and let this happen? I should've been there."

Gertie walked over to James and looked him straight in the eyes. "I don't know the answers to none of that, but yo' business is with Herb, not Billie, and not Lilly Ann. You understand?"

"Yes ma'am. Where's the package?" James asked.

"You the package." Gertie quietly replied.

James cocked his head and stared intently at Gertie, his usual restraint gone. "What the hell are you talking about, old lady?"

Gertie reached into the pocket of the apron she perpetually wore, and pulled out a small, aromatic gingham pouch filled with herbs. "Just funnin.' If you have a mind to, put this under Herb's bed." She took a brown paper bag from the shelf over the sink, tore off a piece, wrapped the pouch in it, and handed it to James. "Now son, be on yo' way."

* * *

James walked back to his car with more determination than when he arrived. Like a man possessed, he got in, gunned the motor, and headed for Baltimore and Provident Hospital. The route was a familiar one, and James sped by the myriad cities and towns on auto-pilot.

Nine road-weary hours later, James pulled into the hospital parking lot. By the time he walked from the parking lot to the front door of the hospital, his anger had reignited. He was light-headed from fatigue, and the hospital's antiseptic smell jarred him as he walked up to the information desk and asked for Herbert Brown's room number.

Too wired to be confined in the limited space of an elevator, James crossed the linoleum lobby and bolted up the steps to the fifth floor. When he walked into Room 550, he was taken aback. His raging anger abated when he saw Herbert Brown laying in his hospital bed. He was frail, and connected to an intravenous drip, a heart monitor, and a respirator. Red lights blinked and machines hummed in the background.

James walked to the bed, gently shook the rail, and waited for Herb to open his eyes. Even in his weakened state, Herb's eyes registered surprise, then fear. He stared at James and said nothing.

James lifted Herb's oxygen mask and Herb gasped for air. "I wonder how long it would take for you to die without this thing?" James asked through clenched teeth. "Or this?" he said as he squeezed shut the IV tubing. "You know you deserve to die, but it's not my right to send you to hell. You've done that yourself. Your sins have found you out," James said as he released the tube, and let the mask snap back on Herb's face.

Herb's lips moved in noiseless words. Then James said things that surprised even him. "Where will your soul spend eternity, Herb? Are you saved? Have you confessed Christ? Do you believe Christ died for your sins, and was crucified and rose again?"

The look in Herb's eyes changed from fear, to contempt, to anger. He raised a bony hand and pointed to the door.

"Out … Out," Herb croaked with as much strength as he could muster.

James stood there for a moment, shaking his head. Herb managed to lift his mask and made a feeble attempt to spit at James. James smiled and quietly walked out of the room.

* * *

James was bone-tired. He had foolishly made the drive round-trip without stopping except to relieve himself, refuel, and grab snacks and sodas from gas station vending machines.

Now he knew why Gertie had sent him. He *was* the package. He was to offer salvation to a man whose moral compass was out of whack and rendered inoperable by unnatural urges in overdrive. He also would have never forgiven himself if he had not confronted Herb before he died, but in his anger he thought, *I did not sin. That is, beat Herb within an inch of his wretched life.*

James couldn't fathom how Gertie could dabble in ungodly things and still have compassion for Herb's soul. Maybe she just wanted to confirm his trip to hell.

James figured that the packet of dried, unidentified weeds she had given him was harmless, but good for mind games. Then he remembered. He patted his pant pocket, and yes, he had forgotten to leave the pouch. James chuckled to himself, rolled down his window, and tossed the pouch into a thicket of bushes growing along I-295.

When he glanced into his rearview mirror, he was sure his tired, over-wrought mind was playing tricks on him. Because surely he imagined seeing smoke rising from the thicket.

53

Billie and Lilly Ann were in the third Eastern Avenue bridal shop, trying to find *the* dress. Billie shunned fluffy, frilly gowns, and was looking for something sleek, sexy, and sophisticated. Billie told her mother she also had to find a dress for the reception.

Billie overheard an eavesdropping saleswoman say, "Blacks are the only people I know who change dresses for the reception."

"Guess we'll be just fine then," Billie's mother retorted. "Since we be Black." The red-faced woman quickly walked away.

Billie laughed and took her mother by the arm. "Momma, you're a mess. We haven't had this much fun since you helped me buy my senior prom dress. Let's go get some lunch."

Arm-in-arm, they left the store and walked to Haussner's, one of Baltimore's premier restaurants. Haussner's was known as much for its massive collection of 19th century European and American artwork, as it was for its extensive menu and strawberry pie. When Billie and Lilly Ann got to the restaurant, they were quickly seated and ordered ice tea to drink while they perused the menu.

"How many more shops do you think we have to go to?" her mother asked, stirring her tea.

"Dunno. Until I find the dress I really want. Momma, you know you love this. You and shopping? A match made in heaven."

"You got me pegged," her mother admitted. "But I'm just a little tired, with running back and forth to the hospital, and all. The doctors say they think the cancer has gone to Herb's brain. He was agitated, and trying to tell me something the other day. Seemed like he was outta his head. I didn't know what he was tryin' to say. Speakin' of the hospital, why you ain't been over there to see him?"

Billie chewed on her bottom lip. *Maybe it's now or never, but I don't want to mess up this moment.* "Momma, you know how busy I've been."

"That's no excuse. Herb's your stepfather—"

"Please, no speeches about how good he's been to me, okay?"

"I don't understand you—"

"You don't understand *me*? You—"

Her mother shrieked as her hand hit her glass and sent tea trickling across the table and into her lap. She jumped up and futilely dabbed at the stain on her dress. "This is one of my favorite Butte Knit dresses," she lamented. An apologetic waitress scurried over to apply club soda to the stain and clean up the spill.

For the duration of lunch, her mother complained about ruining her dress. The moment was lost, and Billie and her mother ate lunch in silence.

* * *

Since their engagement, Billie and Tom always had dinner together in her tiny kitchen. Although Tom often stayed late, he never spent the night.

What Billie most enjoyed about the evenings was the twenty or thirty minutes she spent curled up on Tom's lap with her head on his chest while he read the newspaper. She couldn't bring herself to tell him how satisfied and utterly at peace she was when she did it.

She was sure he would attach some psychological significance to it or call it a syndrome with some Latin name. It had nothing to do with an absent daddy or longing to be daddy's little girl, but she had to admit that on some level, it was very gratifying.

On the evening after the shopping trip, Tom raised the issue of whether Billie had talked with her mother about the sexual abuse she had suffered. That topic, and whether or not she should tell her father and confront Herb, had become a bone of contention that threatened to drive a wedge between them.

Billie always gave what she believed to be rational responses to Tom's concerns. It would be unfair and pointless to burden her father with the guilt. Her mother would never believe her. It was long ago, so forget it. And Herb was probably on his death bed. Despite that, Tom was relentless on the subject.

After dinner, Billie took the dishes to the kitchen and put them in the sink. She went back into the living room and sat on Tom's lap. After a few minutes, he folded the newspaper and dropped it on the floor next to the armchair. "How did shopping go? Find a dress yet?" he asked.

"Nope. When I do, it'll be a secret."

"Is that how it works? What about your mother. You talk to her?"

"Of course I talked to her."

"Don't be flip. You know what I mean."

"You're messin' up my moment, Tom. No, I didn't talk about Herb."

"Why not? You said you would."

"I know, but the time just wasn't right."

"I don't think there'll be a right time. You just have to do it."

"Do we have to add this drama to everything that's happening right now? Give it a rest."

"You need to do this, Billie, so the healing process can take place."

"Really? I don't see how talking about it to them will heal anything. And I'm a little tired of hearing it from you. You know what? You need to stay out of it. May be you should go home."

Tom gave her a gentle nudge. "Get up," he told Billie, and then he stood. "Let's get something straight," he said staring her in the eye.

"I'm not going home until I'm ready. Since you let me in your life by agreeing to marry me, you don't get to just blow me off whenever you feel like it. Not anymore. Got that?"

Billie had not seen an angry Tom in a very long time, and she remembered how ugly it could be. But she noticed his eyes were still soft while he spoke.

"Hmm," Billie said. "How does that work? You don't live here, and we're not married yet, but you're not going to leave *my* apartment even if I ask you to go. I get your point, Mr. McNeal. Sounds like I'm stuck for life, papers or no papers," Billie said to diffuse the situation.

"Smart girl," Tom said, easing back down in the armchair. "Now assume the position."

"No thanks, Billie replied. "Think I'll finish in the kitchen."

* * *

Eventually, Tom admitted to himself that he couldn't be Billie's soon-to-be husband and her therapist too. After some coaxing and his promise to give the subject a rest, Billie promised him that she would talk to Dr. Kaufman, though she didn't say when.

Tom intended to honor his promise to Billie, but he didn't say he wouldn't talk to her mother. He felt compelled to do it. He knew it would be risky, and that Billie might feel betrayed, but that was a chance he was willing to take.

A few days later, while Tom tossed and turned after one of their routine bedtime calls, the obvious solution hit him. He hadn't referred Billie to Dr. Jesus. He dialed her number right away, and a sleepy Billie answered.

"Hello," she whispered.

"Baby. It's me. Let's pray."

Tom prayed for peace, patience, and guidance. After they exchanged I love you's, Tom hung up and peacefully drifted off to sleep.

54

The day had finally come: August 13, 1966. Even though it had been only four months from Billie's engagement to the day of the wedding, it seemed like an eternity to her.

Her mother didn't share her opinion. She had been frantic that they would not be able to pull it off successfully—that is, host a wedding that would get rave reviews from her friends and acquaintances—in such a short time. What her mother's peers thought was the least of Billie's concerns.

Billie wanted a simple ceremony. She didn't know when she changed her mind, but she wanted to be Tom's wife, and all that came with the role. She left the wedding details to her mother, while she was busy merging two apartments, and essentially two lives. For the immediate future, they were going to live in Tom's apartment, the bigger of the two.

On the day of the wedding, Billie dressed at her mother's house with Carletha, her matron of honor and only attendant, and her mother fussing over her. Billie was stunning in a strapless satin gown with a fitted beaded bodice, accented with rhinestones and sequins.

The fishtail gown flowed into a short train, and she wore opera length, fingerless gloves. Her hair was swept back in a French roll, accenting her exquisite cheekbones, and at her mother's insistence, her shoulder-length veil was attached to a garland of gardenias in homage to Billie Holiday.

"Will you two stop?" Billie asked, flicking her hand at the two of them. "You're making me nervous. I'm ready."

"All right," her mother said, adjusting Billie's veil. "I'm just so excited. You are just beautiful, honey."

"You are, cuz," Carletha chimed in. "I'm happy for you."

"Me, too. My stomach is full of butterflies. The limo should be here soon. Let's go downstairs," Billie replied.

"Uh, Billie," her mother said hesitantly. "You and Tom will be real tired tonight. You know all this excitement will wear you out. Just rest tonight, you know what I mean, so things will be right in the morning—"

"Momma, I hope this isn't the birds and bees talk we never had. You're a little late if it is," Billie said, a little irritated.

"Yeah, Aunt Lilly Ann. You *are too late*. Billie and Tom did it when they were kids," Carletha laughed.

"Stop, Carletha," her mother firmly said. "Why are you always so disrespectful and coarse? You know that's not true."

Billie and Carletha headed down the steps, giggling like schoolgirls. "Don't make me laugh, Carletha," Billie said. You're going to make me mess up my makeup."

The door bell rang and Carletha answered it to find the limousine driver, dressed in a black tuxedo, ready to take them to church. A few of the neighbors, who were curious about the limousine, stood on the sidewalk waiting to see the passengers. When Billie, Carletha, and her mother appeared, the onlookers cheered as the driver helped the three ladies into the vehicle.

He whisked them off to the church, where the rest of the wedding party was waiting. Once they arrived, the chauffeur and an usher, who was waiting at the curb, helped Billie out of the car and up the steps to the church.

The church was full, but not because Billie and Tom had invited so many people. As a matter of custom at Baltimore Street Baptist, betrothed couples extended an open invitation to their wedding to the entire church. The guests included family, friends, well-wishers, and the curious. But the congregants knew that without a personal invitation, they were not invited to the reception, which was often held in the fellowship hall or somebody's home. Billie and Tom had planned an hors d'oeuvre reception at the church and to host friends and family at Lilly Ann's.

Baltimore Street Baptist was made up of mostly transplanted southerners, which gave it a down-home feel. There was no baby grand piano or huge pipe organ to usher in the bride. The choir director played by ear, so there would be no Mozart, Beethoven, or Bach to accompany the wedding party. None of that mattered to Billie or Tom.

Billie, standing in the narthex of the church with her father, shifted her weight from foot to foot, and willed herself calm while she waited to hear the Wedding March.

"Calm down, honey," Billie's father nervously whispered in her ear.

"You, too," Billie said, looking approvingly at her father in a white dinner jacket.

The music started, and Billie stepped onto the white runner on rubbery legs, tightly clinching her father's arm. The short aisle might as well have been a mile. She was sure she would never make it to the end of it. After gazing over the crowd, her eyes rested on Tom, and she wondered what he was thinking. She wasn't sure, but he looked like he was swaying until his brother John, his best man, clamped a hand on his shoulder. He was breathtakingly handsome in a white dinner jack, with black pants, bow tie, and cummerbund. Finally, Billie and her father reached the altar.

The minister began, "Dearly beloved, we are gathered together here in the sight of God, and in the face of this company, to join together this man and this woman in holy matrimony: which is an honorable estate, instituted of God ..."

Billie saw the minister move his lips, but she wasn't sure what he was saying. Carletha nudged her at the appropriate moments, and whispered what she should say in her ear. She tried to focus and caught snatches of the ceremony.

"Who giveth this woman to be married to this man?" the minister asked.

Her father answered, "I do," and took his seat.

The minister put Billie's hand in Tom's. Her heart rate started to return to normal, and she was suddenly in the moment.

She heard Tom say, "I, Thomas McNeal, take thee Billie Cunningham to be my wedded wife, to have and to hold from this day forward, for better or for worse, for richer or for poorer, in sickness and in health, to love and to *cherish* ..." The tears started. It was surreal.

She could hardly believe it until the minister said, "Having taken these pledges of your affection and vows of fidelity, I do therefore, by authority of the laws of this State, sanctioned by divine authority pronounce you, Thomas McNeal, and you, Billie Cunningham, lawfully married husband and wife, in the name of the Father, and the Son, and the Holy Spirit. Amen. What, therefore, God hath joined together, let no man put asunder. The Lord bless you and keep you. The Lord make his face to shine upon you, and be gracious to you. The Lord lift up his countenance upon you, and give you peace. Amen. You may kiss your bride."

The church erupted in applause and amen's as Tom lifted Billie's veil and gently kissed her. The music started again, and the wedding party recessed to the church hall for the receiving line.

* * *

The reception at Lilly Ann's turned into quite a party, with plenty of food, lots of dancing, and surreptitious drinking. When Tom and Billie left early, they were hardly missed. Since they couldn't book their wedding trip, as Billie insisted on calling it, until later in the month, they were going to spend their wedding night at a hotel in downtown Baltimore, then head to the Poconos for a few days.

When Billie and Tom arrived at the hotel, the valet parked the car, and they went hand-in-hand into the lobby. The lobby was illuminated with sparkling chandeliers, and the sound of the cascading waters from the fountain in its lush atrium was soothing and peaceful. David had pre-registered for Tom and had given him the key, so Tom led Billie directly to the elevator. They got in, and he punched a button for their floor. As soon as the elevator doors closed, Tom put his arm around Billie's waist, pulled her toward him, and kissed her.

"You're trembling," Tom said, concerned. "What's the matter?"

"Just a little. Nothing. Excited. Nervous. Happy. Giddy. All of the above. I've never been married before," Billie said.

Tom didn't know how to respond and mumbled a feeble, "You're in good company. Me neither." The ding of the elevator bell signaled that they had arrived at their floor and the doors opened. "Hang a left to 704," Tom said, and Billie exited the elevator. He unlocked the door and let her in.

"Oh, nice," she said as she surveyed the room.

"Glad you like it," Tom replied, his mind racing as he tossed his jacket across a chair.

There was a knock at the door, and Billie jumped. "I think it's just the bellman with our overnight bags," he said as he answered the door. Tom let the bellman in, and he put their bags on the luggage rack. Tom handed him a tip and closed the door.

Billie walked across the room and looked out of the window. "Nice view."

"From here, too," Tom said, taking in the silhouette of the woman he had committed his life to.

Billie hadn't noticed, but there was bottle of champagne chilling on a small round table in one corner of the room, compliments of David and John. When Tom popped the cork, Billie jumped again.

"Billie, baby, what's going on?"

"Going on? Nothing."

"You sure? You're a nervous wreck." Tom poured two glasses. "Come here, and let's toast." Tom raised his glass. "To my wife, my new life, I'll cherish you forever."

"To my husband, my new life, I'll love you forever."

After they clinked their glasses, Tom put his down on the table, picked up a surprised Billie, and walked to the door. "I forgot to carry you over the threshold. Can you get that door?"

Billie laughed, reached to open the door, and put the guard on so they wouldn't be locked out. "You know this doesn't count," Billie said. "You'll have to do it again when we get home."

"With pleasure," Tom said. He stepped into the hallway, turned around, stepped back into the room, and put Billie back on her feet. "Whew. Girl, I didn't know you were that heavy," he joked and sat down on the loveseat. "Come here," he said softly, patting his lap.

Billie walked over, sat on Tom's lap, and snuggled against his chest. She could hear his heartbeat and feel the warmth of his body. He gently stroked her arm. "Did I tell you I like this dress?" he asked.

"Tell me again."

"I like this dress. I like the neckline. What do they call it, boat-neck?" Tom asked, kissing Billie's neck. "I like the material. It's soft." He rubbed his hand across Billie's thigh and slowly inched up the dress. "I even like the zipper," he said, reaching around her to unzip her dress.

He pulled the dress off her shoulder, and caressed and kissed her breast. This time, she trembled with desire, not anxiety.

Tom kissed her passionately, and Billie returned the kiss as his hands explored her body. After a few seconds, she got up, shimmied out her dress and went to turn the bed back. Tom followed her, unbuttoning his shirt. *Yes, there is a God!*

55

The article on the obituary page of the August 23, 1966 *Afro-American* newspaper read:

Herbert Brown, Co-owner of Brownies Social Club, Dies at 53. Herbert Jerome Brown, co-owner of the now defunct private social club, Brownies on Edmondson Avenue, died on Sunday, August 21, 1966, after a prolonged illness. Brown and his brother, Leon, who preceded him in death, opened the after-hours club in the late forties. Before it closed in the late fifties, the club was a popular night spot for Baltimore's black elite. The brothers also owned a grocery store and barbershop on Edmondson Avenue. Brown leaves to cherish his memory, his wife, Lilly Ann Cunningham (nee) Brown and stepdaughter, Billie McNeal, and one sister. Homegoing services will be held at the Baltimore Street Baptist Church on Saturday, August 27th at 10:00 a.m. For more information, contact Miles Family Funeral Home.

Except for a dim light at the top of the stairs, the house was dark and deadly quiet. A light rain beat a rhythmic cadence on the roof. Lilly Ann sat at the dining room table, twirling an unlit cigarette and swinging a crossed leg, with the paper folded on her lap. She was exhausted, mentally and physically.

Believing Herb would someday come to no good end, Lilly Ann had purposely not divorced him, and out of a sense of duty, had taken him back when he became seriously ill. His condition, spoken of in hushed tones, was rumored to be the big C. Out of fear and lack of knowledge of the disease, people were reluctant to call it by its name: cancer.

He was hospitalized when he had finally gotten too sick to be cared for at home. The running back and forth to the hospital had worn out Lilly Ann and wreaked havoc with her emotions, in part because she felt he didn't deserve her devotion. She tried to comfort herself, believing she was heaping coals of fire on his head.

To add to her exhaustion was the confrontations with the girlfriend-de jour, who finally got the message and stayed away. Lilly Ann had told her that no matter how many years they had been together, when Herb died, she would play the dutiful wife. She would occupy the first seat on the first pew at the funeral, receive mourners, and be rewarded with everything the law allowed. Most of the women of her day did as she did in her situation, so she sucked it up, and acted like everything was normal.

She was happy for Billie and Tom, but had been suspicious of why they wanted to get married in such a hurry, hoping nothing was baking in Billie's oven. Even James had questioned Tom when he asked James for his daughter's hand in marriage. She had been in no mood to help with another wedding and its concomitant drama so soon after Carletha's, but she managed to get through it.

Because of problems with scheduling, Billie and Tom postponed their wedding trip until the end of August.

Billie had also told her that if Herbert Brown's death would be so inopportune as to occur in August, she would not be at any of the services. Lilly Ann had never understood why her daughter hated her stepfather so much. After all, he had provided for the two of them, fed them, clothed them, and put a roof over their heads. But then she had a strange conversation with her new son-in-law.

"Mrs. Brown, I'm sorry to have to ask you this, and I mean no disrespect, but has Billie ever been sexually molested?" Tom had asked.

Her response had been immediate. "What do you mean? Of course not! How did you fix yo' lips to ask me such a question? You having problems with yo' marriage already?"

Tom had apologized, but persisted. "No ma'am. I'm sorry, but she probably wouldn't have told you if she had been, and you wouldn't have known necessarily. Given a second thought, can you think of any suspicious incident? Did Grandma Gertie ever tell you anything?"

Then a light bulb went on in her head and her heart raced, but she didn't give voice to the revelation. "No, of course not. I would know about such a thing," she had insisted.

She knew Tom had not believed her. And sitting in the dark, she thought if Herbert Brown wasn't already dead, she would kill him— twice.

56

As Billie moved away from the casket and back up the aisle, she surveyed the mourners and smirked. *Old Herbert never wanted to join Baltimore Street Baptist, or any church for that matter, but here he is, laid out to a packed house. He would be proud. A crueler ending couldn't have happened to a nicer person,* she thought with sarcasm.

Any thoughts of Herbert Brown were permanently sealed in that dark vault of her mind where nightmares go. She had a new life with a man who loved her unconditionally, and she was happier than she could have ever imagined.

Billie slowly moved toward the rear of the church, nodding in recognition of familiar faces as she went, and she observed the male ushers, in black suits, flanking the back wall. Her mother had put them on alert to remove any hysterical woman whose grief might cause her to swoon into the casket, or any man, buoyed by Herb's passing, who might have the nerve to curse out his corpse.

Included in the ranks of the black-suited men was a good friend and potential suitor for her mother. On her way out the door, Billie handed him a pale yellow envelope. "Give this to Momma later," she whispered.

Billie slipped out of the sanctuary and into the narthex. She spied a pay telephone in a far corner, fished some coins from her purse, and dialed long distance. She held the phone away from her ear in anticipation of her grandmother's greeting.

"Hello," Grandma Gertie shouted.

"Hello, Grandma Gertie. It's me. I'm on my way," Billie replied.

"Good, baby. Everything gwine be all right. And went you git back, your momma will be ready to talk. You understand? You talk, hear me?"

"Yes ma'am. I hear you. Gotta go. Love you. Bye."

"Love you too, baby. Now, go get yo'self in some trouble!" Grandma Gertie laughed, and the call disconnected.

After exiting the church, Billie paused at the top of the steps and took a deep breath. She felt like a load had been lifted from her shoulders.

A sudden August shower had quickly passed through, leaving the air fresh and the asphalt steaming and shiny. She bounced down the steps, and caught a glimpse of her own reflection in the asphalt as she was about to step off the curb. Amused by the memory of her childhood fear, she hopscotched in place, then ran across the street to the waiting car.

Tom reached across the seat to open her door and kissed her on the cheek as she climbed into the car. "You okay?" he asked. Billie nodded and punched him on the arm. "Aruba, here we come!" he said. He shifted into gear and went south on Monroe Street to I-295, heading for Friendship Airport.

Billie leaned back on the headrest and closed her eyes. She rubbed her husband's leg and smiled. All was right with her world. Right as rain.

ACKNOWLEDGMENTS

First, I thank God for the gift of writing. Secondly, I am grateful to the Enoch Pratt Free Library for all the reading programs that enticed me to read dozens of books during the summers of my youth. I am convinced that reading is the foundation for good writing.

For as long as I can remember, I wanted to write a book—just for the sheer joy of writing a book. I had a basic plot in mind, but could not have imagined how that plot would play out on paper. I found out, thanks to Lauren Smalls, who taught the one and only creative writing course that I ever took, that once you begin to write, the plot takes care of itself. I also thank Lauren for the writing assignment that actually launched the book. Lauren is the author of *Choke Creek*.

I am also indebted to members of my writers' group—my son, Everett Adams (author of *The Tricky 'S'*), Aurisha Stanley, Wanda Kimball, Marcia Wagner, and Joyce Smith—who encouraged and supported me, as well as edited and provided feedback on installments of the manuscript. Special thanks go to Wanda, dubbed the "technical advisor" for her attention to detail and for her penchant for always researching best practices, standard procedures, and writing techniques.

In addition, special thanks go to Marni Graff, author of *Blue Virgin*, for her attention to plot and character development, and for helping me to finally wrap my head around "point of view." She even took the manuscript on vacation with her! Her edits were invaluable. Also, thank you, Mattie Riddick, for sharing your Baltimore memories, which helped to add texture to the narrative.

I can't forget Dorothy Morris, author of the *Fatal* Trilogy (*Fatal Rebound, Fatal Vengeance,* and *Fatal Blow*) for making me rethink the title and suggesting that my original choice was not strong enough for the story. Dot, a stranger to me when she read the manuscript, had questions that helped me bring more clarity to some of the dialogue. I am also appreciative of Dot's encouragement, and her willingness to share her writing and publishing experience.

I thank those "one-off" readers—those who did not know me personally—for taking their time to edit and provide unbiased feedback. Thank you Lisa Brown, Linda Bowie, Sylvia Mack, and Pearl Kirby. Extra thanks go to Pearl for double-checking some cultural and historical facts, and for corroborating the authenticity of some sub-plots based on her professional experiences.

Finally, I thank Tieffa Harper and the Plenary team for plucking my story out of mounds of deserving manuscripts and whipping my talent into shape to make my dream a reality.